Cultivating the relationship since 1891

Events   Education   Publishing

Find out more at

www.japansociety.org.uk

THE JAPAN SOCIETY

GRANTA

12 Addison Avenue, London WII 4QR | email editorial@granta.com
To subscribe go to www.granta.com, or call 845-267-3031 (toll-free 866-438-6150)
in the United States, 020 8955 7011 in the United Kingdom

ISSUE 127: SPRING 2014

ISSUE EDITOR	Yuka Igarashi
ONLINE EDITOR	Rachael Allen
DESIGNER	Daniela Silva
PUBLICITY	Aidan O'Neill
MARKETING AND SUBSCRIPTIONS	David Robinson
EDITORIAL ASSISTANTS	Louise Scothern, Francisco Vilhena
TO ADVERTISE CONTACT	Kate Rochester, katerochester@granta.com
FINANCE	Morgan Graver
SALES	Iain Chapple, Katie Hayward
IT MANAGER	Mark Williams
PRODUCTION ASSOCIATE	Sarah Wasley
PROOFS	David Atkinson, Katherine Fry, Jessica Rawlinson, Vimbai Shire
PHOTOGRAPHY CONSULTANT	Ivan Vartanian
PUBLISHER AND ACTING EDITOR	Sigrid Rausing
CONTRIBUTING EDITORS	Daniel Alarcón, Mohsin Hamid, Isabel Hilton, A.M. Homes, Blake Morrison, John Ryle, Edmund White

Granta Japan

EDITORS	Makoto Ichikawa, David Karashima
CONSULTING EDITOR	Elmer Luke
EDITORIAL ASSISTANTS	Mina Kitahara, Tatsuya Kuboki

Translation Support by The Nippon Foundation

This selection copyright © 2014 Granta Publications.

Granta, ISSN 173231, is published four times a year by Granta Publications, 12 Addison Avenue, London WII 4QR, United Kingdom.

The US annual subscription price is $48. Airfreight and mailing in the USA by agent named Air Business Ltd, c/o Worldnet-Shipping USA Inc., 156–15 146th Avenue, 2nd Floor, Jamaica, NY 11434, USA. Periodicals postage paid at Jamaica NY 11431.

US Postmaster: Send address changes to Granta, Air Business Ltd, c/o Worldnet-Shipping USA Inc., 156–15 146th Avenue, 2nd Floor, Jamaica, NY 11434, USA.

Subscription records are maintained at Granta, c/o Abacus e-Media, Chancery Exchange, 10 Furnival Street, London EC4A 1AH.

Air Business Ltd is acting as our mailing agent.

Granta is printed and bound in Italy by Legoprint. This magazine is printed on paper that fulfils the criteria for 'Paper for permanent document' according to ISO 9706 and the American Library Standard ANSI/NIZO Z39.48-1992 and has been certified by the Forest Stewardship Council (FSC). Granta is indexed in the American Humanities Index.

ISBN 978-1-905881-77-2

CONTENTS

THE WRITER'S FOUNDRY MFA

to be, not to seem.

GRANTA

A CLEAN MARRIAGE

Sayaka Murata

TRANSLATED FROM THE JAPANESE BY GINNY TAPLEY TAKEMORI

M y husband emerged from the bedroom, woken by the beeps at the end of the washing-machine cycle.

'Morning . . . Sorry I overslept. Shall I take over?'

The weekend laundry was his job, but since he'd had to work late at the bank and came home on the last train, I decided I'd do it that day. 'Don't worry about it,' I said. 'Oh, I washed your green shirt. Hope you don't mind.'

'Not at all. Thanks.'

While I was hanging the washing out on the balcony, he used the bathroom and got dressed. Then he put bread into the toaster, wiped the table and sat down to breakfast.

Living with my husband is like living with an exceedingly clean, smart owl. It's good to have a tidy animal around the house. We've been married three years and that hasn't changed. A friend who married for love around the same time tells me she's developed a visceral aversion to her husband, but that's not at all the case with me. My husband has orderly table manners, and the toilet and bath are never left with evidence of his bodily fluids and excretions. I sometimes wonder whether we shouldn't have put him in charge of cleaning when we divided up the household chores.

After finishing with the laundry, I mentioned this to him and he laughed. 'So you're saying I'm like a Roomba?' Actually, that wasn't so far off the mark.

'On the other hand,' he said, 'you, Mizuki, are more like a rabbit, or a squirrel. Quiet, sensitive to noise, and you never jump on me or lose your temper.'

'Don't squirrels ever lose their temper?'

'I don't think so. You and me, we're both clean animals and don't get in each other's way. Which is a good thing, right?'

It really is. Of course there are little things that bother me about him, like his putting in a new roll of toilet paper before the old one has run out, or stacking the dirty dishes by shape rather than by how greasy they are, the way I like it. But they don't stress me out, and that's probably because of the judicious distance between us.

We met through a matchmaking website. As I'd read through the various listings by guys of their 'ideal marriage' – 'I want to raise a loving family' or 'I want to have lots of children' – I'd come across: 'Seeking a clean marriage.' When I looked at this man's profile, this is what it said: 'I'm seeking an amicable daily routine with someone I get along well with, like brother and sister, without being a slave to sex.'

I was intrigued. We exchanged messages, and eventually decided to meet. His silver-rimmed glasses made him look nervous, and I wondered if a 'clean marriage' actually meant an 'obsession with cleanliness'. When we started talking, though, I learned that 'clean' was on another plane altogether.

'I want my family life to be a calm space, the kind you have hanging out with a room-mate you get on really well with or with your favourite younger sister while the parents are away.'

'I see. I can identify with that.'

'The fact is, I feel uncomfortable with the idea of family as an extension of romantic attachment. A family should not have anything to do with feelings of love between man and woman – it should be a simple partnership.'

'I agree,' I said. 'I've lived with several men, but there's always a point where it falls apart. We're supposed to be family, but they expect me to be both a woman and an understanding friend, which is a contradiction, isn't it? I'm supposed to be wife, friend *and* mother . . . I would much rather live as brother and sister.'

'That's precisely what I mean. But nobody understands – not even that matchmaking site. They have these questions about the man's income and what the woman likes cooking – but that's not what a family is about to me. I want a partner, not all that man-woman stuff.'

He had become quite worked up from this outburst, and took out a blue-striped handkerchief to wipe his forehead. Then he gulped down a glass of water and sighed. 'I'm happy you understand how I feel. But it may be a bit idealistic . . .'

'Not at all. We'll never know unless we try it.'

'Huh?' He gulped, pushing his glasses back up his nose.

I looked him straight in the eye and said, 'How about it? Will you enter into a sexless marriage with me?'

'Isn't it about time we went to the clinic?' asked my husband, looking up from the newspaper he was reading while he ate his toast.

'Ah, the clinic . . .'

'You're already thirty-three, Mizuki. It's about time you had an egg fertilized.'

'That's true.' I nodded, staring at the slice of lemon floating in my tea. I'd been thinking more or less the same thing. 'Now that things are settling down at work, I suppose the time is right.'

'Shall I make an appointment for next week?'

'Hang on a minute. I'm still taking the pill. Even if I stop taking it tomorrow, it'll take time for my body to prepare for ovulation.'

'I see, yes, I suppose next week would be premature,' he said, looking uncharacteristically embarrassed. 'But then, I don't think they actually carry out the fertilization on the first visit. You probably have to go through some tests, too, so how about an appointment once you've had a bleed?'

'OK.'

I usually had a withdrawal bleed a couple of days after I stopped taking the pill. It would be much lighter than a normal period, and it'd be over within two or three days. I explained this to my husband, and we decided to make an appointment for a Saturday two weeks later.

A marriage that was far removed from sex was more comfortable than I'd ever imagined. I earned a salary of ¥4 million, my husband ¥5 million. We each paid ¥150,000 into the household account every month, and the rest we managed in bank books under our own names. This ¥300,000 covered our living expenses, while the rest went into savings. We decided against owning a home or any other assets jointly.

Since we were contributing equally to the finances, we also decided to split the housework. Unlike money, housework cannot be split in half precisely, but since my husband was good at cooking, he took care of that while I took care of the laundry and cleaning. On weekdays we both worked late, so we took care of our own evening meals. This meant that I had the heavier burden, and to compensate we agreed that he should do the laundry on weekends.

This much was simple. Sexual matters were trickier.

My husband wanted to ban all sex from our home. That was fine by me.

'As far as I'm concerned, sex is an act you indulge in alone in your own room, or deal with outside. In some homes the partners come home tired from work and have sex together, but I am completely averse to this,' he said.

'So am I,' I said. 'Sex is fine during the early stages of a love affair, but as time goes on and you're living together, it's horrible when your partner feels you up when you're asleep, or he suddenly comes on to you when you're relaxing. I want to be able to turn my sexual desires on and off when I please, and to keep the switch off at home.'

'That's precisely what I think. I'm relieved to know I'm not the only one who's abnormal.'

And so from the start ours was a completely sexless and sex-free marriage, but somewhat inconveniently we both wanted children.

Before we married, we had searched the Internet and discovered a clinic that specialized in the needs of sexual minorities: homosexuals wanting children, asexuals seeking to conceive, people unable to afford artificial insemination or to find a doctor sympathetic to their situation.

'If you decide that you do want children,' the woman on the phone had said, 'please do come to see us. We will be happy to work with you.'

'Um, but we are an asexual couple . . .'

'Not a problem. We treat many such people here. We have couples coming to us with all kinds of unusual circumstances and tastes. Our service provides sex as a medical treatment for people like this.'

We didn't have a clue what 'sex as a medical treatment' meant, but felt reassured that there were options open to us.

Having finished his toast, my husband started playing a video game. I watched his progress as I dialled the clinic's number to make an appointment for a consultation.

The clinic was in a well-appointed white building in the exclusive Aoyama area.

The place oozed wealth. The waiting room was lined with plush, pale beige chairs, with relaxing music playing in the background. Besides ourselves there was a woman sitting alone, who eventually received some medication from the receptionist and left.

'Mr and Mrs Takahashi, please come through,' the receptionist then announced, and we were ushered in to meet a female doctor with short hair.

'You've made an appointment for our Clean Breeder, I see.'

'Excuse me?'

'Our Clean Breeder. As the name suggests, it is a means to facilitate, in the purest sense of the word, reproduction. The aim of sex as a medical treatment is not to provide pleasure.'

'Ah.'

The doctor glanced over our medical questionnaire and nodded several times. 'Yes, yes. I see. "Frequency of sex since marriage: zero." "Reason for interest in the Clean Breeder: we want a child." So that's your purpose for coming today, is that correct?'

'Well, we haven't decided . . . I mean, we don't know what the Clean Breeder is, or what it involves, so we'd like you to explain it to us, please,' my husband said.

The doctor nodded, crossing her legs. 'Well, if you look at our home page you'll find it's pretty well covered there, but I'll run through it again for you.

'These days, an increasing number of people experience psychological issues that prevent them from having sex with their partner. The person who suits your sexual orientation is not always the best partner to have a family with, and quite often the reverse is true. Not everyone is sexually aroused by the person with whom the usual conditions are right for them to start a family.

'For starters, the traditional way of thinking that a couple would have sex to conceive a child is outdated. It is not at all in tune with the times. Sex for pleasure and sex for pregnancy are two completely different concerns, and it's absurd to lump them together. It's out of sync with how people live their lives these days.' With this, the doctor handed each of us a pamphlet bearing the title 'The Clean Breeder and the New Family Image'.

'Sexual orientation is becoming much more diverse,' she went on. 'Is a man attracted to young girls going to get an erection with his thirty-five-year-old wife? Can a woman who only gets aroused by two-dimensional men have sex with a living three-dimensional man without pain? Nowadays, your partner is not necessarily a sex object – this is a wonderful advancement. It means you can choose to have a family by rational means, thinking with your head, not with your loins. Couples who come to us can avail themselves of our experts and leave their superior genes to posterity by means of the Clean Breeder, our pure facilitator of reproduction . . .'

As the doctor droned on, I leafed through the pamphlet. It contained an endless array of phrases like 'couples for the new age' and 'a graceful, non-erotic experience with our state-of-the-art technology'.

'According to the questionnaire here, you made the decision to keep sex and marriage separate even before tying the knot. That's wonderful. It's precisely what we mean by a state-of-the-art marriage.'

'Oh, it's not all that special.' I really didn't like women like her,

I thought uncomfortably, and glanced at my husband. He looked bored and was focusing on the ballpoint pen the doctor was twirling in her fingers.

'Our Clean Breeder advanced medical treatment is exactly right for couples like you. It is not covered by national insurance, however, and the fee is 9,500 yen per treatment. Mrs Takahashi, we will ask you to track your basal body temperature, and we'll carry out the treatment during ovulation. If after several tries you fail to conceive, we suggest infertility counselling. You are still young, and I'm sure that if you keep trying the Clean Breeder you can expect to conceive without infertility treatment. But if you'd like, you can undergo a fertility test before starting.'

'That's pretty damn expensive!' blurted out my husband under his breath.

The doctor beamed at him. 'We're using cutting-edge treatment, Mr Takahashi. Even in Japan very few hospitals have it available, and it's difficult for us to keep up with demand. Just yesterday a couple who came all the way from Tottori told me how so very impressed they were by it. When would you like to make your first appointment? You can try it out now, if you like – in which case you can choose the music you'd like to have playing during the procedure. The normal practice is to make an appointment when your body temperature indicates ovulation, but conception is also possible on other days –'

'We're here just for the consultation today,' I interjected before things could go any further. 'I'll talk it over with my husband.'

The doctor nodded, smiling. 'Of course, please take your time to discuss things. But please bear in mind that the Clean Breeder is extremely popular and an appointment may not be available on your day of ovulation. Things are relatively quiet now, so I suggest you make your decision sooner rather than later.'

'I understand. We'll talk it over and call back.'

My husband stood up, irritation on his face. I quickly followed him out of the consulting room.

We were unfamiliar with the Aoyama area, so upon leaving the clinic we walked towards Omotesandō and went into the first cafe we came across.

'What do you want to do?' I asked my husband as he drank his *café au lait*.

'There's something fishy about the whole affair, isn't there?' he replied, frowning. 'The Clean Breeder treatment – it can't be artificial insemination, and that must mean we do it ourselves?'

'I guess so,' I sighed, stroking my teacup with my index finger. 'So, what shall we do?'

'What do you mean?'

'Our child . . . Shall we do it ourselves? The two of us, at home?' Even before I'd finished talking, a wave of revulsion washed over me. Without raising my head, I leaned back in my chair to put more distance between us.

'I . . . *er* . . . I don't . . .'

Apparently my husband felt the same way, and as I looked down, I saw his feet hurriedly pulled back under the table and out of view.

Reassured by this evidence of shared revulsion, I looked up and saw him scowling.

'Artificial insemination would be harder,' he said, 'but perhaps we should try it. Asexual couples use it, so there must be some understanding doctors out there. If we're talking about 9,500 yen anyway, we should consider this option.'

'I suppose so.'

Relieved, he finally raised his eyes from his coffee and looked out the window. There was a woman walking her dog, harried office workers checking their watches and youngsters fiddling with their mobiles. How many of them, I wondered idly, were the result of sperm ejaculated during sex between people who loved each other? Had they been conceived spontaneously, without any thought of ovulation days? Or by artificial insemination? Or even rape? Whatever the circumstances of their conception, the sperm had reached the egg, and the fertilized egg swelled into a human form.

I looked under the table again. My husband's feet were still out of sight.

I was in the ladies' room at work, brushing my teeth after lunch, when my mobile rang.

The call was from a number I didn't know. I hesitated for a moment, then answered.

'Are you Mizuki Takahashi?' It was a woman's voice.

'Who is this?' I asked, a bit irritated by her forthright manner.

'I'm a friend of Nobuhiro's,' she answered.

'Ah. You're his lover, aren't you?' I said stupidly.

My husband and I kept sex out of our marriage, but that didn't mean we didn't feel sexual desire. We were free to enjoy sex elsewhere. We were like an adolescent brother and sister, having secret sex partners while behaving like we didn't understand the meaning of the word. To outsiders, our sexual relationships might seem like infidelity, but from our point of view it was perfectly natural. Until two months ago I too had had a lover, someone I'd met on Facebook, but we'd grown tired of each other and split up.

It turned out that my husband had used the prospect of us having a baby to break up with this woman. I first thought he was being overly serious, given that I was simply the owner of the egg to be fertilized and he could spread his seed as much as he liked, but when the woman became hysterical on the phone, I realized he might be using me as an excuse to get away from her.

'Are you going to sue me?' the woman screeched. 'Go ahead – you'll be the laughing stock, not me.'

'No, I'm not going to sue you. I'm not going to leave him either. Listen, can't you talk it over with him directly? Your relationship has got nothing to do with me.'

The more unconcerned I sounded, the angrier she became.

'You don't have sex together, right? What kind of a woman are you? I always satisfy him, and we love each other.'

'Of course you do – you're his lover, after all. We're family, so we don't have sex. Look, my lunch break is over, I can't talk.'

'It's because you can't give him the type of sex he wants. He can't get it up with you!'

'That's right. That's why we're family.'

I hung up and blocked her number.

'Mizuki, what's up?' As my husband came out of the bath, he found me sitting on the sofa, mobile in hand. 'You're always checking that phone lately.'

'Mmm, I've been getting a lot of spam. Maybe I should change my email address.'

'You can adjust your settings, you know, and stop things like that. You really are hopeless when it comes to anything technical.'

The emails were from my husband's lover. She must have found my address on his phone and she was sending me daily emails. At first I thought of blocking her email address too, but then, surprisingly, I'd found myself intrigued. She was sending me photos of them having sex.

It felt a bit like walking in on my little brother masturbating. The photos were embarrassingly graphic. It seemed my husband was into age play – acting the baby and sucking at her breast or having his nappy changed. He was apparently so turned on that his erection was plainly evident even beneath his nappy. It was the first time I'd seen even that much of his penis.

The photos were accompanied by messages such as 'Only I can be his mama', or 'He fondles my butthole and begs me to do the same to him', or 'You are such a loser of a woman' – all of which made me think that her brain was addled by lust and love.

The pictures of my husband on hands and knees with a dummy in his mouth and wearing a drool bib were fascinating. But I was seriously glad I wasn't his sex partner.

'Umm . . . ' I started.

My husband was towelling his hair and watching TV, but turned to look at me. 'Um what?'

'I've been thinking about things. Shall we give it a try?'

'Give what a try?'

'That clinic. After all, artificial insemination will probably be even more expensive, and it won't be easy to find a doctor who understands our situation. With the clinic we won't have to worry about that at least, and we won't have to pay for a medical exam either. Also, it seems that the process is close to natural sex, which will be easier on my body.'

'Really? Well, I don't know anything about the physical burden for a woman, so I'll take your word for it.' He looked rather uncomfortable, but apparently hadn't taken so great a dislike to the female doctor as to dismiss my proposal out of hand.

'Actually, since that consultation I've been tracking my temperature. Shall we make an appointment for my next ovulation day? Just to see how things go.'

'All right. If I can get the day off, let's go,' he said, nodding distractedly and turning back to the TV. Playing on the screen were scenes of some distant foreign country, accompanied by the strains of a violin.

M y next ovulation day was luckily on a Saturday. We headed to the clinic together.

'We'd like to undergo the treatment,' I said, bowing to the nurse who came out to greet us. My husband hastily followed suit.

'Please take off your clothes and change into these,' the nurse said, handing each of us a white gown. 'Remove all your underwear. You can put your valuables in the locker. Once you're ready, please let me know.'

We went into our separate cubicles, pulled the curtains and got changed. The women's gown, with long sleeves and a long skirt, left surprisingly little uncovered. I actually thought the gown would get in the way, but I didn't say anything.

'Well, then, Mr Takahashi, please come this way,' a nurse was saying.

When I opened the curtain, I saw my husband wearing a gown similar to mine. He seemed uncomfortable with the skirt and evidently found it hard to relax, and as we followed the nurse into the room, he protected his private parts with his hands. The room was windowless and white, furnished only with two large white reclining chairs, larger than dentist chairs, that faced each other. Two nurses wearing surgical masks were standing beside them. The scent of lavender oil choked the air as classical music played in the background.

'Please lie down on this chair.'

My husband was guided to the chair farther away. The backrest was almost horizontal, so that he looked as though he was lying on a bed.

'Mrs Takahashi, over here, please.'

I sat down on the white chair facing my husband, as indicated. It felt soft, and was a little higher than his chair.

'Place your legs here.'

As instructed, I placed my legs on the rests on either side of the chair, which forced them wide apart as if for a gynaecological examination. Thanks to the long gown, I felt no embarrassment.

'Now, Mr Takahashi will produce the sperm.'

At some point the nurse who brought us to the room had also put on a surgical mask. All three nurses slipped on thin surgical gloves as if they were about to start an operation, and, nodding, they reached under my husband's long gown. They appeared to be touching his penis in time with the music.

'Is it OK like this, Mr Takahashi? Please do your best.'

My husband had taken off his glasses and his eyes were tightly shut as he submitted to the nurses, his face ashen. Eventually one nurse proclaimed solemnly, 'The life flow has entered your husband's body.'

I had just realized what that meant when she came over to me and said, 'Now, Mrs Takahashi, we shall apply this.'

The nurse's gloved hand came under my gown and up between my spreadeagled legs, and she applied some kind of jelly that smelled of herbs around my vagina. I flinched at the cold, but it didn't feel any different from a gynaecological examination and it wasn't unpleasant.

'Now we shall prepare to connect the life flow with the egg,' the nurse announced, and produced a silver tube with what looked to be an electric cord attached to one end. From a brief glance, the tube appeared to contain a jelly-like substance, and I assumed it was something like a masturbation device.

With the practised moves of a medical operation, the nurse lifted my husband's gown and slipped his penis into the device.

'Mr Takahashi, please tell us when life is issuing. Raise your hand! Do you understand?'

My husband nodded wordlessly. He was tightly gripping the hem of his gown, his face growing paler.

'Mr Takahashi, your life flow is being facilitated by electromagnetic waves. Do you understand?' the nurse explained, although from what I could see of her hand movements, it was she who was doing the facilitating, moving the silver tube over his penis up and down. Nevertheless, the tube appeared to be well made, and upon closer inspection I could make out CLEAN BREEDER engraved on it. The cord swung about as the nurse carried on, absorbed in her work. Some of the cold jelly-like substance in it flew out and landed on my leg.

'It's the latest model, Mr Takahashi. I'm afraid it's a bit cold, but please put up with it. You're almost there!'

My husband was sweating profusely and letting out the occasional groan as if his sperm was being sucked out of him by force.

'Mr Takahashi, give it all you've got!'

'It'll be any moment now! The life flow is welling up!'

'Mrs Takahashi, a little closer, please. Hold his hand, yes, like that.'

Bewildered, I leaned forward and gripped the hand my husband held out feebly.

'One last little push, Mr Takahashi!' cried the nurse, pumping his penis with the machine.

'You're almost there, love!' I said, adding my voice to the chorus, at which moment he raised his left hand shakily.

'The life flow is being ejected!' the nurse shouted, and suddenly the backrest on my chair slammed down and the chair began to move.

I was left looking at the ceiling and couldn't see what was going on. It was all happening so fast. I felt cut off from reality, almost as if I were in a video. I gathered that I was being propelled toward my husband, my legs still splayed apart. When the chair came to a stop, something was inserted into my vagina, as if being plugged in. I had a vague sense that it was my husband's penis entering me, still cold from the jelly, but it felt more like a machine transmitting his sperm.

'Ejection has occurred!' A faint warm feeling spread through my loins. My husband had apparently managed to ejaculate.

'Well done, Mr Takahashi!'

'Congratulations, Mrs Takahashi.'

The nurses wiped us down with warm damp flannel cloths as we lay staring at the ceiling.

'Please use this,' said the nurse, handing me a sanitary towel. I slipped on my knickers and put the towel in place. The other nurses were congratulating my husband and wiping the sweat from his forehead. It really was just as if he had given birth, and I had accepted his progeny.

'Just in case, please be sure to wear a sanitary towel and avoid washing your genitals. If you must wash, please wait until you get home to take a short shower. That's all for today, Mrs Takahashi.'

I nodded, feeling it had all been pretty anticlimactic. It had evidently been tougher on my husband, who was breathing heavily and looked exhausted after having been forced to ejaculate despite his utter lack of arousal.

'Nine thousand five hundred yen for that! What a rip-off,' fumed my husband on the way home.

I suppressed a giggle. 'It really was awful, wasn't it? I didn't have to do anything sexual, though . . . Was it OK?'

'I've never in my whole life felt so violated! They did offer me Viagra – I should have taken them up on it.' Getting more and more agitated, he muttered, 'I couldn't tell any difference between entering you or entering that weird machine, and I still don't know if I came in that machine or in you.'

'But that's good, isn't it? That way, we managed to keep our marriage sexless.'

'Well, yeah, but . . .'

We stopped by a small park.

'Do you mind if I go to the toilet? I want to change the sanitary towel.'

'Uh, sure,' he said, nodding, and gave me an odd look, as if uncomfortable about the fact that it was his spunk seeping out of me.

I went into the public toilet in the park and took down my knickers to find my husband's semen all over the sanitary towel. It was like having a white period. I changed it for a fresh one, and went back outside. He was sitting on a bench, waiting.

'Hope I wasn't too long.'

'No, no. Everything OK?'

I sat down next to him, and said, 'I'm fine. A bit tired, though. Shall we have a little rest before going home?'

We sat for a while gazing at the park, which was full of children.

'Oh well, maybe it wasn't such a bad experience.'

'What? You were furious a moment ago.'

'Yeah, well, it's good that I haven't had any form of sexual contact with you. Because we haven't brought sex into our relationship,' he said softly, watching a little girl playing in the sandpit.

'If we manage to have a child, which would you rather have, a boy or girl?'

'A girl, I think. A boy would be fine too, but I can imagine really doting on a girl.'

'Yeah.'

His eyes half closed, he watched as the girl in the sandpit stood up and ran off.

'Mama!' the girl called out, and a young mother stood up, smiling.

He watched the mother stroke her daughter's head affectionately, and the little girl smiled and hugged her mother back. As he stared at them, beads of sweat appeared on his forehead and a look of sheer panic crossed his face.

'What's up?'

He didn't answer. Suddenly he clamped his hand over his mouth and squatted, retching. He hadn't eaten anything since morning, and was bringing up only gastric fluid. I gazed down at him as he crouched, riding out the nausea. It struck me this was just like morning sickness.

Mama, Mama-a-a! The little girl's innocent voice echoed around the park.

My husband's nausea welled up again, and his back started trembling. I reached out a hand to comfort him. At that very moment, I felt his semen gush from my vagina. ■

BREAKFAST

Toshiki Okada

TRANSLATED FROM THE JAPANESE BY MICHAEL EMMERICH

© SOHEI NISHINO
Detail from *Diorama Map, Tokyo*
2004

M y wife Arisa was on a plane bound for Tokyo, only I didn't know it because she hadn't told me, we hadn't seen each other in more than a year and her biggest reason for coming to Tokyo was to see me, talk things over, still, there you go, not a word. I know what she was thinking, she could get in touch after she arrived, whatever plans I might have, anything, I'd postpone it, sure I would, that's the kind of guy I am, if that's what it took to see her. And she was right, I went, past midnight, to her hotel in Shinjuku, to see her. And I'm not going to be annoyed, being on a string like that? She said she had only seventeen hours in Tokyo, though, had to be on a plane at noon tomorrow, so what choice did I have?

The plane had initiated its descent some time ago. She could see they were dropping lower and lower, because she had a window seat over the wings, and she was gazing out. The light was dusky. Night was easing down over Tokyo, but I was riding the subway, dozing, so that light, I hardly ever feel the light in Tokyo, that there is any beauty in the light, this was one of those rare occasions when I could have, only I wasn't there to see it. Faintly purple clouds spread beneath Arisa's gaze, covering the whole sky, breathtakingly flat, at least from up there, hardly a hill or a valley, making the most of a limited range of purples, different shades. And that made it easy, since the clouds covered everything, obscured the ground, for her to go on thinking as she always did, to feel she had been right, here was the proof, that's what she was thinking, that it was true, Tokyo had ceased to exist, all those clouds could dissolve into nothing right now and there would be no Tokyo below. She had made it a kind of habit to think this way, it was how she saw things, one day she'd told me, out of the blue, I can't do this any more, I can't keep living in a city just 250 kilometres from Fukushima as if nothing is wrong, I can't stay with all these people who have no problem with that, who just do it, live their lives, if I have to go on like this I'm going to lose my mind even before it starts physically wearing me down, and not long after that she told me she was leaving Tokyo, and she left, and so basically our marriage was over. As far as she was concerned, Tokyo was gone, but only because she had loved the city, living here, and because if none of this had happened she would still be living here, because it hurt to have to admit that Tokyo could never be home again, that was why, without fully knowing it, but half consciously, she had flicked a switch in her head, quietly substituted one thing for another, making it a matter of the city, of Tokyo's disappearance. Or maybe she had come to think, made herself believe, not only that the city was gone, but also that even if some shell had survived, it was populated by zombies – people neither wholly dead nor wholly alive.

So she couldn't help feeling jittery, now that Tokyo was so close. Something very peculiar was about to happen, after all, for her if for no one else, she had come to a non-existent city, and she would be spending time there, if only seventeen hours. She would have to confront the overblown reality of the place, people coming and going, people who took their coming and going for granted, in a city that should not be there. So she was feeling jittery. Could she, in the face of all that reality, still regard those people as zombies? No, that isn't quite right, I shouldn't say *those people*, I should say *us*, that was the question, could Arisa hold fast to her perception, for the seventeen hours she was in Tokyo, that *we* were zombies, did she have the perseverance, the stubbornness, the willpower to stick to that vision no matter what she saw, what she felt? She herself was confident that she could, it wouldn't be that hard, it was only seventeen hours, she could believe it. If I had known she were heading for Tokyo then, and if I had known she thought of Tokyo as a city of zombies, I would have wanted to know, of course, whether she saw me that way, too. Could she have made an exception for me?

As far as she was concerned, I suppose, I was a zombie.

The plane was skimming the blanket of clouds. Then it plunged into it. The body of the aircraft began to shudder, as Arisa half expected it would. Such shaking did not scare her in the least. There were three seats in her row, the middle one empty, the other seat occupied by a businessman. He stared directly ahead, superficially nonchalant, at the back of the seat in front of him, at the tray that flipped down to become a table during meals but was now fastened in place. Arisa could tell that the shaking unnerved him. She could see that he was struggling not to betray his fear. She did not feel superior to him, quite the opposite, she pitied herself for her fearlessness. The plane emerged from the clouds and finally Tokyo, an endless sprawl of man-made structures, covering everything, lay spread below. Artificial lights everywhere, on the ground, on high-rises. As night fell, their numbers would increase, more and more, they would thrive. The rivers of yellow headlights and red tail lights flowing against each other on all the roads and highways should have shown her that Tokyo was alive, functioning, its blood circulating, that it was breathing, even, its diaphragm rising and falling. But Arisa kept telling herself it wasn't true, the city might look the same from the sky, yes, but appearances deceive, Tokyo was but a shell, unlived-in rooms and deserted offices lit by fluorescent bulbs, cars controlled by computers, a city of zombies.

As the plane touched down with the soft shock of the landing, Arisa was gripped at last by a sort of resignation, a feeling stronger than anything before, the realization that she had actually arrived in Tokyo. She sat dazed, hollow, as the plane slowly rolled toward the gate. It jolted to a stop and suddenly all the passengers stood, the aircraft was filled with that familiar fidgety energy, like the moment before a marathon gets under way, but Arisa was in no rush to insinuate herself into Tokyo, she needed first to prepare herself, she had to put in her earphones – equipment that cancelled noise. She could not imagine hurling herself into Tokyo without earphones. So before coming she had selected a good pair, she needed them, at the very least, as protective gear. I would rather not have known that earphones served as protective gear for her. I would not have minded if she had just worn them without telling me about this, I was wearing my own now, on the subway – who doesn't wear earphones? The whole time, once the jet bridge was attached to the plane and the door had been opened, as passengers began filing slowly out from the front of the cabin, Arisa had her earphones plugged into her iPhone. She had lots of music, Japanese folk and rock from the 1970s. Much more than seventeen hours' worth, no worries on that account. Her ears, and by extension her entire being, protected by the music, she ventured into the airport. From here she would go downtown. She would text me a little later, she decided, to tell me she was in Tokyo. She would get in touch with me, meet with me, sit across from the real, living me and look at my face, gaze into my eyes, and we would confirm, once and for all, together, that our relationship had ended, this was what she wanted. Once she had done this, she would have no reason to come to Tokyo again, and for the rest of her life she probably never would.

The airport was filled with people, crowds of real, living people, they were not zombies, they sat on benches in the boarding area waiting for flights, their faces glowed blue-white as they peered at the screens of their laptops, they napped. They stopped walking and let the automatic walkway carry them along, or stepped to the side and hurried past the others. They ate curry rice and tempura udon, and drank beer from paper cups and green tea from plastic bottles. They reached out to each other with their cellphones. All these people were real, alive, of course they were, but seeing them here in front of her was like some half-baked nightmare. In part it was their overwhelming numbers, but even more, the thing that crept inside her, into her body and heart, that slowly drained the heat from her body and her mind, pulling her toward stillness, was something else, it was, above all, the flood of advertisements. Posters and billboards, the usual kinds of ads, there were plenty of those, but then there were the new varieties that caught her eye, messages in the form of words and photographs and drawings that had been pasted directly to the walls and floors and columns all over the airport, directly on the escalator handrails, ads like these, this was what oppressed her, because they were so much more cloying, so much hungrier than posters of the old type. Ads copywriters had wrung desperately from their weary brains, the products of a threadbare creativity. What's the point, Arisa asked herself, the people looking at them are all zombies anyway. And then there were the stores, places trying to sell food or drinks or souvenirs or medicine, anything, anything, scattered throughout the airport, the lights that shone in these places, special bulbs that created a mood, that entered her field of vision irrespective of her will, that made her remember, gradually, as the light washed over her, this feeling, yes, this is what it is like to be in Tokyo. This awareness of the particular spot in people's hearts that these ads are appealing to, aiming so carefully to hit, trying to worm their way into . . . yes, this is the feeling. You feel it in the airport because this is what Tokyo is, the city itself, and it comes in concentrated form here. Arisa had lived in Tokyo until recently so she knew this feeling, she could not have forgotten it, not even three years had passed since then, and that's short enough that you could call it recent.

Arisa realized she was feeling somewhat tired, it was from the travel, she could feel the exhaustion, whether it was physical or mental she could not tell, it was only twenty minutes after she had disembarked that she noticed it, while she was waiting on the underground platform for the train that connected the airport to downtown. The train glided in, the doors opened, an announcement going on about this and that, she didn't understand what it was saying because she had her music turned up and she felt no inclination to pay any attention. She stepped jerkily into the train, sucked in by a sort of gravity, it seemed, and lowered herself into a spot at the end of the seven-seat bench, resting the full weight of her body against the railing. She positioned her small suitcase at her feet, her arms went limp, she was tempted to go straight to her hotel in Shinjuku, a high-rise hotel known for its magnificent night-time views, check in, stretch out on the bed, only that would defeat the purpose of this trip, she hadn't come to relax. She had come to do what needed to be done, to see me, that is to say, to talk things over. Not that talking would do much, we already knew how it would end, we could not go back to our old life together. Arisa had come to Tokyo to perform a sort of ritual. A necessary ritual, though perhaps no ritual is unnecessary, it must be done because that is what a ritual is. She would remain in Tokyo only seventeen hours, she could get by that long without sleeping, she could sleep as much as she wanted after she left. She decided to ring me before the train started moving. So she paused the music for a moment, interrupted the stream of sound entering her ears, but I had fallen into a light sleep, I didn't realize she had called until a few minutes later. It has been my habit, for a few years now, as soon as I awake, to grope for my phone in my jacket pocket, pull it out, stare at the screen. I had a message from a number I didn't recognize, I didn't know when she had changed numbers but now this was hers, she had left a message, it was her, her voice. Right before the train doors slid shut, she had said into her phone, Uh, hi, it's me, I know this is totally out of the blue but actually I'm in Tokyo right now, and I'm hoping maybe we could get together, actually I'm leaving again tomorrow, around lunchtime actually, so I was hoping I could see you before then, before I go, and she almost laughed as she pictured me, how startled I would be to hear this message, coming out of nowhere. But she mustn't laugh, if I heard her laughing in the recording I might think she was kidding around, toying with me, that it was a sort of prank call. I was stunned by her message, as stunned as she had expected, no doubt. The music on Arisa's phone was still on pause because I called back soon enough. But by then the train was moving, she couldn't pick up, it would have been rude, on a train in Tokyo. Though I was on the subway myself, and I was phoning her, I didn't care. I heard her phone ringing, I don't know how many times, then the voice asking me to leave a message, so I gave up, hung up. Ten seconds later, the music frozen in her iPhone, Japanese rock performed and recorded more than thirty years earlier, started up where it had left off. I would call again, she knew.

Somehow it felt wrong to Arisa to get together with me so soon, when she had just arrived in Tokyo. Or even to make plans, figure out when and where to meet. She was glad I hadn't answered when she rang. She wanted time, half an hour, to wander around on her own. Or rather, she didn't really want to walk but it seemed like the right thing to do, it was not a desire welling up from within but a sense of necessity, almost an obligation. And besides she'd had an idea, she would get off at Shinbashi, the train would be stopping there, and it was one of those typical areas of Tokyo, Shinbashi. She wanted to walk around someplace like that, typical Tokyo, like a foreign tourist visiting for the first or maybe second time, because she would probably never have another chance to do this. To see the people living here, real live Tokyoites, not zombies at all, and burn the memory into her mind. As long as she blocked out the sounds with her music, she could endure it. When the train was still seven minutes away from Shinbashi she got another call from me, but she didn't answer this time either.

The first thing Arisa did after stepping out onto the platform was crank up the music, the second was click up the handle on her rolling suitcase. Shinbashi was not crowded, not enough to make dragging a suitcase more than a pain. But all along the main street, and even the side streets, any number, yes, there were enough that you could say that, any number of electric lights were shining, even now. Points of light forming bits of words, bits of logos, bits of shining background, all this illumination, even now, here in Tokyo. And yet somehow it was entirely different, utterly unlike before, when she had lived here, when she had inhabited this city without thinking anything of it, there seemed to be just slightly less light than before, maybe, she thought, people were trying to keep their energy consumption down, or maybe not, maybe it only seemed that way because she herself had changed. A woman in a skintight black dress that traced the curves of her back and her large ass stood outside a building, her legs terminating in high heels. A parking attendant perched on a pipe chair outside an elevator parking garage, legs crossed, smoking, eyeing the woman in the dress, who had to be a professional. An ashtray on a stand beside him. Behind him a garage-like space with two turntables on the floor, each large enough to contain a single car, behind each an electric door that would deliver the car onto a carousel so it could be lifted up into the building, until the carousel stopped and the car was parked. The turntables were level with the floor but detached from it, they revolved on their own, this took electricity, these turntables that rotated the cars to face the doors before they entered, to rotate them back to face the street when they came out. Arisa wanted to believe that everything before her came as a set, to think these people were actors, each playing a role, she wondered to what extent this feeling had to do with the music coursing into her through her earphones. Just then her stomach growled. She didn't hear the sound, but she felt it. She had made up her mind to do nothing about her hunger, to ignore it, she would eat nothing in Tokyo. Only I didn't know that, so when I finally got through to her, and was heading for Shinjuku, which was past midnight, I assumed we would get something to eat, go out for a drink, we were married, after all, and we hadn't seen each other for more than a year. I had interrupted her music again when I called this time, although an iPhone doesn't rudely cut off the music, it executes a gentle fade-out, it's over in an instant, it happens just like that, but still that is what happens, and then she hears the ringing. They value that kind of smooth flow, and so, even if it only lasts a second, I have to wait an extra second, but maybe this time it was worth it, because at last she picked up, and we were talking. Where in Tokyo are you? I asked, and she said Shinjuku, why did she tell that lie? There was no reason, it seemed like a pain to explain that she was in Shinbashi, and anyway she was on her way to Shinjuku. I had to go back to the office, I had work due that day that would take about an hour, but after that, around nine, I would be free. I told Arisa this, and she said she was busy until just after eleven. I couldn't imagine what she might have to do, or rather I knew she had nothing to do, but I let her have her way.

Arisa caught a cab. She couldn't bear riding in another train, she couldn't bear the thought, she didn't care how many thousands of yen it cost, she would spend the money, and she needed the music flowing through her earphones in order to endure. The taxi passed Hibiya Park, drove along the moat around the Imperial Palace, passed through Sakuradamon, Miyakezaka. The ads on the train had been more than she could stand, the flyer for a manga dangling from the ceiling the worst, that girl in her teens, still a child, her breasts pushed up and spilling out of the bikini they'd put her in. Yes, Tokyo was just as Arisa had expected, it conformed so perfectly to her expectations that it was startling, really, nothing was any different. Still, being here wasn't as bad as it could have been, because at least the music kept the city out of her ears. What if she hadn't taken this small protective measure, the sounds, too, would be the same, overhearing a conversation on the train would have brought on an even harsher sadness, the realization, resigned, deep, how little Tokyo had changed, that the will to change had not been widely enough shared to matter. All of a sudden Arisa remembers that she must be sure to charge her iPhone at the hotel. Having more than enough music to fill the space would be useless if the battery died. A moment ago, when she got in the taxi and told the driver the name of her hotel, she had removed one earphone, but they were both in again, even here inside the car. The music made her nostalgic for the city, folk songs three or four decades old, those voices, those guitars, those drums, moving through the city with these sounds, waiting for the lights to change, getting caught up again in slow traffic and then darting over to another lane, it tore at her chest, the nostalgia toyed with her. They went left at Hanzōmon, they were going down Shinjuku Dōri now, no longer skirting the palace, Yotsuya was coming up, as they passed the intersection by the station the nostalgia intensified. An awareness of how impossible it was for her to visit Tokyo without marking out the beginning and end of her stay, anger at the circumstances that made her feel this way, a wrenching sense of guilt toward Tokyo and all the people who lived here, this tangle of emotions bore down on her relentlessly, crushing her. She felt a helpless fury at how it crushed her, but she was not the one who had caused it. It wasn't my fault, either. Arisa had to be careful, otherwise she might tell me how guilty she felt. Please, please don't tell me, find someone else to confess to, hold in those emotions these seventeen hours and then go tell someone else, anyone else, outside Tokyo. Do not allow me to see that you feel that way, not for a moment, just talk with me about what we must talk about, pile on no more extra troubles, and then if you must go, go, that is all I ask, losing Arisa was devastating enough, it would take time to get over it, ups and downs over and over again. Now the taxi was passing another park, Shinjuku Gyoen. She had the music turned up so loud the driver could hear snatches of it coming out of her earphones. On the back of the driver's seat, hung so that the passengers could see, was a picture of the driver with his name, Mr Kazama, she read, that was his name, it didn't say how old he was but he was fifty-five, Mr Kazama could tell from the faint snatches of music he heard that this woman in her early thirties was listening to songs he himself knew well, and from time to time he found himself glancing at her in the mirror, couldn't help it, because old songs like that, it was kind of unexpected for her to listen to that kind of stuff, Arisa paid no attention, instead thinking I'm going to have a shower first thing, soon as I get to the hotel, before I look at the scenery, and after that I'll look outside, I wonder if my room will look out on one of the parks we passed, Hibiya Park or Shinjuku Gyoen or the enormous grounds of the palace? Of course, even if I can see one of the parks, all it will be is a strange blank in the city's glittering landscape, a black emptiness in the middle of all Tokyo's glittering.

Why would Arisa want to stay in a hotel, and *that* hotel, I hardly knew what to think when she said it, why would she choose such a lavish place, unless she meant it as some kind of subtle dig at me? Part of me was able to consider things objectively, though, and that part understood that she had come to Tokyo and gotten a hotel room because the apartment where I lived, where she herself had once lived, where I was still living now, I had taken out a loan and bought it the year before the earthquake, was out of the question, she had never for a moment considered coming to see me there and certainly wouldn't spend the night, it was only natural, and that was the smart thing to do, for both of us.

There was no way I was going to take a taxi from my office in Roppongi to the hotel where Arisa was staying, because I wasn't like her, for me this was the same Tokyo as always, an ordinary day almost indistinguishable from any other, so I took the Ōedo line, which ran deep below the earth. Riding the subway, I found myself wanting to shout at her, I pictured myself doing it, What, you think you'll be safe from the radiation if you stay shut up in this fancy hotel? Give me a fucking break! I'm shouting so loud, my voice booming, that no one around us in the hotel lobby can help glancing over. But I knew there was no point, none, and that wasn't what I really wanted to say. I called her when I left Tochōmae Station, as I was passing Shinjuku Chūō Park, I'll be at the hotel soon, I told her, and she said OK, I'll go downstairs in just a bit. Have you eaten? I asked. She hummed a no. Are you hungry? I asked. No, I'm OK, I don't need anything. Meaning she wasn't going to eat while she was in Tokyo, I could have guessed that much, I had already guessed as much, but I asked anyway.

She'd said she'd be down soon, so I expected her to show up in a minute or two, even though I should have known she wasn't that kind of person, I couldn't help getting my hopes up, but by the time her elevator finally descended to the ground floor and slid open and she stepped out, Arisa and not someone else, ten minutes had gone by. She didn't have her earphones in then, she had left her iPhone in the room, plugged into the outlet on the desk. She looked thinner than the Arisa I had known, but I couldn't tell whether she had lost a healthy or an unhealthy amount of weight, or rather I didn't want to be able to tell the difference.

I hated myself then, I did, for being unable to recognize that there was zero chance that Arisa might invite me up to her room, how much easier it would have been if I could have cut that part of me right out. Sitting in this insistently luxurious hotel, on a comfortable sofa in the lobby, was no consolation, pure comedy, and I was just as ludicrous myself as I started a fumbling conversation, but I had no choice, even I was long past the age where I wanted to run away. The discussion we had to have was had, just like that, no differences of opinion stood in the way, and we were equally eager to get it over with. What separated us was our attitude toward Tokyo, the fact that hers had changed so drastically that day.

My apartment, mine, not ours any more, was within the city, so there was no need to keep an eye on the clock, to make sure I could still get home, but I had no reason to linger. All I had to do was find a good moment to end the conversation and I could stand up, leave. But then it came, almost right away, from somewhere in the space between us, that rumbling, I knew immediately what it was, and that it had come not from me but from her, there was no mistaking that. For a moment after we heard the sound neither of us reacted, but then it was too much for Arisa, a puff of laughter escaped from her lips, and she started laughing so hard, so loud that everyone around us, that's an exaggeration, some of the people around us couldn't help glancing over. I laughed too, and then we both stood up. Arisa went back up to her room in the hotel, I went back to my apartment, stopping in at the 7-Eleven next door to my building for a package of microwaveable pasta and a beer. The next morning, not that early, Arisa checked out of the hotel, took a shuttle to the airport. Sometime, somewhere, maybe on the plane, maybe after the plane had reached wherever it was bound for, Arisa would get something to eat, but that was no longer any concern of mine. ■

VARIATIONS ON A THEME BY MISTER DONUT

David Mitchell

1

Well, if this is a Mister Donut, then in my opinion, Mister Donut is a disgrace. Where's the service? When I was at the company, the department head used to take his inner circle to a coffee shop by the main gate every Friday. Now the master of that place, he remembered our names, our ranks and what coffees we like. There were rumours he was Korean, but they were nonsense. His manners were impeccable. He didn't leave you sitting in the corner all day like that girl behind the counter. The older man – surely not her boss? – looks around the place, looks straight through me . . . and vanishes into the back! An utter disgrace.

I ask my wife, 'What's the time now?'

My wife shows me her empty wrists.

'How many times do I have to tell you to wear your watch when you leave the house?' I look at the Seiko presented to me by the president of the company himself. I started at Iwakura Engineering two summers after the war. A few beers, a few women, one marriage and a short time later, it was my retirement party. My Seiko says it's 21.45, so it's 21.45. The idiot with the earring at the place where I'm living until something more permanent comes up, the 'warden', he offered to 'keep' my watch in the office safe, but I wasn't born yesterday. It stays on my wrist. I don't trust any of the residents, either. There are two other men and three women. They range from mildly gaga to mad as a tree of screaming pink-arsed monkeys. What sort of warden wears an earring? I tell him, 'Shouldn't you be working in a queer bar with a dog collar round your neck?' Instead of answering

me like a man, he just says, 'That's not very friendly, Kaneda-san.'
He left the keys on the table when he went to answer the phone.
Why thank you, 'Warden', I'll borrow these. Outside, it was evening.
Plenty of commuters about. I joined them. The lights flashed and
I got brushed by a, a, a thing, with wheels.

I didn't rush, I didn't look back, the sky was inky.

My feet got sore. It got harder to breathe.

People rushed past me, jostling, running . . .

Did I, too, go at that speed, once upon a time?

My wife tells me the warden will be worried.

'When I want your opinion, I'll ask for it.'

Well, if this is a Mister Donut, it's a disgrace. That waitress isn't only bone idle – she's deliberately ignoring me. The other two customers are both women and they've both got their orders, even though they arrived after I sat down. The Kyoto man in the room next to mine, at that place, he said, 'If you want to become the Invisible Man, just live to be eighty.' The Kyoto man wasn't a total idiot, even if he did come from Kyoto. We played go, until the board started going wrong. We talked. The others just jabber about the old days and moan about the food. It's true about going invisible. Waitresses, pedestrians, drivers: they look straight through you. I want to tell them, 'Your turn'll come. You just wait.'

'In one minute' – I check my Seiko – 'I'm kicking up a stink.'

My wife makes a face to say, *Oh I do wish you wouldn't.*

'This place is an utter disgrace. I'm not standing for it.'

An American walks in. They were supposed to leave with MacArthur in 1953, but so far as I can see, they're still everywhere. Black ones, even. When I worked at Iwakura Engineering, I used to walk across the park from my bus stop to the downtown office. Sometimes earnest young men would ask me to sign a petition to 'protect the Peace Constitution'. I'd tell them right out: that so-called Peace Constitution is an American document, forced on us by Americans, so we stay dependent upon Americans. They had earrings too, those petitioners, those idiot queers. They'd say, 'But don't you want peace?' And I'd say, 'Who doesn't want peace? The question you ought to be asking is, "Whose peace?" Your peace? Kim Il-sung's peace? Deng Xiaoping's peace? Shoko Asahara's peace?' I turn to my wife and I tell her, 'If you're not prepared for war, you can't control the peace!'

She gives me a look like I'm talking too loud. I don't care. The next generation needs to know this stuff. They're not taught modern history. They walk around with wires trailing out of their ears, staring goggle-eyed at their phones, like that woman by the window. Who's looking after her children while she's sat here? Disgraceful.

My own sons don't even visit me. Well, one can't. 'That was your fault,' I tell my wife. 'I raised him to be strong and gutsy, the same way my father raised me, but you had to mollycoddle him, and undermine my authority.' After the funeral, Japan Railways came after us for two million yen for 'disruption to the schedule'. Bastards. Bastards. My idiot lawyer could only get it halved, so that was three years' bonuses down the drain.

Now my wife's about to cry.

'Why must you *always* make a spectacle of yourself, woman?'

M y Seiko says the girl's time is up. I go to the counter. She has the cheek to smile and ask, 'Would you like to order now, sir?'

'No. I want to know why you've been ignoring us.'

The smile fades. 'Sir, I wasn't ignoring you, I was –'

'My wife and I have been waiting hours.'

Now she acts confused. 'Sir, you haven't been here that long –'

'You served those two' – I point to the dolly bird in her fancy clothes at the window, then at the frumpy woman at the table next to me, who has scuttled away, I see – 'who came in after I did. And then, then, then you served that one.' I glare at the American who's acting all studious with his book and his pen. He doesn't fool me. I'm old enough to remember them swanning around our country as if they owned it, throwing sweets at malnourished orphans – as if that made up for incinerating their parents. I was there. I saw. Them and their sluts.

'Sir,' says the waitress, who actually meets my eye instead of looking away embarrassed – it wouldn't surprise me if she's Korean or even *buraku* – 'Mister Donut is actually a self-service cafe. But to make up for the confusion, I'd be happy to give you a coffee –'

My shout's a bit croaky: 'I wouldn't *spit* in your coffee!'

Now the whole place is watching. Suddenly it's full.

An idiotic pop song about donuts won't – shut – up.

My wife is saying we should leave now, let's just go.

'Will you *all'* – I despise them – 'stop inter*rupt*ing me?'

2

My watch says 21.45. Good, a few more minutes. The elderly gentleman at the next table is mumbling to himself. He's too well tended to be homeless, but I suspect he's gone walkabout. Somewhere, a relative or nurse will be going frantic. There are some sheltered housing units between the railway and the river. Maybe he's wandered up from there. I ought to do something. It's easier to say 'it's none of my business and I'm too tired to bother', but nursing is all about being bothered.

I yawn, enormously. Quite a day. Four deaths, four loads of paperwork; the staff assessments; a department meeting; and the computer system crashed.

Sasaki-san's manning the counter tonight. A daughter like her would have been lovely, if we'd been able to have children. She's one of the few who smiles like she means it. She works here full time, so she can't be attending college, not like the other one. Every April, when a fresh batch of trainee nurses start at the hospital, I know within a day who'll excel, who'll muddle through and who'll fall by the wayside. Young women like Sasaki-san are the right sort. It's the way she keeps the tables spotless, or chases after customers who leave umbrellas behind. Little things that speak of the big things.

Her future's none of my business, but I'd like to ask her if she's ever considered nursing. The nurse who looked after my father planted that same seed in my mind when I was Sasaki-san's age, and that's the only reason I have my career now. Nursing is messy and demanding, of course, and it's the male doctors and surgeons who get the glory and the packets of cash from scared relatives before surgery. But it's us nurses who keep hospitals running. If it's your vocation, it's a great job. A noble job. It matters.

Fujiwara-san was one of the four who passed away on today's shift. She lived alone on a widow's pension, and hobbled into A & E one morning last month after the pain of going to the toilet had become too great. Bowel cancer. It had spread everywhere, treatment was pointless and she was admitted into Palliative Care that afternoon. Aoko-sensei prescribed morphine-based painkillers and gave her a prognosis of six weeks. She reacted calmly, as if a mechanic was describing a broken-down car – until her eyes opened wide in panic and she clutched my sleeve: 'Who'll take care of Ai-chan?' I asked if Ai-chan was a relative. 'My budgie,' said Fujiwara-san. I suggested someone in her family could take Ai-chan in, but it turned out there was no family. No children, her father died years ago, and her ninety-five-year-old mother had Alzheimer's and was dying in a care home in Sendai. A cousin in Kagoshima was eventually located, but there had been no contact for years, and the cousin declared that 'now isn't a convenient time'. Fujiwara-san wasn't upset about the cousin, but it was clear that the idea of Ai-chan starving in her cage would destroy any hopes of a peaceful end to her life. So that evening, after work, I went with a trainee to rescue the bird. We could hardly bring a budgie into a hospital, so Ai-chan now lives with me and my husband. She has a view of our little garden. Every morning, while I ate breakfast, I'd record a few minutes of Ai-chan on an old phone of my nephew's. Fujiwara-san replayed it over and over, all day long. She lasted three weeks in Palliative Care, not six. A junior nurse caught me as I left this afternoon's meeting and told me Fujiwara-san was waiting for me, so I went straight there. My nephew's phone was propped up on her bed tray, so she could watch the budgie from her pillow. No doctor was around, or needed. Doctors tend to avoid dying people, I've noticed. The room filled with the musky smell of a person in their final minutes. I put my hand over Fujiwara-san's, and we watched Ai-chan trilling away, while my husband clattered about the kitchen at seven this morning, frying eggs for us both.

Fujiwara-san slipped away and I noted the time of death.

The fashion at nursing college nowadays is to hammer into trainees the notion that forming friendships with patients is unprofessional, and puts you at risk of 'continuous bereavement syndrome'. I disagree. It's bad enough that most of our old people spend their last years feeling shut out and ignored – why must they spend their last days, hours and minutes lonely too? Would you rather be nursed by a professionally aloof robot or by another human being who'll miss you when you die, remember you from time to time and take care of your budgie?

I'd like to tell Sasaki-san this: nursing is a way of living.

The elderly gentleman on the neighbouring table snarls at empty air. 'If you're not prepared for war, you can't control the peace!' Bang on cue, a young man in a uniform walks past the cafe. He's not a policeman, but maybe he'll do. Grabbing my bag, I hurry out of Mister Donut and catch him up. The words 'Station Ranger' are emblazoned on his hat. He mumbles into his phone, 'Gotta go,' and asks me, 'Yes?'

'Excuse me, but what does a Station Ranger do?'

He looks very young indeed. 'Help police if there's an emergency . . . Tell people where the toilets are . . . Pick up lost property . . . Help blind people, people in wheelchairs . . . Why?'

A job creation scheme, then. 'Do you help confused old people?'

The young man looks dubious. 'Ye-es. Possibly.'

'Perfect. Follow me. There's a job for you.'

I re-enter Mister Donut not a moment too soon: the old man's at the counter haranguing poor Sasaki-san: 'I wouldn't *spit* in your coffee!'

Sasaki-san swallows nervously. Her manager reappears.

'Will you *all*,' the old man snaps, 'stop inter*rupt*ing me?'

'Certainly, sir,' I say. 'How about we sit down and go through your complaints point by point with my colleague?' I step aside to reveal the Station Ranger. 'Then we can address your grievances promptly, and file a full report with the company president.'

He peers at me. This might work. If we can get his name, the Station Ranger can contact the police and we'll see if he's been reported as missing. Unfortunately, something catches his eye: the young woman by the window has had the bad taste to start filming us all. He shouts, lunges and swings his metal stick at her. The phone rockets through the air. The young woman shrieks and clutches her hand, unable to believe that such a thing could be happening to her. She tries to get off her stool, but her high heel catches in its footrest, and over she topples, slamming into the floor.

3

I check the time – 21.45 – and pour myself another coffee. 'I'm just going to grab a breath of air on the veranda,' I tell Sasaki, but she's gazing into the distance, even though the place is too tiny to have any distance to gaze at. 'Sasaki? You OK? Do you want to sit down? Are you feeling dizzy?'

She comes to, as if a hypnotist has clicked his fingers. 'No, I'm fine, thanks. I just thought I had a migraine coming on.'

Huh? 'So . . . Have you a migraine, or not?'

A customer comes in and Sasaki issues a cheerful '*Irasshaimase!*' I do a quieter echo. She tells me, 'I might take a painkiller later, but I'm fine.'

I sense she's embarrassed, so maybe it's a girl thing. 'If you need to knock off early, Wada-kun and me can handle the last hour.'

'I'm grateful for the offer, Kojima-san, but I'll be fine.'

'OK. Keep an eye on the coffee, we may need a third jug. I'll just slip out the back, then – if you're sure you'll be OK piloting the ship on your own for a minute?'

Sasaki says, 'I'll try to avoid the icebergs, Captain,' which reassures me. I go through the kitchen where Wada is loading up the dishwasher. The rear kitchen door's propped open for ventilation, so I step through and park my bone-tired backside on the fire-escape stairs – our veranda.

I wipe my face on my sweaty handkerchief, light up a Marlboro and suck in its smoky soul. A Shinkansen glides into the station at about eye level. Wonder if my son's in the driver's seat. Improbable, not impossible. It's been a couple of New Years since I heard from him, and I have no idea which route he's assigned to. His mother'll know, but she only contacts me through the lawyers now. So stupid, the money those parasites charge. Down below, on the humbler JR tracks, a regular train trundles around the curve, into the night. All these arrivals and departures, they're beautiful and sad and I'll never know why, even if I live to be a hundred.

S asaki's too good for a working life in Mister Donut. She hasn't had one sick day since she started here over a year ago. Unlike Osawa, who phoned up this morning forty minutes before her shift starts with yet another case of mystery food poisoning. She's 'studying' Fashion and Media or something, and seems to think she's doing the rest of us a favour by showing up. I'll show her the yellow card tomorrow. It isn't on. She's why I haven't had a break all day.

When I worked for Embassy Hotels, I had every third weekend off plus ten days' holiday a year plus rental subsidy. I met my wife at a company-sponsored trip to Okinawa. *We're not just a company, we're the Embassy Hotel Family*, went the company song. We owned two hotels in Waikiki and my wife was forever trying to get me transferred there. She dreamed of a house by the beach and our son growing up, chattering away in English with all his blond- and red-haired little friends. Her and every other Embassy Hotel wife. Then the bubble times ended and the company found itself with a property portfolio acquired at 1980s prices now worth shit, and a debt mountain to match. I survived the first cull, but when Embassy was bought by the Royal Nippon chain, downsizing began in earnest. One day the executioner called me in and said, 'Change can be a positive thing, Kojima, don't you agree?' Not that they chopped you directly. You got assigned to a Regional Headquarters in Hokkaido – aka the Gulag – where you did meaningless admin jobs by day and froze your tits off in the company dorm (no family allowed) by night. Winter lasts eight months up there, and absolutely everyone quits. That's how the Harmonious Embassy Family wriggles out of paying proper severance. Who says that Japan has lost its entrepreneurial edge?

A Shinkansen departs, heading west. My son's train, maybe.
Is loneliness a disease? Are all our messy human ties a sort of cure?
Or is loneliness life's default mode, as inevitable as suffering?
I slurp my coffee. The one decent perk of my lowly job.
Wada calls Sasaki 'Miho-chan', which he can, them being the same age, but it still pisses me off. The other day I think he made a pass at her. She was just leaving. Wada said something, Sasaki flushed and then hurried off. Osawa saw I'd seen and looked smug. I was seized by a strong desire to slap Osawa's stupid face and sink my size 9 shoe deep into Wada's donuts to teach him a bit of respect.

Look. Three floors down, in the shadows of the bins. They're gathering. Their cigarettes glow in the garbage-ripe dark. Feeding the homeless isn't official Mister Donut policy, but I can't dump bags of unsold donuts into a locked bin instead of handing them to a hungry human being. I just can't. So I give the bags to Kurosu-san, their sort of shop steward, and he distributes the donuts to the neediest in Tent City. Kurosu's predecessor, Sonada-san, died of appendicitis last year because each hospital he went to said, 'We're full.' When I have to clean a shitty toilet, or work all day because of an unreliable counter girl, or get a bollocking from the franchise head because the profits are down (as if it's my fault that the new Starbucks and Krispy Kreme and Café Du Monde sell nicer stuff than we do), I think of Sonada, I think of Kurosu, and I think, *you're one of the lucky ones, Kojima,* and my little apartment with no view, my YouTube sex life and lack of free time to see the friends I don't have anyway, it all feels more bearable.

'Kojima-san?' It's Wada, looking worried.

'What's up?'

'Quick, you'd better come.'

So I follow Wada into the shop, and find an old guy bellowing at Sasaki: 'I wouldn't *spit* in your coffee!'

OK . . . an old guy with ants in his pants about something. And look, a handy Station Ranger arriving in case Grandad turns violent with that walking stick.

'Will you *all*,' the old man demands, 'stop inter*rupt*ing me?'

I exchange a look with Wada to double-check that nobody is interrupting him, and that the poor old boy's hearing voices in his head. Yep, Grandad's definitely lost it. But then another customer, a woman, starts speaking to him, softly. I can't catch what she's saying, but it seems to calm him – until he spots the customer in a Burberry suit filming him on her phone. Now he goes bananas. He swings that metal cane at her, quick as a golf club – smash 'n' crack goes the phone against the far wall. Miss Burberry shrieks and falls to Earth. *Shit,* I think. The paper, the claims, the reports, the police! *Shit.* Station Ranger just stands there, mouth open, as useful as tissue-paper underpants. Miss Burberry is crouched on the floor, in too much pain to be embarrassed that a foreigner is gathering up the spilled contents of her bag. The Mister Donut music burbles on. I click into action and walk around the counter. 'You'd better sit down,' I tell the old guy, 'I'll have to report this to the police. The *real* police,' I tell Station Ranger.

But I've underestimated the old man: 'Don't address *me* in that manner, you sweaty little shopkeeper! Get back! Get back! All of you.' He glares at me like I, me, personally, am the reason everything in his life's gone wrong, from the day he was born until now. Then he swings his metal cane like a kendo master and it whooshes straight at my face.

4

Well. 21.45 – my train's not until 22.00, so I have enough time to text Tomomi: *Hiro proposed between dessert and coffee! Face red as a tomato and hyperventilating. Thought he was puking up the oysters. Stammered out the question. Ring at the ready. Wanna know Part 2? x Yukiko.* I press SEND – and since I have my smartphone out, I check in on my Heart Heart Sweet Shop. My Blueberry Bonbons are ready, so I move them across to the counter, and pick up some poo my mascot plopped to fix the damage to my Popularity Score. I harvest the lemons from my lemon tree and get some Lemon Drops cooking on the spare stove. They sell for less than the bonbons but they'll be ready before I have to catch my train. Back in the real world, I stir my sweet iced tea. Hiro handled the rejection well, though he may not actually notice he's been rejected until he speaks to his mother. First, I told him how flattered I am that a civil servant would propose to a humble ink-cartridge saleswoman. Then I told him to keep the ring until I'd had the chance to discuss his proposal with my uncle, the head of our family. 'Right, fine, I see, good,' he said, firing a worried glance at the sommelier, who then wagged a finger at an offstage underling to send the champagne back to the fridge, methinks. Hiro said it was very wise of me to discuss his proposal with my uncle, saying that love marriages are all very well (Love? First I'd heard of it!) but these big decisions in life shouldn't be rushed. How very true, I replied. Hiro said he'd be happy to provide any information to my uncle to prove there was no bad blood in his family tree. I'll mention it to Uncle, I said, and smiled. Then the coffee arrived.

Poor Hiro asked for the bill.

'Right away,' said the waiter.

I'm choosing new wallpaper for my sweet shop when Tomomi's message flashes up: *C the ring? Did H take Big No like a Big Boy?*
I text back: *Only 1 diamond. How u know I said no?*
A young foreigner sits near me. Big nose, nice bum.
Only 1?! TIGHT-ASS. U said earlier u'd say no if H asks.
Oh yes, so I did. C u Saturday, g'night, x Yukiko.
Tomomi's one of my best Facebook friends, though face to face she gets tiring. She's got this really annoying laugh like a chimpanzee. You can see right down her throat. It's impossible not to look.
The foreigner opens a notebook, and smiles at something in it.
Secretly, I take a side-on photo of him. Just because.
He opens a book, but soon his mind wanders, and he stares out at the flow of people, the salarymen, students, Office Ladies, criss-crossing . . .
. . . all the tribes. What's he looking for? A girl, probably. Why else do foreign guys come here? Not to teach English.

There's a lot of talk on TV with pop idols and professors about why women in Japan don't have babies – as if it's the greatest, darkest mystery of our age. But it's obvious. If I'd said yes to Hiro tonight and drunk his champagne, I'd be kissing goodbye to my job, my shopping trips, my meals out with Tomomi and the girls, my annual trip to Hawaii, my independence. And in return? I'd get an apartment in a thirty-year-old company block on the edge of town where I'd cook for Hiro, clean for Hiro, iron Hiro's shirts and pour Hiro's beer; swim in the shark pool of Hiro's colleagues' wives; and give Hiro sex when he comes home drunk. I'd have to wear one of those stupid housewife aprons with Minnie Mouse on it. Arguments would be settled by Hiro yelling 'WHO EARNS THE MONEY ROUND HERE ANYWAY?' one inch from my face. When the baby arrived, I'd have a year of bitten nipples and three years of my apartment ponging of dirty nappies. A day out would mean a trip to MaxValu Supermarket, and holidays would mean Golden Week at Hiro's parents' place in Niigata, who – just as Son of Hiro leaves for university – become weak and infirm, handing me the privilege of changing their diapers and being their human punchbag when they feel angry or obnoxious. The question isn't 'Why are so few Japanese women getting married and having babies?' The question is 'Why on Earth would we?' I'll buy my own champagne, thank you very much.

My mother asks me if I'm not afraid of being old, lonely and childless. But so far as I can see, husbands make you grow old faster. Babies on TV are cute enough, but real live ones are pretty revolting, really. As for lonely, the loneliest people I come across are housewives. Trapped, put-upon women whose husbands think, *I'm paying for this, so I should get what I want.*

My train of thought is abruptly derailed by the mumbly old man from the corner up at the counter shouting at the Mister Donut girl, 'I wouldn't *spit* in your coffee!'

Few sights in life are as amusing as a geriatric goblin with tufty eyebrows and nasal hair. I access the video function on my phone and start filming. I'll show it to Tomomi and the girls before the movie on Saturday. It'll be a hoot. The manager and a zitty-looking kitchen kid appear. 'Will you *all*,' the old man demands, 'stop inter*rupt*ing me?'

Perhaps that's his way of shutting up the counter girl, or maybe he's shouting at people in his head. Amazing! This is what YouTube was invented for. Then this frumpy woman starts talking to him. I can't quite catch what she's saying. I zoom in on the guy's face . . .

. . . and my phone flies from my hand with supernatural force, and my stupid heel's snagged over a crossbar on the stool, and I lose my balance and suddenly the floor's slamming the breath out of my body, and my bag's spilt open, but my hand and my knees and my side are absolutely *killing* me. I'm dimly aware of the foreigner gathering up my lipstick and keyholder and my breath-freshener, and I don't want anyone touching them, but my hand's broken, it has to be, the bones are crunched into little pieces, and from outside the fog of agony the manager's talking, and the demented old bastard's waving his stick, shouting at the manager, and a boy in a toy uniform steps back, and I cower because the crazy guy's coming nearer but not looking where he's going, heading straight towards where the foreigner's bending down to get my stuff, and . . .

. . . oh please, I know exactly what happens next.

5

This being Japan, the station master's whistle blows exactly as the platform clock switches from 21.44 to 21.45. The doors hiss shut. The train pulls away. She gives me a final wave. Last impressions count. I replicate the wave. The ghost of a smile? God, she looks beautiful when she's not crying or angry or sulky. I watch until the last carriage is gone.

That's that then.

Walk, Luke. Attack the stairs, two at a time. Let the ache in your legs muffle the ache in – yes – your heart. Dodge the drunk salaryman hurtling past, his briefcase flapping, still hoping to catch the 21.45. Too late now, matey. Give your ticket to the JR man in the summer uniform and . . . where now?

Mister Donut. Why not? I've got nowhere to go but my tenth-floor 3.5-mat room. I could go to a bar and try to pick up a gaijin groupie but that wouldn't be very clever, not in this mood, not with an 8 a.m. class to teach at the Tax Office tomorrow morning.

I stand for a moment in the blast of cold air below the air con, just inside the automatic doors. Normally I hate air con, but this evening it's delicious and baptismal. Maybe because tonight's so damn sticky. Or maybe it's because I just said goodbye to a girl I still love but have to say goodbye to. Or maybe it's just me, maybe I'm changing.

I point to the green-tea donut because the kanji for 'tea' is one I know, and hold up a finger for 'one'. I ask for an iced coffee, too. The Mister Donut girl seems a bit jumpy. I want to find out if the place closes at 10 p.m. or 11 p.m., so I ask '*Sumimasen, nanji aite imasu ka?*' in my best growly male Japanese voice. She freezes like a rabbit in headlights but luckily the kitchen guy behind her understands and tells me they close at eleven.

I sit by the window and start munching my donut.

My throat's tight. The donut's OK. I smell perfume . . .

. . . has to be that woman in Burberry gear, three seats away.

At the grand old age of twenty-five, I've come to understand that while 'All You Need is Love' isn't a lie exactly, it's not the whole story either. You can only gaze adoringly into the eyes of a beloved for so long before you need to get up, shower and think about dinner, about what you'll do with your life. The girl now hurtling away from my future at the speed of a JR local train was – is – totally perfect in loads of ways, but the fact is our futures lie down different tracks. There's also the small matter of her parents, who'd prefer her to marry a mortician than a foreigner. So why spoil our fabulous romance by staying together? This way we get to part as friends.

In my backpack I find *Kanji ABC*, an anthology of Japanese short stories and – to my surprise – a Moleskine notebook. She must have slipped it in, clandestinely. The wrapper's off and the 'Return to Sender' box has been filled in in her careful handwriting. NAME: *Luke Stringfellow*. ADDRESS: *A Long Time Ago in a Galaxy Far, Far Away*. REWARD: ¥ *10 only – I grew up in Wales*. There's funny for you.

I'll miss her. I miss her now. That's the price. That's the point.

I find my bookmark in the anthology, and read the short preface to 'Fushinchū' by Mori Ōgai, translated as 'Under Reconstruction'. The story is set around the turn of the twentieth century in a noisy hotel where builders are replacing the decor and fittings from Japanese to Western. An Ōgai-shaped protagonist meets his German ex-lover in the hotel, and the hotel symbolizes the state of late-Meiji Japan, caught between its samurai past and industrial future. That nation-as-building metaphor is rather tasty. What might a twentieth-century equivalent look like?

How about a Mister Donut, instead of a hotel?

Nah, it wouldn't work. Modern Japan's too multiplex.

Try anyway. You're twenty-five years old, Stringfellow. Teaching English in Japan is a section of track, not a destination. Two years away from the UK may qualify as 'seeing the world' but a three- or four-year hole on your CV smacks of reality avoidance. Think about those EFL lifers you meet here in bars. Some have decent jobs in universities which isn't such a bad gig, but most have a Robinson Crusoe-ness about them. There's no return to the job markets and property ladders of Milwaukee, Coventry or Melbourne for them. Ever. If you really want to be a writer, Stringfellow, you'd better wake up and get serious about it. Now. Tonight. So what if coming to Japan and writing a book is a cliché in a hi-vis vest? So what if you're girlfriendless, if your gaijin friends have found real jobs back in their own countries? Befriend loneliness. Put it to work. Don't go to bars. Erase your time-wasting apps. You may be talented, but talent's not enough in this world. Millions are talented, and an ever-increasing number'll be younger than you.

Success = Talent + *Discipline.*

I'm snatched back to the here and now by an old man having a right go at the girl behind the counter. His dialect defeats me and the only word I get is '*kōhī*': what, didn't Mr Angry like his coffee? Hang on, now he's pointing at me! What did *I* do? What's going on? The girl's trying to get a word in edgeways but Mr Angry's still bellowing his tits off. The manager comes out from the back, thank God – just as an older woman arrives with a station guard of some sort, but he's hardly Robocop. I don't think he's even started shaving yet. The older woman starts addressing Mr Angry in a horse-whisperer voice, which seems to work – until he notices that Miss Burberry filming him on her phone, and he goes absolutely apeshit. He strides over and swings his metal cane and the phone goes flying out of the woman's hand. She shrieks, tips over, falls, crumples and her handbag's innards spill out. Without really thinking about it, I get down on the floor to salvage her lipstick and stuff. The manager's having words with Mr Angry – bloody hell, the old guy's swinging his stick at the manager now; it misses him by a fraction and hits the rack of robot toys they give away as points card prizes. The Burberry woman's lipstick is rolling under a chair, and I crawl after it and –

Fuck that hurts! A bony shin rams my side, but I don't work out what's happened until Mr Angry's fallen over right by me, smacking his head on the floor by my elbow. Crack, like a teapot in a cloth bag, dropped.

The old man's face is unnaturally, horribly still.

Time's stopped. I'm unnaturally, horribly hollow.

Move. Please. Christ. Move. Groan. Anything . . .

Look at his twisted glasses. One lens is smashed.

6

'Sasaki? You OK?' It's my boss, Kojima-san, peering at me. 'Do you want to sit down? Are you feeling dizzy?'

I haul myself back from the bad place. 'No, I'm fine, thanks, I . . . just thought I had a migraine coming on.'

My boss is confused. 'So . . . Have you a migraine, or not?'

I'm saved by the doors shuddering open, and I call out '*Irasshaimase!*' Without my contact lenses the customer's just a blurry guy in a blue shirt, but I bless his timing. 'I might take a painkiller later, but I'm fine.'

Kojima-san looks a bit uncertain. 'OK. Keep an eye on the coffee, we may need a third jug. I'll just slip out the back, then – if you're sure you'll be OK piloting the ship on your own for a minute?

I say, 'I'll try to avoid the icebergs, Captain.'

Kojima-san sort of smiles, and goes into the kitchen. I see Wada the donut chef through the window. He sees me. I look away.

My backflashes are getting worse, not better. My aunt's doctor in Nagano said that I've been through a very tough time, of course, but that I'm still young with my life ahead of me, and if I did my best then what I saw that day would fade. *Do your best.* Doctors, teachers, everyone loves telling me that.

The customer in the blue shirt comes up to the counter, and I realize it's a foreigner. I seize up, as usual. Rie-chan's taking English at college and she's not shy like me, she actually enjoys handling them, but today she's at an *onsen* with her boyfriend. This foreigner's a marine, I think – his head's shaved. The ones who helped after the tsunami were kind, but the marines in Okinawa did terrible things. We don't say it aloud but we don't forget. Then there's the language. We studied English in high school, but when I hear them talk in films or on the subway, it's like they're speaking Martian. They never want to know, 'Is this a pen?'

The marine points to a matcha donut and indicates 'one' with his finger. Should I ask him if he wants anything else? A drink? But what if he answers in Martian? I'll die.

I put his donut on a tray and he taps a cardboard promo cut-out of an iced coffee, and says, 'Ice coffee.'

'One ice coffee.' I manage to scoop ice into a glass, pour the coffee and place little cartons of syrup and milk on the saucer. Drink plus donut comes to ¥490. I point to the total on the till and swallow. He puts a ¥500 coin on the coin tray. ¥10 change. Almost done. I tell him to take his time, like we do with all our customers. He sort of bows a little with his head, then turns away.

I breathe. But just when I think I'm safe, the marine turns back: '*Smissu-san, Nanjee Aitery Massker?*'

A bicycle tyre that can't take any more air: that's how I feel. Who's Smith? What's Nanjee? Why me?

'Until eleven,' says Wada at my shoulder – in Japanese.

'Thanks.' The foreigner nods at Wada and takes his tray to a seat by the window.

Now I'm staring at Wada in astonishment. 'C'mon, Miho-chan,' he says. 'His pronunciation wasn't that crap. "*Nanji made aite imasu ka?*"' Then he understands and a big fat smirk spreads over his face. 'Don't tell me you thought he was actually speaking English just then?'

I'm blushing so hard my earlobes throb like I just had them pierced, so I pretend to look for something in the storage cupboard, just to hide my face. Wada takes a couple of the empty trays into the back for the dishwasher, pleased with himself. If he tells Rie she'll never let me live it down. Wada asked me out on a date a couple of weeks ago, but he seems to think 'no' means 'keep asking'. At least Kojima-san didn't see my mistake with the foreigner. What about the customers? There's that nice lady who's often in at this time of day. I've got a feeling she's a nurse too, like Mum was. I ought to ask. The old man in the corner probably didn't notice. He's just been sitting there since I came in. Maybe I ought to check that he knows Mister Donut is a self-service place, but what if he thinks I'm telling him to place an order or leave? The woman in the Burberry outfit by the window, though, she's tapping on her smartphone with a quiet smile on her face. She saw, all right. I bet she's writing all about the dozy Mister Donut girl for her blog right now.

What's the time? Still only 21.47?

I need a new job. I need a new apartment. 35,000 yen a month and no deposit sounded too good to be true and it was: my 'room' is half a room curtained off from Momoe's side, and now she's got a boyfriend, it's getting impossible. She snores, too, which isn't her fault, but my nightmares aren't my fault either. I haven't told her why I have them. Or Kojima-san, or Rie, or Wada, or anyone. I can't take the look you get when you say yes, you're from *that* Fukushima, *the* Fukushima that'll be contaminating the Pacific for the next 40,000 years. First their jaws drop, like you just sprouted an extra head; then it's pity; then they want to know about my family, and at that point I just want to walk out 'cause otherwise my mind'll zoom back in time to the roof of the city office. And I'll remember the sea, pouring over the sea wall . . . and the fires flaring up and vanishing. And the car alarms and klaxons blaring, until they fell silent too. And the oily surge, spilling uphill, scummed with roofs, boats, vans, pushchairs. And the dead dialling tone when I called Mum at home, or Dad at his office, or what had been his office, by the mouth of the river.

Last of all, people remember the reactors. They don't say anything, but you can see it in their eyes. Pregnant women edge away. I'm lonely all the time, and I'm used to that, but the way people treat you like you're leaking caesium through your skin pores makes it all ten times worse.

Still, no point feeling sorry for myself. Do your best.

The old man's walking over with his walking stick. I smile and ask, 'Would you like to order now, sir?'

'No. I want to know why you've been ignoring us.'

Who is 'us'? 'Sir, I wasn't ignoring you, I was –'

'My wife and I have been waiting *hours*.'

Wife? 'Sir, you haven't been here that long –'

'You served *those* two' – he tosses his head at the fashionable woman on the stool, then glares towards where the nice lady was sitting just now – 'who came in *after* I did. And then, then, *then* you served *that* one!' The old man jabs his finger at the marine.

I'm starting to understand. 'Sir, Mister Donut is a self-service cafe. But to make up for the confusion, I'd be happy to give you a coffee –'

The old man hollers at me. 'I wouldn't *spit* in your coffee!'

I flinch like I've been slapped. The fashionable woman and the marine are watching. I don't think he knows what 'self-service' means. How can I get out of this without him losing face? 'Will you *all*' – he's ready to explode – 'stop inter*rupt*ing me?'

Wada arrives with Kojima-san through the kitchen door, and the friendly lady – the possible nurse – enters with a Station Ranger. She starts to speak to the old man about listing his complaints for the president of the company: great, she's humouring him. For a few seconds he cools down, but then he notices the woman in Burberry filming us, gawping into the screen. What happens next is like a weird, violent dance. The old guy roars at her, and swings his metal cane. Her phone flies away, but the cane must have smashed the woman's hand because she's clutching it and half faints, falling off the stool. Kojima-san snaps into life, stepping out from behind the counter, but the old guy swings his cane at him, and misses my boss's nose by a millimetre. A row of Ursa the Robot Bears – this month's movie tie-in promotion – go clattering all over the floor. The old man then shuffles backwards, trembling, not looking where he's going. 'Hurry up,' he snarls at nobody in the corner. 'We're leaving. Now. Now! This place is a disgrace. It's time. It's time. It's time.' ■

ARVON

RESIDENTIAL CREATIVE WRITING COURSES 2014

STARTING TO WRITE, FICTION, POETRY, NON-FICTION & LIFE WRITING, THEATRE, FILM, TV, RADIO, WRITING FOR CHILDREN & YOUNG ADULTS

"There are plenty of newcomers on the scene offering short courses for writers but Arvon remains in a class of its own. An Arvon course can change your life. It's as simple as that."
—Andrew Miller

www.arvon.org

LINKED

Ruth Ozeki

Once, when I was a little kid, I tried writing a haiku. I must have been seven or eight years old, and some well-intentioned English teacher must have suggested I try my hand at it. Perhaps she thought I'd be good at it, that being half-Japanese I would have a special aptitude for the form. Perhaps the rest of the kids were writing limericks and sonnets, and I wanted to write limericks and sonnets too. I don't recall why, but for some reason, probably having to do with resentment or indignation or stubbornness, I baulked. I remember the baulking. I remember what it felt like to sit with a pencil gripped between my fingers as my knuckles turned white and my mind refused to cooperate. It was my first experience with writer's block. I remember my mother's frustration as she tried to help me. Seventeen syllables! How hard could it be? Her own father was a haiku poet, so perhaps she, too, thought I would be a natural.

Her father, my grandfather, was a complicated man, with three names and as many identities. He was born in Hiroshima in 1880 to a farming family named Yokoyama. Although they owned land, they were not wealthy people, and my grandfather, Ken'ichi, was the second son. Unable to ensure a good future for him, his parents gave him up for adoption to a wealthy family named Maehara, who had no male heir. He took their name, and became Ken'ichi Maehara, the first in line to inherit the estate.

I'm not sure what happened next – perhaps he didn't get along with his adopted parents, or maybe the Maeharas eventually had a son of their own – but in 1896, at the age of sixteen, my grandfather signed on as an indentured labourer, boarded a ship and emigrated to the island of Hawaii to work on the sugar-cane plantations. It took several years, but he eventually made enough money to pay off his contract and secure his freedom. He got a job in the post office and bought a camera. He opened a photography studio, and using the name Maehara, he became the first official photographer for Volcanoes National Park. He later opened a second shop just inside the entrance to the park, which happened to be adjacent to the Kilauea Military Camp.

When he married, his wife and children – including my mother – all took the name Yokoyama. When he wrote haiku, he published under the pen name Shōsei. When the moon was full, he and his poet friends used to gather at night for *haikukai*, when they would drink sake and write poems.

On December 8, 1941, the day after Pearl Harbor was bombed, the FBI came to his house and questioned him. A few months later, they arrested him under suspicion of organizing secret meetings, owning surveillance equipment, spying on a military facility and operating under three aliases. They transported him to a Justice Department prison camp in the middle of the New Mexico desert, where he was incarcerated for the next four years. During this time, my grandmother supported the family by printing his negatives and then hand-colouring the photographs, making souvenir postcards of paradise, which she sold to the American GIs stationed in Hawaii.

After my grandfather was released in 1945, he went back to Hawaii and tried to resume life there, but he'd lost his business and his home, and many of his friends had moved away, and he no longer felt welcome in America. He and my grandmother decided to return to Japan, but before they did, they came to visit my family in Connecticut. I was three years old. I remember the first time I saw him, he was sitting cross-legged on the floor in my parents' bedroom, doing zazen meditation. When he raised his gaze to look at me, our eyes were level, and he was my height exactly. This is the very first memory I have, so it must have made a strong impression.

It was also the only time we met. My grandfather died in Japan three years later. When I was seven, I visited my grandmother in the coastal town of Atami, where she lived alone in a little house on the side of a mountain, next to a bamboo forest. Inside the house was a small Buddhist altar with a candle and incense and a framed photograph of my grandfather, and every morning my grandmother used to make a cup of hot water and leave it next to his picture. When I asked her why she did this, she explained that he preferred it to tea.

I grew up surrounded by my grandfather's things: his photographs, cameras and stamp collections, the furniture he made from twisted driftwood, the rocks he collected in the New Mexico desert. The prison camp had a workshop with a rock tumbler, and he used to cut and polish agate, jasper, quartz and bits of petrified wood. When he went back to Japan, he left them with us. I believed they were priceless gems.

Eventually I got over my writer's block and started writing – not haiku, but stories. Later on I got a camera and started taking pictures and making films. My mom used to shake her head, mystified. You're just like your grandfather, she would say, and this made me terribly proud.

I have a strange photograph of my grandfather as a young man, in which he's standing, barefoot, on the upturned blades of two short unsheathed swords, holding the blade of another, longer sword pressed hard against the flesh of his cheek. His trouser legs are rolled up slightly, and his sleeves pushed back, and if you look closely, you can see a long metal skewer pushed straight through his left forearm. My mother once explained that he could stand on swords and not be cut, and he could pierce his forearms with spikes and not bleed. It was mind over matter, she said.

I can't really judge the quality of my grandfather's poetry. I'm not a poet in English, never mind in Japanese, and the spare, concise haiku form continues to confound me. But I had an idea of translating some of his poems (loosely), and responding to them (roughly), in order to make a kind of *renga*, a linked verse, across time.

I remember the look my grandfather gave me, when I was three, as he raised his gaze from zazen and our eyes met. If I were to depict this as a manga, I would draw a sparking blue bolt of electricity travelling from his old eyes to mine. A kind of mental transmission. Mind over matter.

then   now

Another London air raid,
reflected in
a Hawaiian moon –

                    the moon wanes, and the earth
                    unwinds through time, and still
destroyers, restless,
come and go, grumbling,
like winter thunder,

                    massing, always within range,
                    droning, out of earshot.
We knew it was coming,
and it's happened at last –
December 7th.

                    You knew? Of course, and we did, too.
                    Pearl Harbor, New York, Baghdad.
Hunted down, captured,
but my old wife escaped –
day fifteen

                    and losing count, in desert prisons,
                    poets, terrorists, grandfathers, spies
look up,
above the stockade, I see
a bird fly by –

                    look down, lose sight,
                    what bird, what fence, what paradise?
Autumn of sand,
accustomed now to living here –
pitiful

                    old poems, like polished stones,
                    tumbled words to break my teeth on. ∎

THINGS REMEMBERED AND THINGS FORGOTTEN

Kyoko Nakajima

TRANSLATED FROM THE JAPANESE BY IAN M. MACDONALD

Masaru Masaoka, in the passenger seat of the silver Lexus, sneezed nervously. His wife Yumi was driving, and they were on the western outskirts of Tokyo.

'Must be the fall pollen – lots of ragweed out here in the sticks. Put up the windows, will you?' he said.

Yumi pressed the power window switch, and Masaru tilted his seat back, shutting his eyes.

'Are you going to take a nap?'

'I'm not sleepy. Anyway, we'll be there soon.'

'You know, dear, we haven't seen your brother in almost forty years. Not since our wedding. I'm feeling a little awkward.'

'You shouldn't. It's not like he's ever expressed any desire to see us. And, considering his condition –' Masaru paused and tapped his temple with his index finger – 'he probably won't even recognize me.'

They crossed a bridge and turned off the highway onto a narrow road. Soon they arrived at their destination: a single-family house remodelled to serve as a group home for the elderly. The Masaokas were shown through to the lounge where a man sat watching television and four women were gathered around a table folding pieces of fabric. Two other women sat dozing, each in her own chair, their bodies slumped to one side or the other. Just then a thin elderly man came shuffling in.

'Takashi,' Masaru called out.

The man responded with a friendly salute and a bow. The women at the table stopped what they were doing and bowed politely.

'Takashi, it's me, Masaru. You remember Yumi.'

'I'm sorry we haven't seen you for so long,' said Yumi, bowing deeply to her husband's elder brother, who nodded his head and smiled.

Everything in the room – from the artlessly arranged cabinets to the *kokeshi* dolls and knick-knacks inside them – were of considerable antiquity, just like the home's human occupants.

'This really takes you back, doesn't it, Takashi?'

In response to Masaru's remark, a staff member volunteered that the home was equipped with all the latest modern conveniences, including an elevator and newly remodelled bathrooms. But, he said, the furniture, paintings and other items had been deliberately chosen to evoke an 'old-time' atmosphere.

'It makes our patrons feel at home,' explained the staff member. 'And, just between you and me, I picked these things up for a song at a thrift shop.'

Masaru took his brother's arm and led him over to the window, then pulled open the lace curtain.

'*This* takes me back, too,' Masaru said.

The window looked out onto a flood plain where children were playing baseball, the wide Tama River flowing by. Masaru's brother sat down in an armchair nearby.

'There's a bird,' he said to no one in particular.

'You're right. How unusual. Is it an egret? It *is*, isn't it? Hey, Takashi, doesn't it remind you of Tsukishima? Doesn't it?' Masaru felt a wave of nostalgia washing over him.

But his elder brother was absorbed in the graceful white bird that had alighted at the river's edge, seemingly uninterested in any distant memory. He moved his head up and down as though he were tracing the bird's movements with his chin.

Yumi broke in. 'I didn't know you and Takashi had lived in Tsukishima.'

'Yes. A long, long time ago.'

'You never told me that.'

'Didn't I? Maybe not. It was nearly seventy years ago.'

'We should have asked Takashi to come visit us there – for old times' sake.'

'That's a laugh. Nothing but high-rise apartment buildings there now. This place is more like Tsukishima was in those days.'

'I suppose you're right.' Yumi shrugged her shoulders.

'Are you getting tired, Takashi?' Masaru spoke, more loudly now, into his elder brother's ear.

'Yes. I suppose I am.'

Takashi set off, leading his little brother by the hand.

At the end of the narrow alley lined with flowerpots, they came to the grassy expanse alongside the Sumida River. To their left they could see the huge Kachidoki Drawbridge opening and closing.

Beyond it, across the river, stood the hospital requisitioned by the Occupation Army and Hongan-ji with its Indian-style main temple hall. Straight ahead, across Mihara Bridge, stood the old clock tower building in Ginza that now served as the military PX. Takashi, who was eight, and Masaru, who was three, had heard that there were lots of American GIs there who handed out chocolates and chewing gum to children. But their mother had warned them: 'Don't go near the drawbridge or the GIs will grab you and line you up for target practice.' So they had never crossed the river.

The bridge was used by American soldiers going to the PX or GHQ from their barracks in Harumi, on the east side of Tsukishima ('where the World's Fair would've been if it hadn't been for the war', people muttered), and was said to be teeming with drunk GIs who caused all kinds of trouble. So whenever Takashi's mother suggested he take Masaru outside, they headed either west to the river to stare off toward Ginza, or north across the scorched grassland that Tsukuda had become, to sit at the foot of Aioi Bridge.

As Takashi and Masaru returned to their neighbourhood dotted with the skeletons of burnt-out houses, a sudden gust of wind knocked over the washboard and bucket that had been left out to dry. The bucket came hurtling toward the smaller boy. Takashi jerked his brother out of the way, and Masaru spun, pivoting on one foot with his arm above his head like a young woman in a dance hall twirling in the arms of her beau.

Masaru was wearing baggy trousers, hand-me-downs from his big brother. Takashi's were too short and had been worn for so long they were tattered and threadbare.

'Back so soon?' said the old lady who lived on the first floor, peering over spectacles perched on her nose. 'Well, come in and sit with me, boys. Your ma's not home yet.'

Takashi nodded, urging his little brother forward, and together they went in and plopped themselves down in a corner of the small sitting room.

The old lady turned to the gasman who had come about a leaky valve. 'You lied to me last month,' she said.

'How so?' replied the man, fiddling with the rubber hose.

'You said since Japan surrendered "unconditionally", the Americans wouldn't take our land or force Japan to pay reparations. Because it was "unconditional". That's what you said. Now look at all that land across the river they've gone and taken.'

'It hasn't been *taken*,' said the man, who was in his late fifties. 'It's just been requisitioned.'

The old lady tilted her head to one side, repeating *rek-we-zish-und* under her breath. She didn't understand the meaning of the word any more than she knew what 'unconditional surrender' meant, and in truth the gasman didn't either. He replaced the old gas hose with a new one and left the old lady frowning at the receipt.

'My,' she said, clicking her tongue, 'what things *cost* these days!'

No sooner had the gasman left than the boys' young mother slid open the front door.

'How'd it go?' asked the old lady.

'Bad – really bad,' Tomiyo replied, waving her hand emphatically over her head. 'It wasn't what I expected at all. I couldn't believe it.'

'In what way?'

'In every way. I was completely floored.'

Kneeling down on the tatami, Tomiyo reached over and gave each of her sons a pat on the head. 'Did you two behave yourselves?' she asked. 'I'll steam some sweet potatoes for you later.'

'This is what I went to see about,' she said, seating herself on a cushion at the low dining table and smoothing the curled edges of something she'd cut out from the newspaper. She read aloud to the old lady:

URGENTLY SEEKING QUALIFIED FEMALE STAFF
Excellent pay and benefits – food, clothing and lodging provided; salary payable in advance upon request. Will reimburse applicants' travel expenses from anywhere in Japan.

'Sounds too good to be true, doesn't it? Well, when I told them I had two kids they told me this work was unsuitable for married women.'

'Smells fishy if you ask me,' said the old lady.

'Yeah, *real* fishy!' Tomiyo replied, pinching her nose. 'I should've consulted you before going. Want to know what they asked me? "Are you prepared to serve as a sexual breakwater to protect and nurture the purity of our race for the next hundred years?" Imagine!'

The old lady – comprehending this even less than she understood 'unconditional surrender' – gave the younger woman the blank look of a Noh mask.

Tomiyo frowned and shook her head. 'In other words, you know . . .' She paused and glanced at her two boys. 'Doing *it* – with American GIs. Can you believe it? I was in shock. I ran straight out of there.'

'Did they pay your travel expenses at least?'

Tomiyo shook her head again. Just then she noticed a small child with a runny nose standing outside the front door.

'Who's that boy?'

'No idea. He's been hanging around since morning.'

'Looks about the same age as Masaru.'

'Well, so long, Takashi. We'll come again.'

Masaru Masaoka rested a hand on his elder brother's shoulder. Takashi patted it several times.

'Take care of yourself, Takashi.'

Together Masaru and Yumi walked toward the front door. Takashi, shuffling from the lounge, softly called out Masaru's name.

'What is it?' Masaru asked, turning around.

Takashi just smiled and waved.

The Masaokas bowed to the staff and walked to their car.

'Your brother remembered you, dear. He said your name.'

'Some things you remember, others you forget.'

Masaru took the car keys from his wife and climbed into the driver's seat of the Lexus.

'Well, well. This is a change.'

'What is?'

'You driving – and taking a day off, for that matter. I never expected you to be so busy in your retirement.'

'What did you think? I'm learning a new job. It takes time to get up to speed.'

'Is it going well? It's so different from what you used to do.'

'Yeah, well, I was in the wrong field before. After all, I studied humanities, remember?'

'So why did you stay at the power company for forty years?'

'Back then the best and brightest were all going into nuclear energy, even if you didn't have a science background. That's just the way things were.'

'Where was it your brother worked?'

'Why do you always make a point of asking me that?'

'Do I?'

'You do. He dropped out of school after junior high and got a job in a factory. I don't remember where he ended up. A small book bindery or someplace like that.'

'I can never remember – not unless I have a name to latch on to.'

'Not everyone works for a blue-chip company like in your family.'

Feeling slightly chastised, Yumi shifted her gaze out the window. They were stuck in a traffic jam on the Chūō Expressway and had only got as far as the turn-off for Chōfu Airport.

'When did you and Takashi live in Tsukishima?'

Yumi took a sip from a bottle of green tea and placed it in the cup holder behind the gear shift. Masaru reached over and grabbed the bottle.

'Want a sip?' She took the bottle from him and unscrewed the cap, then handed it back to her husband.

'Let's see. Not that long. We went there to stay with a family friend when the air raids got really bad. I must've been two at the time, not that I remember. Then the year after the war ended, we moved to Chiba.'

'Your father fought in the South Pacific?'

'Yeah, but he never came back – not even his ashes.'

'You were twelve when your mother died, right? So Takashi would have been seventeen.'

'Sounds about right.' Masaru took a sip of tea, then muttered, 'An accident – so that's what it was.' Once they passed the scene of the crash, the traffic started to flow again.

'I suppose he looked after you most of the time growing up.'

'Are you kidding? I looked after *him*. Takashi was kind of a screw-up. He did badly at school. Always near the bottom of his class.'

'And I suppose you were near the top?'

'Not *near*.'

'What? Oh, meaning you were *first* in your class? You shouldn't brag, dear – that's what annoys Masato.'

'I guess Masato takes after Takashi, then.'

'*Really*, dear. Don't start!' said Yumi. 'So how long did you and your brother live together?'

'He moved into the factory dormitory the year I graduated from junior high.'

'And you lived with your aunt and uncle in Chiba while you went to high school . . . I know the rest by heart.'

'Those were the good old days. It didn't matter if you were poor. So long as you had brains, there were plenty of opportunities.'

'Please don't go into *that* all over again,' said Yumi, rolling her eyes. 'Did you see Takashi often?'

'From time to time.'

'Such as when?'

'Weddings, death anniversaries – that sort of thing.'

'He didn't come to either your aunt's or uncle's funerals.'

'Didn't he? Well, brothers are like that.'

'You know, I don't think Takashi is as senile as you think, dear.'

'How so?'

'He knew exactly who you were.'

'Memories come back when you see someone face to face.'

'He's been alone all his life.'

'Since his wife died anyway. That was before you and I were married. Look, I'm not as heartless as you make me sound. I chose that home carefully after talking to the long-term care manager.'

'Which way *are* you going, dear?' asked Yumi, glancing at her husband. They had come to the Hamazaki Bridge Interchange and he had headed off to the right.

'Darn. I didn't mean to do that. It's because I haven't driven for so long.'

'I'm glad even *you* make mistakes sometimes. Isn't this fun!'

'Fun – how so?'

'It's a nice day. Let's take the Rainbow Bridge over to Toyosu and go home that way. It's not much longer anyway.'

'Wow, this area has completely changed.'

'Has it?'

'None of these buildings were here before.'

'You mean when you lived in Tsukishima with your brother?'

'Yeah.'

'Well, things change. Anyway, do you really remember? You were so little at the time.'

'I remember. Better than Takashi, anyway.'

'Do you? You've forgotten a lot of things. Things from before we were married.'

'Don't be ridiculous.'

'Some things you remember, others you forget – isn't that what you said?'

On another day, Takashi took his little brother to Aioi Bridge. It was fall and the tall grasses along the riverbank were turning brown and smelling wonderful. Takashi took a deep breath, filling his lungs with the cool air, and ran through the grass with his arms spread wide, making a droning sound. 'Brrrrrr.'

Masaru ran along behind, mimicking him. He copied everything Takashi did.

'Brrrrrr,' he droned in his high voice.

The next moment Takashi cried out in alarm. Masaru was no longer running behind him. He'd tripped and was rolling down the embankment. Takashi broke into a cold sweat as he imagined his brother ending up in the water. But just then, with a thud, Masaru collided into another child.

It was the same little boy who had been hanging around outside their house all morning. Takashi looked fiercely at the boy but gave up and went back to running around with his arms outstretched, droning like an airplane. Masaru started running again, too, in imitation, and then the other little boy took up the game as well, until all three were running around and going, 'Brrrrrr.' The boys played like that until the sun went down. There was nothing else for them to do.

At dusk the two brothers returned to their cramped neighbourhood of ramshackle row houses to find that the old lady's granddaughter had dropped by with some canned meats and fruits.

'I've applied for a job as a maid in one of the requisitioned houses,' said the young woman, who was wearing a bright-coloured dress.

'Are you crazy?' said her grandmother angrily. 'You mustn't take a job like that. What will you do if something happens? "Science for boys, etiquette for girls" – that's the motto these days. A woman has to guard her virginity.'

'Don't worry, Grandma. It's for a married couple. They've even got kids.'

'But don't you have to be able to speak English?' asked Tomiyo, a bit childishly.

'Not really. All I need to do is keep saying "Yes, sir" and "Yes, ma'am". It's a great big mansion in Ōokayama. I met the husband today. He wants me to start next month after his wife and kids arrive. Then I'll be able to bring you jam and canned food all the time, Grandma.'

'Sounds too good to be true if you ask me.'

'It isn't. You'll see,' said the girl smugly.

Tomiyo sighed. 'Perhaps *I* should take English typing lessons or something,' she said uncertainly.

'What for?' asked the girl.

'Every day the newspaper's full of help-wanted ads for people who can type in English.'

'Don't bother with lessons – just go ahead and apply.'

'But nobody will hire me unless I can type.'

'Just act like you know what you're doing. You'll pick it up as you go along, even if you have to hunt and peck at first.'

'I suppose so.' Tomiyo stared down at her fingers dubiously.

From the entryway came the sound of the front door opening, and in stepped the upstairs lodger. He was leading a little boy by the hand.

'And what do we have here?' asked the old lady suspiciously, a proprietary tone in her voice.

'I found him wandering around outside,' the lodger said. 'Since it's late I thought he could stay here tonight. In the morning I'll take him over to the police station.'

'I've seen him before – he's been hanging around here a lot.'

'I can't get much out of him. Maybe he's lost or maybe his parents are dead.'

Just then the two brothers, noticing the boy, called out to him.

'Do you know him?' asked the lodger.

The boys nodded.

'Where's he live?'

They both shook their heads. The little boy rushed over to his new playmates.

'All right, he can stay,' said Tomiyo, on behalf of the old lady. 'But just for tonight.'

'Hey,' said the lodger, changing the topic, 'about that job you were just talking about – I think you should give it a go.'

'You see?' said the girl, pleased with herself.

'As a matter of fact, I found something in the newspaper too. Take a look.' The lodger slipped his hand into his trouser pocket and took out a clipping for Tomiyo to read.

> The editors of *Bungei Shunjū* request that anyone who has ever contributed a story to our magazine contact our offices and let us know your current address. We would also be glad to receive news about how you are doing.

'Their records must've been destroyed in the war,' explained the lodger. 'I was thinking of contacting them and trying to sell them a story.'

'Ha!' interjected a second lodger, an ex-soldier, who was standing in the entryway listening to the conversation. 'Good luck with that. Records or no records, a magazine editor can tell the difference between a writer and a wannabe.'

'But,' protested the would-be writer, 'it says "anyone who has *ever* contributed a story" to the magazine.'

'Yeah, it doesn't say "anyone who has *never* contributed a story".'

'There isn't much difference between "ever" and "never".'

The ex-soldier didn't bother replying. He lowered a sack from his shoulder and placed it in front of the old lady.

'You're too kind!' The old lady beamed.

'It's just some sweet potatoes. A contact got them for me,' he said.

'So how's business?'

'Not bad.' He massaged his shoulder. 'Things have picked up since I started selling those pictures of Mount Fuji.'

'That's great,' chimed in Tomiyo. In addition to her work sewing clothes by the piece, she made paper fans, which the ex-soldier, a struggling artist, painted with scenes of Mount Fuji and sold to souvenir shops catering to American soldiers.

A strong gust of wind buffeted the front door, rattling the glass.

'Lot of typhoons this year,' said the would-be writer.

'Yeah, but where was all that "divine wind" when we needed it?' the ex-soldier said sarcastically.

'But it did come. They say the divine wind delayed the Americans' arrival by two or three days.'

'Really? A lot of good *that* did.'

'It bought the authorities enough time to destroy a bunch of documents they didn't want the Americans to get their hands on.'

The old lady nodded seriously. 'That's what all that ash was,' she said.

Toward the end of the year in which the war ended, Masaru died. He caught a cold that turned into pneumonia, and he was too malnourished to recover.

It was something Takashi remembered but Masaru had forgotten.

Takashi and his mother cried all winter long. They were still crying when the little boy, the playmate of the two brothers, reappeared at their door.

Takashi quietly slipped his hand into the little boy's and led him inside. ■

FINAL FANTASY III

Tao Lin

From *Tokyo Twilight Zone*
Kabukichō Shinjuku-ku, 2005

November 11, in the afternoon, I rode the F train from Manhattan to Brooklyn and walked six blocks to my brother's apartment, where my parents were staying while visiting from Taiwan. I would be eating dinner with them that night and the next two nights. My brother, who was at work and whose wife was on a business trip, would stay home each of the three nights with his one-year-old son, who was on the carpeted floor – across the room from where my mother and I sat on a sofa facing a large-screen TV – playing with toys in a determined, slightly bumbling manner, as if simultaneously exerting a set amount of effort and absorbing a set amount of pleasure. I hadn't watched TV in around a year, and it seemed utterly insane. The same pre-recorded segment of local news showed repeatedly, on a loop, with only the commercials changing. The singer, it seemed, of a heavy metal band, which had moved from Iran to Brooklyn a few years ago, had reportedly killed three of his band mates, then himself, with a shotgun, that morning. I'd stayed awake the previous night, in my room, working on an essay that I'd come to associate, over the past month, almost exclusively with a feeling of being unable to write anything satisfying. It was currently around 6,000 words, which I'd separated into forty to sixty groups of disconnected texts, which I'd then organized, with feelings, at times, of despair, into four different files.

I could feel myself staring at the TV screen. I was intermittently grinning in a way that I'd sometimes notice at a delay, as if my face was operating independently of myself. My brother's son, I noticed at some point, had walked to where I sat and was holding a large, unwieldy children's book toward me while staring pragmatically at my face. He stood motionless in a vague, inhuman way, like he wouldn't get tired – or would, but in the way a tree might. He seemed exclusively distracted by what he was doing. I accepted the book, and he walked away. Later he seemed less purposeful, almost confused, when I noticed him looking at me from four or five feet away. I realized, as we stared at each other, that he wouldn't remember this moment, or day, or probably any of the next one to three years, after which, for the rest of his life, he wouldn't know why he has certain likes and dislikes, fears and desires, nightmares and dreams, fantasies and neuroses. He would always seem – in an undetectably pervasive manner – otherly and slightly incomprehensible to himself, because his unconscious and subconscious and autonomic nervous system would remember what he would not.

I was surprised I'd never viewed anyone, it seemed, in this manner. I'd never thought 'he doesn't remember the three years of his life when, to those interacting with him, it was apparent he wouldn't remember anything he was experiencing', for example, about myself or someone else.

At dinner, a few minutes after being seated, I was surprised to hear myself say 'I don't know what to write' while thinking vaguely about my essay, which I hadn't planned to discuss. Substituting in English what I didn't know in Mandarin, the language I used, not fluently, with my parents, I explained I was writing a 4,000-word essay about Japan that was due November 25. I didn't think they, or anyone, could say anything I'd use in my essay, but I was enjoying the conversation, so I began asking my parents, who I'd asked for writing advice probably zero to four times in the past ten years, what I could write about Japan.

My father said he would tell me if I took notes. 'Keywords,' he said in English. I opened Notes on my iPhone. My father shifted a little and, after a pause, in a voice that unintentionally, it seemed, sounded like what one would stereotypically use to half-earnestly quote Confucius, said it was a good sign in Japan if your husband stayed out late every night after work because that meant business was doing well. He stopped talking. I stared at my iPhone. I was considering typing 'husband' as a keyword.

'Did you write it down?' said my father.

'Not yet,' I said. 'Say more.'

My father said that was all he had to say.

'Huh?' said my mother in a surprised tone.

My father asked if I'd taken notes.

'That isn't enough,' I said, grinning.

'Of course it isn't,' said my father. 'After you take notes, I'll tell you more. You'll write a little about each item.' Closing Notes on my iPhone, I told him he was saying things everyone already knew. My mother said Japanese people were patriotic and, without using the word kamikaze, explained that every Japanese pilot, when attacking Pearl Harbor, sacrificed their life by using their plane as a weapon.

'Not every,' I said.

'Right,' said my mother, mishearing me, it seemed.

'You said every. It wasn't every.'

'I did?' said my mother, then made a noise indicating she'd realized, with some amusement, she'd been unconsciously exaggerating in a tone of authority. 'Right, it wasn't every,' she said. 'Many,' she said in a slightly tentative voice. My father, who had been quiet for some time, seated beside me, both of us facing my mother, said in a convictionless voice that Japanese people loved sushi.

I asked where their ancestors were from, and my parents said China. I questioned their certainty. My mother seemed to relent to the possibility she had one or more Japanese ancestors.

'In Florida there were no Japanese people. Right?'

My mother, sounding almost bored, said there'd been some.

'But I didn't know any. There were none at school.'

'There were many Koreans,' said my mother, and my father strongly agreed in a sudden, exaggerated manner, as if the Korean population in Florida was completely, reprehensibly out of control. The only Japanese person I remember from Florida was a woman in her fifties or sixties who owned or managed Yae Sushi, a restaurant my family dined at around ten times a year. I don't remember learning about Japan in elementary or middle school. I remember learning about Japan in high school, but only in the context of World War II. I remember feeling confused when looking at photos in textbooks of Japanese generals with moustaches and form-fitting uniforms and perfect posture, standing or sitting. When I left Florida for college in New York City, when I was eighteen, my strongest associations with Japan were World War II and Nintendo games.

'Why did Florida have no Japanese people?'

My parents seemed unnaturally inattentive, as if feigning distraction to gain time to formulate a careful answer to a difficult, sensitive question. They'd focused immediately on Florida's Korean population. Finally, after I stressed my focus was on Japanese people, not Koreans, my mother said 'Japanese people are a little' and hesitated, then meekly said 'rare' in English. Later I noticed her miming seppuku in an exact, assured, nonchalant manner while also talking about what she was doing, as if she'd once taught a class on miming certain violent customs. I asked if anyone survived 'that'. My mother said 'no' in the confident, alert voice, I thought, she'd used earlier to say 'every'.

'There must be some,' I said.

'Maybe there are,' said my mother.

'Some probably survive,' said my father in a slower-than-normal voice, sounding wise and a little reverent, though he was probably thinking about something unrelated and only partially conscious of what he was saying.

'Japan has samurai,' I said.

'Right,' said my mother.

'What about China?'

'No,' said my mother decisively. 'China doesn't.'

'Why doesn't China have anything like samurai?'

'China just doesn't,' said my mother.

'Why not?' As a child, peaking in frequency when I was nine or ten, I'd sometimes unsolicitedly praise Japan to my mother, feeling satisfaction whenever, at my insistence, she'd agree with me that Japan was better than other countries. I liked Japan, when I was eight or nine, probably simply because I liked comfort and entertainment and convenience. Later, when I was twelve to fourteen, I began to view Japan, or my idea of Japan, as the ideal country, in terms of birthplace and lifelong residence, for someone like myself, to whom most people, especially classmates, seemed incomprehensible and violent; who viewed failure in a social or romantic situation as a clear and welcome message, for at least one person, in one situation, to resign; and who suspected resignation to be what finally all people, taking into account a long enough time frame, would want. But, through high school and college, it became increasingly difficult to enjoy doing things alone, because I'd also feel lonely, depressed, worried about the future. Resignation, which had once felt almost triumphant, became associated, as it was, I think, in the culture I lived in, with defeat.

'I don't know,' said my mother meekly, earnestly.

Before leaving the restaurant, while still seated, I half consciously said 'I don't know what to write' in a soft, simple, disembodied voice, as if quoting a catchphrase from a movie or contentedly humming to myself. My father said I should find information on Google and Wikipedia, mispronouncing Wikipedia five or six times, with some 'z' sounds, in quick succession. He said I should use what he'd said about businessmen, that what he'd said couldn't be found on Wikipedia.

At my brother's apartment my mother and I watched Ashton Kutcher, as Steve Jobs, unveil the iPod to an auditorium of employees in time to inspirational-sounding music, which the characters in the movie couldn't hear. I wondered, in a fleeting way, what stood in relation to people as the music did to the characters. I said something to convey I didn't think the movie would be enjoyable. In kind of a sad-sounding voice, as if wary I might leave now, instead of after maybe an entire movie, my mother said my brother's TV had many movies and encouraged me to choose something different. My father was in view, in another room, working on things on his computer. Around twenty minutes into *Fetish*, the Korean movie I'd chosen, after no one had spoken for some time, my mother asked what the relationship was between the two main characters. I mumbled 'I don't know' and laughed, and my mother laughed. The demeanour, mannerisms, hairstyle, eye movements of the female character, who was maybe the male character's wife for purposes of gaining American citizenship, reminded me of the person I'd thought about most, I think, the past three months, since August, when I met her in London in a bookstore, where she worked. She had a boyfriend. We'd talked in emails, but not for around a month.

My mother, who had left the room, returned to see the male character unconscious for no apparent reason on a sofa. In the next scene he was unconscious on a bed. Then an ambulance was shown outside a house. Next was an open-casket funeral. I watched absent-mindedly, barely conscious of what was happening in the movie, feeling peacefully zombie-like, until my mother said 'he just dies, just like that' in a sceptical, bemused voice, when I laughed suddenly and smiled for some time after.

On the F train to Manhattan I emailed a friend in the UK. I said I couldn't write my essay about Japan. I said 'I don't know what to say at all.' I asked my friend if he'd been to a certain bookstore in London. I said I felt like not writing for two years, but that I would need to get some kind of job. I had enough money for maybe two to four more months. In Chinese cultures, I knew because my parents sometimes paraphrased Confucius, it was widely accepted, or at least widely known, as a considered opinion, that parents should financially support their children until they're thirty, after which their children should begin to support them. My father had said 'everyone' in China knew this, because memorizing Confucius, who was born around 2,500 years ago, when maybe thirty was half the average lifespan, was mandatory in school.

Alone, in my apartment, I read from a posthumously assembled collection of stories by Osamu Dazai, who died at thirty-eight of suicide in 1948. The publisher had titled the collection *Self Portraits*. I'd been surprised, around two years ago, to learn on Wikipedia that Dazai's last completed work, *No Longer Human*, was Japan's second-best-selling novel. I'd thought of *The Great Gatsby*, which features two deaths (one arguably manslaughter, one murder) as America's *No Longer Human*, whose protagonist linearly relates lifelong, extreme-seeming, 'no concrete reason'-type alienation and survives a double suicide in which the other person dies. Not counting a brief epilogue, which is from a different character's perspective, *No Longer Human* ends with the protagonist living on the outskirts of a village in a house he describes as 'thatch-covered' and 'rather ancient looking' and these sentences: 'This year I am twenty-seven. My hair has become much greyer. Most people would take me for over forty.'

November 12, at the second dinner, I asked my parents if they knew of any famous people who were Japanese. My father mentioned a famous warlord whose name he couldn't remember. He said there was a Japanese physicist named 'headache', he said in English, who'd won the Nobel Prize. We were in a low-lit restaurant, and I sat opposite my parents. 'Headache,' said my father again while grinning and distractedly rearranging things in front of him on the table.

'China has Confucius,' I said. 'What about Japan?'

My mother, who couldn't think of anyone, said both her and my father's parents spoke fluent Japanese, due to Japan's occupation of Taiwan. Later she said we'd visited Japan twice as a family. She said we'd gone to a sumo museum and a ramen museum. I'd thought, for probably more than ten years, we'd visited Japan only once, when I was ten or eleven or twelve. I had four memories of that visit.

1. Leaving the airport, on an elevated train, I thought Japan looked like how I imagined Atlantis might. My mother was sitting to my right as I looked out the window to my left. I don't remember what I saw.

2. At the first place we went for food, a diner-like restaurant, our waiter, who took orders using what looked like a large calculator that produced paper receipts, didn't understand when we asked for ketchup for our French fries. He returned with a waitress, who also didn't understand. When he finally understood – I don't remember how – he brought it quickly and said 'ketchup' in English in a way that sounded different than how we had said it. I remember we were all grinning a lot, happy at the resolution.

3. Two businessmen were drinking large glasses of beer one night at an otherwise non-bar-like restaurant. They faced each other with straight posture and talked with red faces, seeming uninhibited and out of control. After my parents explained that routinely getting drunk after work was customary – that it was culturally acceptable behaviour in Japan – I saw how, despite being loud and appearing drunk, the businessmen probably wouldn't embarrass or antagonize anyone, and my confusion, with the addition of endearment, resolved into something like intrigue.

4. I saw schoolgirls in uniform one night underground, maybe in a subway station. They wore high socks that were thick at the ankles. I imagined they were going to private tutors and extra-curricular activities throughout the city. I felt myself watching them as they moved away, into corridors and elevators, toward enclosed spaces on other floors in other buildings; there was something role-playing-game-like about it. I had read in video-game magazines that Japanese people loved role-playing games, which was also my favourite video-game genre.

My favourite role-playing game, *Final Fantasy III*, released around this time, in 1994, was set in a world, both fantastical and science-fictional, in which magic and technology – medieval and shamanic past and melancholic, dystopian future – coexist. There were fourteen playable characters, but no protagonist. The geography of the game's world changed halfway through, becoming the World of Ruin, which can be explored leisurely, non-linearly. Kefka, the final boss, whose defeat ended the game, was in a tower near the centre of the World of Ruin, but there was no pressure or explicit instructions to enter. One could forget Kefka, and do other things. This appealed to me in 1994, when I was ten or eleven. I liked not knowing what to do exactly. But I didn't live in the World of Ruin. I lived on Earth, in a suburban neighbourhood, where my strongest memory of rollerblading was also from around this time, one day, on a gently downhill street, when an eighth grader standing alone on his front yard, three or four houses ahead, noticed me and immediately began shouting 'you suck at rollerblading, you're the worst, you look terrible, you can't rollerblade, you're fake', not stopping until I'd passed him and more houses and – focused the entire time on pretending nothing was happening – turned left, out of view.

November 13, at the third dinner, in a darker restaurant, I felt, than the previous two, I asked my parents, seated across from me, if they had more thoughts about Japan. I saw my parents once or twice a year. My father turned his head ninety degrees in facilitation of earnest consideration and suggested after around ten seconds that I type keywords into Wikipedia. My mother asked if I was writing that Japan was good or bad. I felt I lacked the vocabulary to answer. I said I didn't know. I asked if the two women seated by us, closer to my mother than my father, were Japanese. My mother said they were Korean, that Japanese sounded more pleasing than what she heard. 'Japanese sounds better,' said my father idly while looking at his smartphone. 'What else is there,' I said, some time later.

My father repeated what he said about businessmen.

'Is that real?' said my mother in a suspicious voice.

'Go ask anyone,' said my father.

'Is it something you made up yourself?'

'Yes,' said my father, by accident, it seemed. 'No.' In a subdued voice he said that a Japanese businessman he'd worked with, a distributor, had told him.

I talked about Japan's high suicide rate, ranked tenth in the world in 2011 by the World Health Organization. The last sentence of the 'Demographics' section of Japan's Wikipedia page was, I'd noticed, 'Suicide is the leading cause of death for people under 30.' I asked how Japanese people were both productive and depressed. My parents questioned Japan's level of productivity. I realized my idea of Japan's economy (and the economies of other countries, including America) hadn't changed in probably more than fifteen years. My parents followed the stock market and watched TV, so knew these things. My father said it was young people who were depressed, that Japan relied on people in their forties and fifties to do the work. He said 'itchy skin'. I knew what 'itchy skin' meant, but asked anyway, wanting to hear his explanation again. 'As children, many of us had itchy skin, so we needed to be beat,' said my father in a fond, slightly amused voice. 'Children want attention. They have itchy skin.'

I asked about Japan's low homicide rate, which conflicted, in a way, with some of what had been discussed earlier and the past two nights, for example Japan's behaviour toward China during World War II. My father, after saying he'd thought of this himself, explained that Japan, being an island nation, required war to expand its population.

'What's the second reason?' said my mother.

'What second reason,' said my father quietly.

'Didn't you say there were two reasons?' said my mother in a voice like she now doubted herself.

I'd been typing notes on my iPhone as my parents talked.

'Second reason,' said my father. 'Because Japanese migrated from northern China, and those in north China like to fight. Because they like alcohol.'

I repeated that Japan had low homicide, crime rates.

'Because they have self-control,' said my mother.

'If they do wrong, they attack themselves, not others,' said my father, and we laughed in a sympathetic, almost nervous manner. 'With swords,' added my father. My mother said a Chinese woman wrote a book titled *Nanking Massacre* and was depressed and committed suicide. Taiwan, she said, had donated the most money out of any country to Japan after 'the tsunami'. She said this was on public record. She said Taiwanese people liked Japan more than they liked Korea because Japan had occupied Taiwan.

'You said Koreans don't like Japanese people because Japan occupied Korea,' I said, and my mother confirmed. I asked why Taiwanese people liked Japan for occupying Taiwan.

Japan invaded, not occupied, Korea, said my father.

'They keep saying *yong ji*, which is forty in Japanese,' said my mother about the two women by us. 'Why do they keep saying forty?'

'They're both Japanese?' I said.

'Yeah,' said my mother, nodding a little.

'Why did you think they were Korean?'

My mother said one woman had a Korean-sounding accent. My father indicated an amount of time, which I don't remember but was maybe a year, that my mother had been enrolled in Japanese-language classes and laughed heartily. My mother corrected the amount of time, which my father had maybe exaggerated, and I think said something indicating she was no longer enrolled.

November 23, walking at night to a train station, I was thinking about my essay, which at this point was structured around my three dinners with my parents. I'd wanted and had tried for a few days to focus the essay on the topic of my inability to write an essay, but had begun to feel unable to write about my inability to write an essay. It occurred to me to write 'I am annoying' directly in the essay. I thought I'd write 'I know this is annoying. It's annoying to me also. So is this sentence and, if I include it, so will be the next.' For accuracy, I thought, it'd need to be 'I know this is annoying to some people. It's annoying to some of me also,' because part of me liked it, I knew, at least some of the time. I realized, around five seconds later, that I'd stopped thinking. I began typing the first draft of this paragraph in Notes on my iPhone. I crossed a street and descended into the train station.

Around a year ago, in my room one night, I was reorganizing my books, one of which was *Jean Rhys: Letters 1931–1966*, when I remembered in a sudden way – with surprise, because it seemed like I'd forgotten for at least ten years – that, as a child, in Florida, one afternoon, I unexpectedly found and read letters my parents, maybe a decade earlier, had sent each other. I don't remember what the letters said. I remember reading them in a sunny room, sitting on a carpeted floor, aware, on some level, with excitement and nervousness, that I was learning about my parents in a way I hadn't before. It occurs to me they were probably around the age I am now when they wrote the letters.

I'm thirty, and these are some of my thoughts. In seven months, in July, I'll be thirty-one. ∎

SUBSCRIBE

Subscribe to *Granta* to save up to 38% on the cover price and get free access to the magazine's entire digital archive.

UK £36 | £32 by Direct Debit

EUROPE £42

REST OF THE WORLD* £46

*US, Canada and Latin America not included

Complete the form overleaf,
visit granta.com or call +44 (0)208 955 7011

'Still the coolest magazine to have
on your coffee table'
– *Observer*

GRANTA.COM

GRANTA

THE MAGAZINE OF NEW WRITING

SUBSCRIPTION FORM FOR UK, EUROPE AND REST OF THE WORLD

Yes, I would like to take out a subscription to *Granta*.

GUARANTEE: If I am ever dissatisfied with my *Granta* subscription, I will simply notify you, and you will send me a complete refund or credit my credit card, as applicable, for all un-mailed issues.

YOUR DETAILS

MR / MISS / MRS / DR ....
NAME ....
ADDRESS ....
....
POSTCODE ....
EMAIL ....

☐ Please tick this box if you do not wish to receive special offers from *Granta*
☐ Please tick this box if you do not wish to receive offers from organizations selected by *Granta*

YOUR PAYMENT DETAILS

1) ☐ Pay £32 (saving £20) by Direct Debit
To pay by Direct Debit please complete the mandate and return to the address shown below.

2) Pay by cheque or credit/debit card. Please complete below:

1 year subscription: ☐ UK: £36   ☐ Europe: £42   ☐ Rest of World: £46

3 year subscription: ☐ UK: £99   ☐ Europe: £108   ☐ Rest of World: £126

I wish to pay by ☐ CHEQUE ☐ CREDIT/DEBIT CARD
Cheque enclosed for £_____ made payable to *Granta*.

Please charge £ _____ to my: ☐ Visa ☐ MasterCard ☐ Amex ☐ Switch/Maestro

Card No. ☐☐☐☐☐☐☐☐☐☐☐☐☐☐☐☐

Valid from *(if applicable)* ☐☐ / ☐☐   Expiry Date ☐☐ / ☐☐   Issue No. ☐☐

Security No. ☐☐☐

SIGNATURE .... DATE ....

Instructions to your Bank or Building Society to pay by Direct Debit
BANK NAME ....
BANK ADDRESS ....
POSTCODE ....
ACCOUNT IN THE NAMES(S) OF: ....
SIGNED ....
DATE ....

DIRECT Debit

Instructions to your Bank or Building Society: Please pay Granta Publications direct debits from the account detailed on this instruction subject to the safeguards assured by the direct debit guarantee. I understand that this instruction may remain with Granta and, if so, details will be passed electronically to my bank/building society. Banks and building societies may not accept direct debit instructions from some types of account.

Bank/building society account number
☐☐☐☐☐☐☐☐

Sort Code
☐☐☐☐☐☐

Originator's Identification
9 1 3 1 3 3

Please mail this order form with payment instructions to:

Granta Publications
12 Addison Avenue
London, W11 4QR
Or call +44(0)208 955 7011
Or visit GRANTA.COM for details

PRIMAL MOUNTAIN

Yuji Hamada

In March 2011, the Great East Japan Earthquake occurred. Afterwards, everyday life quaked in the unreliable information that was being released. The information that was broadcast by the media, the information that we received, didn't match up to the reality that was before our eyes.

Around that time, one of my good friends sent me a postcard with a photo of beautiful Swiss mountains. It was so picturesque that the more I looked at the photo the more it started to look unreal, to the point that my brain started to register it as a two-dimensional drawing. I thought about how a photograph, which is meant to capture 3D aspects of the world, is perceived as something two-dimensional.

That set me off to find interesting materials that I could easily get a hold of. I settled upon aluminium foil, with its reflective and malleable qualities. From rooftops I started to photograph the foil with the Tokyo sky as the background. The point of shooting under a real sky wasn't to pass off something fake as real. Rather, I wanted to make something that showed 'real' and 'fake' becoming friendly with each other.

With this work, what is most important is the image of a mountain in the viewer's mind. In other words, it is not the maker of the images who establishes and delivers what is to be seen; rather, I surrendered the work to the viewer's first impression, which led me to title the series 'Primal Mountain'. ∎

Translated from the Japanese by Ivan Vartanian

GRANTA

BLUE MOON

Hiromi Kawakami

TRANSLATED FROM THE JAPANESE BY LUCY NORTH

I sometimes think back on certain events and find myself puzzled about when exactly they started.

It was a lovely day without a cloud in the sky, and the seven-storey building, out in the western suburbs of Tokyo, afforded a clear view of Mount Fuji. The air conditioning made the room pleasantly cool. Yet all of the dozen or so people dressed in white gowns and trousers waiting for their medical check-up looked like they had better things to do.

As someone who spends most of her time typing away in a study, I'd begun to think of my annual check-up more as a change of scene than anything having to do with my health. The hearing in my right ear has been muffled for over two decades, and for almost ten years my white blood cell count has been slightly lower than average. 'If there's a major change in your cell count, we might take some further tests. But not to worry,' I am usually told. Small issues like these, it seemed to me, were normal for someone in her mid-fifties; it might be slightly embarrassing if I had nothing wrong with me at all.

After we had completed the tests, we were called in one by one for a chat with the doctor. How have you been feeling? Pretty much the same as last time. Good, keep it up, see you next year. You might try a little more exercise. This was how the conversation usually went, and how I expected it to go this day too. So when the doctor told me, in a gentle voice, 'You have a tumour on your pancreas. You should go in for tests right away,' for a second I had difficulty understanding his words.

That afternoon I made an appointment at the university hospital, and in a daze wrote the date and time in my calendar. I had no way of knowing if this was the start of something life-changing. It didn't feel like anything – there were no signs. My appetite was fine. I wasn't in any pain. I looked well. But malignant tumours are often the tumours that have no symptoms. My pancreas. A part of me that is impossible to see. Or touch. Even though it is so intimately mine. I found that terribly strange.

Several tests were conducted, and then, after reviewing my records from the clinic, the doctor said, 'There's a very high possibility the tumour is malignant. We need to do more tests. You'll have to be hospitalized. When can you come in?'

Why do all doctors talk in that kind, gentle voice? I felt a slight urge to laugh. But I didn't.

So it was that I was hospitalized, the next week, for further tests. Anaesthesia, intravenous drips, X-rays. Becquerel: a unit of measurement I first learned about at the time of the meltdowns at the Fukushima nuclear power plant. How many becquerels are passing through my body at this moment? I found myself wondering dimly. I lay on the bed and waited for the results. In a kind voice the doctor said, There's a 90 per cent chance the tumour is malignant. The stress these people must feel, having to give news like this to patients every day. If it does turn out to be malignant, what's the probability of survival? The five-year survival rate is roughly 10 per cent. I'm supposed to be going to Russia next week, for work, is it all right to go? Yes. But as soon as you get back you need to come into hospital. We'll be performing a surgical procedure. Should I take any precautions, is there anything I shouldn't do, anything I should avoid eating or drinking? No, nothing. Carry on as normal.

As normal. With the thought of that 10 per cent. The probability of the tumour's being benign and the probability of five-year survival after a malignant tumour were the same. 10 per cent. A pretty unambiguous figure. It might be cold in Russia. Must remember to take a warm hat.

Arriving in Moscow, I remember I've forgotten to bring a small notebook. Whenever I'm travelling abroad, I make sure to go to a stationery shop and buy one. I use it to jot down every detail: the number of my air ticket, my daily expenses, schedules, the people I meet, the food I eat, the colour of the sky on any particular day. A week-long trip usually means I fill a fifty-page notebook from cover to cover. When I'm at home, though, I don't keep a diary at all.

I hesitate, wondering whether I should buy one in the airport. But then the thought pops into my mind: why bother? What is the purpose of recording everything like that? When I get back from my travels I rarely open up the notebook to read what's there. All those memories, lines and lines of them, filling a dozen or more notebooks. So, opting not to buy a notebook, I wave at the person from the Japan Foundation who has come to meet me. It's the first heavy snowfall of the year. It might take us a while to get into the city. Really? In Japan, it's still early autumn, still quite hot. We chat in the car. I'm nervous, I'm trembling a little, whether because of the 10 per cent, or because of the darkness of a city I'm visiting for the first time.

But human beings are forgetful by nature. Maybe I shouldn't generalize. *I* am forgetful by nature. I gave a presentation at the Moscow International Book Fair. I enjoyed it: I truly did. I discussed haiku with some Russians who write them. That was fun: I really enjoyed that. And in St Petersburg, believe it or not, I got to hear Ludmilla Petrushevskaya sing. It came about by chance: on the train from Moscow to St Petersburg, Professor Mitsuyoshi Numano, who was part of my group, had a seat next to Petrushevskaya. She invited him to a concert she was giving the next day, and he asked if he could bring a guest, and she said – of course! And so, with a single word from the renowned writer, there I was, sitting in the audience. I really enjoyed myself. In a book cafe, I listened to some haiku composed by Russians. I presented some of my own haiku. It was fun: really good fun.

Maybe I've been concerned with death, all along. That's what you actually do when you write fiction – you think about death. The one thing that no one, absolutely no one, avoids – the single thing that occurs to every human being, without exception. I only understood this is what death is after I'd been writing fiction for a while. I ought to have known it, but I didn't. I only understood it once I'd lived with the people in my stories. I'm amazed that I had to be taught it not by the death of anyone in my life, but by people who hadn't died yet, who existed only in my novels.

In Moscow, and in St Petersburg, I probably spent a total of forty-three minutes each day thinking about death. In the taxi as it waited to continue travelling along the snowbound roads, on the escalator descending into the depths of the metro, in those moments of silence during pauses in the discussions, in the minutes before I fell asleep late at night. It was only a little longer than the time I spent thinking about death in the days before I found out about the 10 per cent. Strangely, when I think about my death, it is as if a blockage intervenes. I only think about it in the abstract.

I walk through the snowy streets, and reach the book cafe. I am going to meet with a Russian haiku circle.

The woman who is to interpret for me has arrived well ahead of schedule, and she is sitting in a corner of the cafe on the topmost floor of the building. Haiku have *kigo*, season words, which say something about the sky, the breeze, the birds, the insects, the plants, the moon and the stars, in a given season. What kind of season words, I wonder, will Russians use when they compose haiku?

Soon, people arrive in twos and threes, and the meeting starts. Japanese is put into Russian. Russian is put into Japanese. The surface meanings come across fine. But I'm not sure about the nuances. The subtle shades of words are intimate to the culture that uses them. Feeling doubtful that anyone can align the nuances in one language with the nuances in the other, with two languages that are so vastly different, and in such a short time, I watch as the interpreter puts

Russian into Japanese, and Japanese into Russian. *All translation is mistranslation.* So says Motoyuki Shibata, a translator and scholar of American literature whom I trust. He says this as a kind of joke, I know, but there's a truth to it too.

The interpreter translates a haiku from Russian into Japanese for me:

> *Konayuki ga futte iru. Nakunatta kyōdai no fuku*
> *o moratta.*
> Powdery snow is falling. I received a coat from
> my dead brother.

The person who composed the haiku is sitting in front of me. A man, probably in his sixties.

I try to make this into a Japanese haiku.

> *konayuki ya naki harakara no fuku o eru*
> powdery snow – receiving my dead brother's
> coat

The man is startled, and stares at me.

Several more Russian haiku are presented, and we each give our reactions. Words: such fragile, small things. I wonder if the man too is facing the possibility of death. Words, life . . . so very fragile, so small and insignificant. I realize I am probably being sentimental. In the beginning, we are cells with only half a set of chromosomes and with no distinguishing characteristics; at some point we become human beings; then we return to being nothing at all. What is there to surprise us in that?

The meeting comes to an end, and the man who composed the haiku about the powdery snow comes up and reaches for my hand. He shakes it, squeezes it tightly. I didn't know anything about Japanese people. But today, meeting you, I knew Japanese people for the first time. I am happy. The interpreter tells me in Japanese what the man said in Russian. The subtler shades of meaning are beyond me. The man smiles; his eyes are grey. What kind of person was your brother? I ask. He was a good guy, he replies. On sleepless nights, I remember the man's grey eyes.

I am not a religious person. I had thought that, when I was to die, not being religious might make it hard to bear. But maybe because I am dangling in the 10 per cent, I no longer fear dying.

Rather than death itself, it is the disappearance of traces that seems unbearable and sad. The disappearance of all signs that I existed. The traces that might linger in a coat I once owned, that would then be passed on to my sibling . . . When the coat got old and tattered, the memories of me would fade too, and eventually be gone. In old family photographs, or on the shelves of second-hand bookshops, my traces would linger, perhaps, for a few moments. Like those grey eyes that now rest briefly in me. It is in brief moments that we are born. All this should be no surprise.

I got back to Japan, and had the operation. The tumour on your pancreas was benign, the doctor informed me. In a kind, gentle tone of voice.

And so the days pass. *All translation is mistranslation.* But maybe there should be a second part to that phrase. All conversation is misunderstanding. I think about the discrepancies that will always exist in the gaps between languages whenever I go anywhere outside Japan, anywhere where Japanese, my native language, isn't spoken. But even when I use my native language, the same thing does apply. All language is misunderstanding. In degrees.

Two months before my trip to Russia, in early autumn, I travelled with Motoyuki Shibata, his wife and some others to spend a night in the country house of Ted Goossen, a scholar of Japanese literature, outside Toronto. I had no inkling at that time of the 10 per cent that I was to know of two months later.

We built a bonfire, under a full moon. Every now and then, there was the small thud of an apple dropping to the ground.

'There is a *kigo* for the full moon in autumn,' I told Ted. '*Jūgo-ya.*
Fifteenth night.'

'In English,' Ted said, gazing up, 'we have a different word: blue
moon.'

When two full moons occur in a single calendar month, he
explained, the second one is known as a blue moon. It's a rather rare
event. After I got back to Japan, I looked the phrase up. The blue
moon we'd seen was in August 2012, and the next one will be in
July 2015.

Human beings have always judged the passing of time by looking
up at the sky. Will I be able to look up at the next blue moon? It might
appear that death has receded into the distance, but it really hasn't,
not at all. I know this now. I didn't know it before.

The universe is said to have been created from a massive explosion
13.7 billion years ago. The earth was created 4.5 billion years ago, and
modern human beings just two hundred thousand years ago. No one
witnessed the beginnings of these events, and no one kept detailed
observations of developments as they occurred. The same with
all existence, from small to large. The universe, I myself, the birds
winging through the skies, the snowflakes swirling through Moscow
. . . No one sees the beginning of these things, and no one can predict
how they will end. How precious it is, how precarious it is to be living.
The skies during my week-long trip to Russia were overcast nearly
the whole time, but there was one day when, miraculously, they
were clear and blue and sunlight sparkled on the dome of St Isaac's
Cathedral in St Petersburg. At this moment, I am alive, I thought.
That is enough. That is all I need. ■

The Japanese Firefly Squid

reminds me of the aging Genji
who, to rid himself of Princess Tamakazura,

arranged to meet her
                in the protocol of darkness,
slipped his brother in,
and, when he untied a brocade bag,

released a glaring swarm

to light her face
              to captivate his brother.
The Princess is nothing like the female

who lays soft strings of eggs

one thousand feet on the Pacific floor;
nothing like the offspring

that hatch into a calm stretch of qualms.

No. They are equipped
to blend into light and squid ink –

nothing like an ancient corridor where a
woman is stripped of resistance.

GRANTA

SPIDER LILIES

Hiroko Oyamada

TRANSLATED FROM THE JAPANESE BY
JULIET WINTERS CARPENTER

The memorial service for my paternal grandmother – how many years this was after her death, I'm not sure – was held in town at a very shiny temple tucked between a brick-red apartment building and a colourful pizza delivery place. Afterwards we went to the cemetery, where even from a distance we could make out a red cluster of something growing by the family plot. It was mystifying, and as we drew closer we discovered it was several dozen spider lilies in bloom – quite as if someone had planted them there. It was the only grave that had them, and none of us could remember having seen any such flowers there before. Mother and Grandfather and I gasped at the sight, but Father turned livid. 'What are these doing here, just on our plot!' He grabbed a handful and tried to yank them out of the ground. They wouldn't come up easily.

'You don't have to do this, not today of all days,' my mother said, distraught.

My father kept saying, 'Why are there so goddamn many of them, just here?' He spat out the words as he tugged on the slender, weak-looking stalks, but they were a match for him. He ended up scattering the crimson petals all about.

'They're called *shibitobana*. Dead man's flower,' my grandfather mumbled.

Once my father got rid of all the spider lilies (he may have gone back later and dug up the roots with a trowel), never again did they appear at the gravesite. 'They're not like dandelions that just pop up wherever the seeds get scattered,' whispered somebody, probably Grandfather. Even after he died and was buried at the family plot in turn, spider lilies never bloomed there again.

The next time I saw spider lilies was in the garden of my parents-in-law. My husband and I were still engaged at the time, so he wasn't actually my husband and they weren't actually my in-laws, but in any case it was the first time I ever visited their home. They lived pretty far from us, while my parents lived nearby, so although my husband had met my folks a number of times this was my first time meeting his. I took the train with my parents so the two sides could exchange formal greetings in advance of the wedding. We travelled over three hours by bullet train, then went a few stations more on the local line, then took a taxi. My husband-to-be had gone ahead the day before.

'Why don't you text Hiroyuki that we'll be getting in on time?' suggested my father.

'Since we're getting in on time, why bother?'

'Yes, but just to be polite . . . Look, a chicken farm!'

'Looks kind of like a city factory, if you ask me.'

'I've never seen one before. Must be noisy in the morning.'

'Yes indeed. Even one chicken makes a racket.'

'Not really,' the taxi driver said in a low voice, and for some reason we all stopped talking.

The closer we came to my husband-to-be's childhood home, the bluer and higher the sky became. We climbed out of the taxi in front of a house with the family's surname on the plaque. The place was bigger than anything he had described or I had imagined. Off in a corner of the surrounding garden was a clump of bright red spider lilies, the stalks thicker than those I remembered from the gravesite. There'd been something creepy about those earlier blooms, but these, set harmlessly in the garden of a traditional Japanese house, struck me as a natural and appealingly simple fall flower. They were clustered at the far edge of the garden, along a narrow path bordering the adjacent property.

But why would anyone plant anything that had the sinister name of 'dead man's flower' and grew at gravesites, a flower that my father, half berserk, had tried to yank out? I looked at my parents – knowing that this day was special, the day the two families were finally to meet.

They were murmuring happily about how big the house was, how luxuriant the garden. 'So spacious!' my mother whispered to me, unable to suppress her excitement.

Father nodded. 'A fine-looking place,' he declared approvingly. 'Fine-looking.'

'All the homes around here are fine-looking, but this one especially!' my mother enthused.

'The houses hereabouts are all old and distinguished,' my father agreed.

'Yes, no high-rises or apartment blocks.'

Hiroyuki came out of the front door and bowed. He'd gone to the trouble of putting on a suit for the occasion. We bowed back. I had on a dress of a shade I seldom wore. I thought it was commendable of me to have selected it on my own, without anyone's encouragement or coercion. I also found it a little repellent.

Beside the front door was a row of large, tall chrysanthemums, each one in a separate pot, clearly the object of tender care. The flowers were still in bud.

'How splendid they are – just lovely!'

Hiroyuki explained: 'This was my grandfather's hobby originally. My dad inherited the plants from him, and then found he really loves taking care of them.'

'One day it will be your turn, then.'

'Not me. Then again, I could be wrong. Dad was completely uninterested at first. So you never know. Maybe I'll even take up bonsai, thirty or forty years down the line.'

'Bonsai is good, too,' said my father.

'Yes,' Mother chimed in. 'Since you grew up surrounded by all this nature, that would be nice, a hobby to keep you in touch with nature.'

Whether either hobby – bonsai, the miniaturization of trees, or raising tall, straight chrysanthemums propped up with a brace – would qualify as keeping one in touch with nature, I wasn't sure.

We were ushered into the parlour and settled formally on cushions on the tatami floor. In the alcove was an arrangement of some pink flower whose name I didn't know, mixed with silvery sprays of pampas grass. I sat between my parents, we three facing the foursome of my husband-to-be, his parents and, seated on a low chair, his grandmother. After tea was served in lidded cups, Hiroyuki's father began:

'On this occasion when by all rights we should be calling on you, bearing betrothal gifts, I apologize for making you travel such a long way. As you see, we have my mother to consider, and she's getting on in years.'

'Sorry you had to come to the middle of nowhere on my account,' said the grandmother, who then giggled unaccountably.

My parents both said, 'Oh, no,' simultaneously waving their hands back and forth before their eyes.

Mother addressed the grandmother with great apparent interest. 'You look so well! How old would you be, if I may ask?'

'Eighty-six,' she replied, and giggled again, covering her mouth with her hand. Her fingers, the back of her hand, and her face all looked as soft and white as if they'd been dusted with flour and polished. 'It's beyond my control, but if I can I'd like to stay well till my time comes.'

'Oh, you have a long way to go, I'm sure,' said my mother. 'And what a beautiful place this is! Why, I'd be embarrassed to have anyone who lives in surroundings like this come visit us. Where we live is just so small and cramped. It's really much better that we did it this way, coming to see you. Sitting in a big spacious room with tatami is such a luxury.'

'Yes,' agreed my father. 'Just like a fancy inn.'

'It's only that we're so far out in the country,' beamed the grandmother. 'You folks must live in a high-rise apartment in the city.'

My father answered, 'Our building has thirty-two floors, and we're on the tenth floor.'

My father-in-law's eyes popped. 'Thirty-two floors! If we went up that high, our heads would spin, wouldn't they?'

'They sure would,' agreed my mother-in-law. 'I'd love to see it myself some day.'

'By all means, you must come as soon as you are able –' My father got this far and clamped his mouth shut. 'As soon as you are able', he realized, meant 'as soon as Grandma dies'.

I looked at my husband-to-be. When the formal pleasantries began, his spine had been erect, but by now he was slumped.

My parents and I had taken two rooms at a hotel by the station, but at Hiroyuki's family's strong urging, I agreed to spend the night. They had plenty of spare rooms, the bedding was freshly aired and they'd even laid in a brand-new nightgown for me. My parents insisted on staying at the hotel.

'Maybe this is how they do things in the country,' my father muttered on the way out. 'On the day the two families first meet, as a token of the betrothal they have the bride-to-be stay overnight.'

'Where's the harm?' said my mother. 'I wouldn't mind staying here myself.'

Father grimaced and shook his head. 'I planned on sleeping in the hotel *yukata* and didn't bring any pyjamas.'

'They said they'd lend you a *yukata*.'

'Yes, but whose? You can bet it belonged to the dead grandfather.'

They left, after ascertaining that in the morning either Hiroyuki's father or mother would drive me to the station. I was unable to relax in the dress I had on, but I finished my tea and ate the sweets I was offered. Hiroyuki's mother then said cheerfully that she was going out to pick up some sashimi. Hiroyuki excused himself to go take a nap, leaving his father to ask me about my work and such. It wasn't long before we ran out of things to say and an awkward silence set in. The grandmother then slowly got up and said, 'Well now, Yuki dear, will you come into my room?'

Her room had sliding glass doors and a good view of the garden. 'What a relief it is to have such a wonderful girl marrying our Hiroyuki,' she said. She'd said this several times before, and repeated it now again while handing me the cushion from a rattan chair.

The only other pieces of furniture in the room were a white electric reclining bed and a small table. I settled into a place on the floor.

'The garden was much better cared for when my husband was alive and could look after it,' she said. 'Lately it's gotten to look a little shabby.'

'I see the spider lilies are in bloom.'

She nodded eagerly. 'Yes! That's a medicinal plant, you know.'

'Medicinal?'

'Yes, but not the flower and not the stalk. It's the root. You grate it and set it on oil paper as a poultice for breasts.'

'For . . . breasts?'

She laughed. 'Yes, breasts. When they get hard and swollen, the poultice works wonders. I always had plenty of milk. Raised six children, too. One died young, but I had so many, one right after the other without much time between them, seemed like I was always nursing for years.'

'Oh, really,' I said. I couldn't imagine what that might feel like.

'Why, I had so much milk, people used to stop by and ask if I had extra to share. Back then we didn't have nutritious baby formula like you can get now. I used to marvel at how much milk I produced, whether it was for my own baby or someone else's.'

She didn't pause for me to respond. 'I hope you'll be the same way, Yuki. It's terrible when the milk won't come. The baby cries in frustration, and you just feel so ashamed of yourself if you have nothing to give. But when there's too much milk, now and again the breasts swell up and turn hard, like there's stone inside. When that used to happen to me, my husband would go out and dig up a spider lily – the root is like taro – and he'd grate up the root real fine and make me a poultice. But you know,' she added, 'spider lilies are poisonous, too.'

'Poisonous?'

She laid a hand on her breast and made a face as if in pain. 'That's right. The root's got poison in it, too. That's what the oil paper's for, to keep it from touching the breast directly. But the one who grates it can't help touching it, you see. My husband's hands would be bright red afterwards, covered with little blisters. Made me feel terrible, but he'd grate away, not worrying, seeing it was for the sake of the milk.'

'And that's why you have spider lilies in the garden.'

She looked out at the flowers, eyes crinkling in a smile. With no leaves or shoots, the stalks topped by a single flower did look both medicinal and poisonous. 'We never planted them. They've just always been there, for as long as anyone can remember. They were a real boon. Probably no one does such a thing any more, but Yuki dear, if your breasts swell up and turn hard as stone, I'll make you a nice poultice. It's all the same now if my hands get rough.'

For some reason she began making massaging motions. I could almost sense her full, drooping breast moving around under her dress with the floral design in lavender and brown.

I smiled vaguely and looked away. 'So even though the root has healing power, it's poisonous, too,' I said, repeating the lesson.

'Oh yes. But then that's true of all medicines. They're all poison, even the pills I take every day.' She pointed to a bag of medicines, overflowing, on the little table. 'If you took those, young and healthy as you are, they'd poison you for sure.'

'Did Hiroyuki's mother also use the spider lilies?' I asked.

'Yoko?' After a little pause, she smiled thinly. 'She used to be skin and bones, so delicate you'd have thought she'd break in two if she fell over. Hips like so.' She made a small circle with her palms. 'I had my doubts when I first saw her, but the two of them were in love and wanted to get married, and who was I to oppose the match? Sure enough, first she had trouble conceiving a child, then she had trouble with the delivery, and then barely a drop of milk. So there was never any question of her using the poultice, since her breasts were dry to begin with. She used formula from the very first. I said to myself, Well, now isn't that handy, but then I remembered the old days and it just about tore me up. I breastfed other people's children, didn't I? I'd have gladly fed my own grandson, but by then I had nothing left to give him. Of course not – I was an old lady by then.'

She smiled, leaning forward and bringing her face toward mine in a way that caused me to lean in toward her as well. I could smell the sweet scent of her face powder. Her eyebrows were filled in with grey eyebrow pencil, and she was wearing a touch of lipstick. 'You know,' she said, chuckling, 'there's something else that's both medicine and poison. It's mother's milk itself!'

'Really?'

She laughed again, shaking all over. 'Yes, and what do you think it's good for?'

'Um, settling the stomach?'

'You don't take it by mouth.'

'No? Then it's an ointment?'

'I'll tell you. It makes good eye drops.'

'Eye drops?' My mouth dropped open, and she laughed, her breasts shaking along with the rest of her. Apparently she wasn't wearing a bra.

'You put it in the eye. And not by first collecting it in a container and then dipping in your finger and letting a drop fall from the tip. You've got to hold the breast close to the face and squeeze – put it straight into the eye.'

I didn't quite follow. *Put it straight into the eye?*

'Freshly squeezed breast milk delivered straight into the eye will cure a sty in no time. The next day you'll forget the eye was ever swollen. But if you let it drop from your finger, the opposite happens. It stings and stings. Just like poison.'

'Would that be because germs from the finger get into the milk? You could use a dropper.'

'I don't know about that. All I know is, put it straight into the eye. That's what my mother-in-law taught me.'

The hair on her head, white and yellowish-grey mixed with black, stirred in the breeze coming through the screen door. The breeze smelled of many things: autumn and earth, the green of the countryside, face powder and old age.

'I know it's strange, and who thought it up I can't imagine, but anyway, like I said I had so much milk that at one time or another I put my breast milk in the eyes of everybody in the family. My children, my parents-in-law, my husband, too.'

'But . . . if you put the milk straight into the eye, then the person would see you. Men, they would see you.'

She shrugged. 'It wasn't nice, but what choice did I have? I did it to cure them. When my father-in-law got a sty, my mother-in-law would come and ask me to do it. She'd do the asking, not him. So what was I supposed to do? I'd get him to lie down flat on the bed with his head on a pillow and then bend over him, lean in just over his face and give my breast a squeeze. It's not easy to get just one drop to land square in the eye, either. I had to be careful not to hit him with a jet of milk.'

I imagined the scene with horror. Even if my mother-in-law begged me, I would never, ever take out my breast, stick it in my father-in-law's face and squeeze out milk.

'But even though she was the one who'd asked me, she'd stand by the whole time, glaring at me with a look on her face like you never saw. All I wanted to do was land one drop in his eye and be done with it, but I was nervous, and the more nervous I was, the worse my aim was. Of course *she* wasn't enjoying it, and there *he* was, stuck, unable to look away. Not only that, I used to do the same thing for my husband, too. Think about that. Her son.'

'Right.'

'She'd glare at me then, too.'

'I'm back!' My soon-to-be mother-in-law's voice rang out from the front door. I excused myself, sliding open the grandmother's door, and went to help. She was standing in the vestibule with the front door still open, the sun behind her still strong this fall day, wearing a dark blue sun visor and holding a big bag of groceries in her arms. The grandmother had disapprovingly pronounced her 'skin and bones', but now she had the physique of any middle-aged woman, I thought, plenty of flesh on her shoulders and hips.

'Oh, Yuki, sorry I was away so long. Where's Hiroyuki?'

'He kind of dozed off.'

She opened her eyes wide and said in a loud voice, 'No! Really? And left you on your own? That's terrible! I'm so sorry.'

'It's fine. Um, let me carry that.'

'No, I can manage . . . but there are more bags out in the car. Would you mind?'

She set down the bag she was carrying, and I followed her through the garden to the garage. She opened the rear door of the car, lifted out another big shopping bag and handed it to me.

It was full of adult diapers. She said, 'Today they were giving double points for purchases, so while I was at it I bought some extra. You'd be amazed how quickly the points add up.' The grandmother had been so alert talking to me, I never would have guessed she wore diapers.

'So you were chatting with Grandma?'

'Yes, she was quite interesting.'

'Oh, no. It must have been tiresome for you, listening to an old lady run on. Let it go in one ear and out the other.'

A paper diaper by itself surely weighs next to nothing, but the bagful was plenty heavy as we lugged the groceries back to the house. I was about to relate what the grandmother had said when Hiroyuki's mother nodded toward the bright red spider lilies.

'You know, those flowers bloom every year without fail.'

'Do they? How nice.'

'Actually, I have to say, I'm not very fond of them. The colour is so lurid. Grandma won't hear of our getting rid of them, though. Once when I was starting to pull them up, she came along and mumbled something about their being poisonous. She said if I touched one, I'd break into a rash.'

'But aren't spider lilies –' I started to say, then thought better of it. She'd never needed the ministrations of the drug, and anyway the flowers were vaguely ominous to me, too.

We went into the kitchen, and the grandmother called out from behind her door: 'Is that you, Yoko?' Her voice sounded blurry in a way it hadn't before. Hiroyuki's mother responded in a high-pitched voice: 'Yes, I'm back!'

The hospital where my husband was staying was large, with every kind of specialty in both surgical and internal medicine. There was even an obstetrics and gynaecology department that for some reason had its own entrance. If I happened to go in the wrong door on my way to see him, my error would be pointed out by a big sign announcing, THIS IS THE OBSTETRICS AND GYNAEOCOLOGY DEPARTMENT, FOR EXPECTANT AND NURSING MOTHERS, PELVIC EXAMINATIONS, ETC., with an arrow directing all other comers to general reception.

I had visited the gynaecology department once. It was before we were married, for a general examination (a 'bridal check', they called it), and at the time there'd seemed nothing strange about the separate entrance. Now that I was visiting someone in the hospital, however, I felt as if I were being treated as somehow unclean. Were they being solicitous, making sure to keep patients brushing shoulders with death away from elevators for young women about to give birth? Or perhaps it was the other way around: perhaps invalids wrapped in pain, suffering and despair felt revulsion at the sight of hopeful young women carrying within them new life. The two areas of the building with their separate entrances seemed to differ in colour, in smell and in the heaviness of the air.

My husband had suffered multiple fractures, but his life was in no danger and he was conscious. There'd been a traffic accident. He'd been a victim, but the identity of his fellow passenger was unknown. He was hurried into surgery, and afterwards his parents hovered over him, having rushed up from the country and gotten a hotel room nearby, so he and I never had a chance to talk alone. Yesterday his parents finally went back home. The other victim had only been slightly injured, so she wasn't hospitalized and returned to work – at the same office where my husband worked – the very next day. She was the one who'd called for an ambulance and notified the police. Some flowers and a fruit basket had arrived from my husband's office. The fruit was still hard and unripe, so it sat uneaten at his bedside, and as my mother-in-law hadn't seemed very happy with the flowers – 'Would you look at these, so pale you'd think they were for a funeral!' – I'd taken them home. I thought they were pretty. It was true that the main colour of the arrangement was white, but it was set off by green leaves and light pink flowers; the effect, I thought, was soft and contemporary, no garish reds and purples. The evident good taste it demonstrated bothered me, but the flowers certainly weren't from that woman alone. They had no scent, not even when I put my face up close to them. My mother-in-law had explained: 'Well, of course not! Sending a sick person flowers with a strong scent would be ridiculous.' The next time I went home, to my puzzlement I found the room full of heady perfume. Several of the flowers soon wilted or shrivelled, but the scent seemed only to grow stronger with the passing days.

'Hi, I'm back,' I said to my husband, and he took out the earphones connected to the TV set, looked up at me and grunted in response. His eyes looked heavy with sleepiness.

'How're you doing?'

'OK.'

'I see they took the bandage around your head off.'

'Yeah, just this morning.' He rubbed his face with his uninjured right hand.

'That's good.'

'How about you? Everything OK?'

'Sure.' *Everything is not OK, how could it be,* I wanted to say to him, but I wouldn't do it. If I probed, he would probably apologize. Probably he wanted to. Once when his parents had left the room for a bit, he seemed about to express some regret. I'd waited silently, but in the end he said nothing. If he was waiting for me to bring it up, it was pretty insolent and arrogant of him.

'Do you have trouble managing without your parents here?'

'No, I manage fine. The nurses come right away when I push the button, and I've got the use of my right hand anyway.'

'Yes, if you'd broken that one, you'd really be up a tree.'

'Yup.'

For the past several days, he'd been in a four-person room. The other occupants were all elderly men, each with his visitors and caregivers, so often the room was clamorous; now, however, it seemed deserted, the cream-coloured curtains drawn around each bed. I sat on the stool provided for visitors. From here, my husband's face was uncomfortably close. On the nightstand was the fruit basket. I reached out to touch a melon with a ribbon attached to the stem. It was still hard, so hard it could have been a ceramic fake.

On the small portable table that extended over his bed were a mug for tea, an array of medicines and some little yellow plastic things. 'What's this for?' I asked, fingering one of them.

'Eye drops,' he said. 'They're single-use dispensers. I got a sty last night.' He pointed to his right eye. The lid was red and swollen. No wonder he seemed sleepy – that eye was swollen half shut.

'The drops don't do a thing,' he said. 'If I were at work I'd probably never notice, but flat on my back like this, I notice everything more than ever.'

'I can imagine.'

'Having something go wrong with your eyes or your ears is way harder to take than pain in the arms or legs. But pretty soon I'll be going to rehab, and that'll take my mind off it.'

We were silent for a time. There were no sounds of snoring or throat-clearing from the other beds. I imagined that people were listening in on us, but there was no reason for a bunch of elderly men to listen breathlessly to anything we said.

'Well, I'll run off and do the laundry, OK?' I said. 'Want me to get you anything?'

'No, I'm good. Thanks.'

Between the patients' rooms was the nurses' station and also a lounge area with tables, chairs and a sofa, a big-screen TV and a microwave, newspapers, magazines and a fish tank. Behind the lounge was a communal sink and the laundry area. The corridor was well lit, and from rooms with the door left open came children's laughter and the voices of women – nurses, evidently – offering cheerful encouragement. Yet the overall atmosphere was subdued. Moment by moment, I got the feeling that the smell of the hospital was becoming absorbed in my hair and skin.

Fortunately, one of the two washing machines was free. I put in the little packets of detergent and bleach I'd purchased at the hospital store and turned my machine on. There was a sudden roar of water that I found disconcerting. For a while I stood and listened to it, so different from my washer at home. The laundry area was clean, but the smell of mouthwash and disinfectant was thick, making it seem as if traces of some dark, watery crime had just been mopped up and everything sterilized. I went to the lounge and sat on the sofa.

Next to the goldfish tank was a large vase decorated with a Chinese-style floral design, holding an arrangement of bright red flowers. Local volunteers supplied the arrangements weekly, according to the sign. The other occupants of the lounge were an old man reading a newspaper and a young man in pyjamas playing Othello with a little boy around eight or nine. Suddenly the boy let out a cry and laid down a stone with a dramatic slap. The young man acknowledged this with an admiring grunt, and the boy giggled while loudly turning over stone after stone. The man's arms and legs were dark and skinny. The material of his pyjamas was worn, testimony to the length of his stay.

I thought of going back to my husband's room, but there would be nothing to say if I did. If I kept on acting as if nothing had happened, would he stay silent?

'You got me!' The young man playing Othello sighed with exaggeration. The triumphant boy laughed out loud. The old man reading the paper shot the two of them a glance. I closed my eyes. All I could hear were the sounds of Othello stones, muffled laughter from the large TV screen and the rustle of newspaper pages being turned. I stayed like that awhile. I might have fallen asleep. All at once I had trouble breathing, and my eyes flew open.

My pulse was racing. I touched my chest, then quickly withdrew my hand. My breasts were swollen, painful and hot. It was a pain

I'd never felt before, as if under my clothes a force were pressing on my breasts, as if something inside them were swelling. It wasn't air, it was more like having concrete poured into me. My body felt moist, heated. My breasts felt transformed, no longer belonging to me. Cautiously I brought a hand to my chest. Sharp pain ran through me. There was something straining against my breasts. Milk, mother's milk, was about to come gushing out of me. Although I'd never experienced such a thing, I could imagine it all too vividly.

I glanced around. Nobody was paying me any attention. The little boy was urging the young man, 'Let's play another game!' The young man shook his head, smiling. Goldfish seemed to hover, poised between strands of dark green seaweed. The red flowers were so still they might have been artificial. I stood up and went back to my husband's room. Every step sent dull pain shooting through my breasts. I was bathed in sweat.

My husband had turned off the TV. The room was silent, as before. Maybe the three elderly men were dead.

As soon as I stepped inside the curtain, my husband said, 'Hey, Yuki.'

I looked at him without a word.

'About what happened . . .'

I shifted my eyes to the turned-off TV, thinking my face might be reflected on the dark, flat screen. It wasn't. But definitely my breasts were swollen. Any second now, warm, fresh liquid would come gushing out of them. From a room down the hall came the sound of a hacking cough.

'I mean, about what happened . . .' My husband was floundering.

'Yeah,' I said. He looked at me expectantly. Looking down at him, I pushed my fingers under my blouse and inside my bra. My breast was swollen hard as stone, rising higher with every beat of my pulse, and when I brushed the nipple, I felt a rush of pain. I pushed down hard. Holding the nipple between two fingers, I squeezed, and slowly, drops of hot liquid emerged and trickled down the slope of my breast. I wet my thumb and finger and pulled my hand back out. It gave off a faintly sweet smell.

'Yuki, I . . .' His gaze wavered, wandered away from me.

I turned to where he was looking, droplets clinging to my finger and thumb. There in the break in the curtains I saw the face of my mother-in-law, who was supposed to have gone home yesterday. On her face was a look I'd never seen before. It was a look of hatred, but her face wasn't contorted. It was a blank. Her face was dark red, and she was looking right at me. But she said nothing. I thrust my breasts out in her direction. By now they were wet all over. Milk came pouring out, overflowing, soaking through my blouse.

My mother-in-law suddenly said my name: 'Tsudamoto-san.' This was of course my husband's name, too. I was completely startled. It wasn't my mother-in-law standing before me – it was the woman who was here when I came rushing to the hospital upon hearing that my husband was in an accident. Her face was familiar and unfamiliar, her clothes fashionable and old-fashioned.

'Tsudamoto-san,' she said again, 'your laundry is done.'

'Huh?'

'You wrote your name on his pyjamas. There were people waiting, so I went ahead and emptied your load into a basket.'

It wasn't my mother-in-law, it wasn't that woman, it was a middle-aged nurse.

'Sorry to touch your things without permission.' She went up to my husband. 'Tsudamoto-san, how are you? Does the eye still hurt? Did you use the drops?'

My husband's eye was more badly swollen than before. It looked like someone had hit him. Maybe I had. If only it were true. There was prolonged coughing coming from the next bed over, and from the one across the way, a clearing of the throat.

In a low voice, my husband said, 'I did, but it hasn't gotten any better.'

The nurse smiled, bemused. 'It's not that easy. You've got an infection, after all.' She turned to me. 'There's a dryer free now, so why don't you go put the clothes in?'

I thanked her and trotted off. I put my husband's clothes in the dryer and pushed the switch, then felt my breasts again. The swelling had gone away. They didn't feel hot or painful or moist to the touch.

When I licked my dry fingertip, it tasted salty.

When I got home, the room was full of the smell of flowers – not the scent of lilies but the organic smell of vegetation, as if leaves and roots and the soil clinging to them had been ground up together. This was the stench of rot. I washed my hands. The phone rang.

It was my mother-in-law. 'How is he?'

I took in a breath. 'Good, I think. He ate all his lunch and had some fruit, too.' He'd watched my hands wistfully while I peeled an orange from the basket. He didn't say a word.

'I wanted to stay with him until he got out of the hospital, but it's hard staying in a hotel for so long.'

'I'm so sorry I couldn't offer you a place to stay.' I repeated the apology I had said many times already at the hospital.

'No, no, it was fine! You don't have lots of room the way we do, and although I shouldn't say so, I can relax more in a hotel. But there are limits. You can never really recover from your fatigue in a hotel.' She made a sound midway between a sigh and a laugh.

'Since you came all the way to the city, I really wish we could have gone around and done some sightseeing . . .'

'Yes, but it wasn't the right time for that, was it?'

My parents-in-law didn't know who'd been with my husband at the time of the crash. There was no way for them to know, unless he'd made a confession while I wasn't around. That he would never do.

'Anyway,' she went on, 'at least he didn't suffer any brain damage. I mean, just think if he had to be bedridden the rest of his life.'

'Yes, I know,' I said, and then thought to add, 'By the way, what do you do for someone who has a sty?'

'A sty?'

'Hiroyuki's got one. They gave him eye drops at the hospital, but they aren't working . . .'

'Oh? He didn't have anything like that when I was there. But you know, he always used to get those.'

'Did he?'

'Yes, for some reason, he's prone to getting them. But all you can do is use the eye drops.'

My mother-in-law hadn't been in the family when Hiroyuki's grandmother produced such abundant milk, so of course she wouldn't know about the cure. And besides, according to the grandmother, my mother-in-law never had any milk, so that method of curing a sty must have died out with the previous generation.

'What do you know about breast milk?' I asked.

'What?'

Outside it was suddenly beginning to grow dark.

'I heard once that breast milk can cure a sty.'

'Really? Breast milk? Who told you that?'

'My grandmother,' I lied. 'She died when I was a little girl.'

'Is that right?' she said, her voice pitched high. 'A kind of folk cure, I guess. I never heard of such a thing. Well, what a shame!'

'What do you mean?'

'Yuki dear, when Hiroyuki was a baby I had so much milk! If I'd only known it was a cure for a sty, I'd have used it. I could have frozen it and saved it for when it was needed. I always had more milk than I knew what to do with.' She was talking faster and faster. 'So much milk that after I fed Hiroyuki, I had to squeeze out the rest or my breasts would ache. Or they'd swell, and they'd hurt, and I'd get a fever. Hiroyuki couldn't keep formula down; he could only take the breast. It was an ordeal. I used to be in an agony until the swelling went away.'

'How did you make it go away?'

Without a moment's hesitation she answered, 'I went to the hospital, or got a massage.'

'What about spider lilies?'

'Spider lilies? What about them?'

The room was now quite dark. The pale remnants of the flowers sent to my convalescing husband seemed to rise up in the dim room.

'My grandmother said spider lilies could cure the swelling of the breasts,' I said.

My mother-in-law's voice rose higher yet. 'Spider lilies can do that? No! Really? Then I should have left them there for you, Yuki.'

'What?'

'The spider lilies in our garden. I had them all pulled up and thrown out just the other day. Not just the lilies, the whole garden. The trees, the plants, everything. I had it flattened. Now some day when you have a child, there'll be space for a pool or whatever you want. There's plenty of room to run around and play catch, too. You know, you could even build a little house there.'

'Oh, really.'

She burst into laughter. 'Don't worry, Yuki, I'm not saying you should move here or anything. I'm just talking about possibilities . . .'

After I hung up, I pulled the dead flowers out of the spongy material they were stuck in, ready to throw them out. Some were dry and cracking, others brown and sticky; pollen fell on the back of my hands. The last one of the batch had a rather thick stalk, atop which were narrow, faded petals that had ridden up and shrivelled, while central stamens wound around like a crown. It was a white spider lily. ∎

OUT OF ARK

Yumiko Utsu

I have been shooting the 'Out of Ark' series since 2006. There were a number of people and various life forms that didn't or couldn't board Noah's Ark, and I imagine them being multifaceted and complex creatures that interbred, which results in the strange life forms that I make and photograph.

How long has it been since Noah and his passengers set off in their vessel? During that time, these abandoned ones flourished into such a world of beautiful and odd creatures, even God would have to feel terribly slighted at the idea of their having been lost.

In the present time in which I live, I want to relish their beauty, evolution and fun.

The activities of the human race have brought about global warming and its ancillary problems. During my life on this planet I have been a witness to the consequences: the extinction of various creatures as well as many peoples and their cultures. I take various things that are common in our environment and set them aside, placing them in a condition that is at times discomforting or disconcerting, in order to show the beauty of their existence, their intrigue, as well as the bounty of the world. My intention is to make work that can, in a small way, facilitate that awareness. ∎

Translated from the Japanese by Ivan Vartanian

1. *Squid Maria*

2. *Eryingi Family*

3. *Sabo-chan*

4. *Squid Mask*

5. *Squilla Girl*

6. *Caranginae Gills Margarita*

7. Banana Eyelash

8. *Pine Owl*

9. *Swimming Dragon Fruit*

10. *Dekopon Pomeranian*

THE BEAUTY OF
THE PACKAGE

Pico Iyer

'It's My Life', by Bon Jovi, is thumping at high volume through the banquet room in the five-star hotel and people are rising from their chairs to shout, 'Hiroko, Hiroko!' This is a summons to my wife, the fifty-three-year-old mother of the groom, celebrated for her love of both Metallica and the Dalai Lama, to get up from her seat and join her son, a frequent companion at Marilyn Manson concerts, in dancing through the room, hands linked together as they punch the air.

The music is deafening in this great space in the Tokyo suburbs and the spirit is freer, wilder than at any wedding I've known. A local girl is clapping her hands as furiously as her Cuban-American husband back in Florida might. The boys in Armani – products of the country's finest universities – are roaring their approval, as if everything is quite normal. It looks to ignorant me as if the whole, immaculately programmed ceremony is coming apart. But what allows everyone to be so uninhibited is that each one has a keen sense of what's coming next. As soon as the song subsides, we'll be back on a fast-moving bullet train that will carry us through moments of tears and quiet laughter, scenes of reminiscence and silent community, aching ballads and rousing photographs, before ending up at a place called Guaranteed Satisfaction.

I look at my wife, the glamorous soon-to-be grandma still pumping her fist, and wonder how one begins to negotiate a society that somehow meets expectation and confounds it in every gesture, sets up a Platonic model and then encourages individuals to flood it with surprises. Her parents, not long after the war, went through more or less arranged marriages, as many Japanese couples did then;

her children are stepping into a world in which one in every three Japanese under the age of thirty has never dated and almost two-thirds of unmarried men between the ages of eighteen and thirty-four are in no romantic relationship at all.

Not long after we met – my third week in the country, twenty-six years ago – Hiroko said to me, 'You're a little difficult, so I'm going to have to change.'

'Change me, you mean?'

'No!' she said. 'I can't change you! I'll have to change myself to make my peace with what's not easy in you.'

I was so moved by that spirit of selfless adaptability – in Japan, I saw, you try to fit yourself to the situation rather than expecting it to adapt itself to you – that I aspired to change myself to live up to her example. Yet even as this dance of harmony-making was unfolding, the larger whole around us was rewriting its script with every hour: when Hiroko got divorced, in 1989, it was such an unheard-of transgression that her parents cut her off for three months and her brother, though long resident in the West, refuses to speak to her to this day. Nowadays, one in three Japanese marriages ends in divorce.

Bon Jovi, meanwhile, is shouting, 'I ain't gonna be just a face in the crowd / You gonna hear my voice / When I shout it loud,' and I recall the neighbour of mine, a single mom with two kids in suburban Nara, who has painted I ❤ JON across her wall, next to the health club with the Easter Island statue outside it that we walk past on the way to the supermarket. She once packed her two kids into a taxi, flew them to JFK, rented a car so that all three could be taken to Bon Jovi's mansion in New Jersey, stood in silent homage outside his gates – 'My heart is like an open highway,' he's now wailing – then headed back to JFK to fly home.

You can throw yourself into any fantasy, she (and her country) might have been saying, so long as you don't mistake it for real life. That part hasn't changed much since Hiroko's day – or, maybe, Genji's.

Soon after breakfast this bright October morning, the bride's family was led into a special waiting room in the many-storeyed Brighton Hotel, separated from our clan by a small, low barrier, as if the two were on opposite sides, negotiating terms. Perhaps they should be: the girl's family is dressed impeccably, according to the classical model – the patriarch's hands squarely on the thighs of his spotless black trousers, his wife in a kimono that chimes with the early-autumn day, nobody in their group daring to efface the dream with the smudge of personality. On our side is a Spanish boyfriend, a daughter who lives in Valladolid and a mother who's done up her hair in the hotel beauty salon to go with a grey dress that suggests she's off to lunch in the 6th arrondissement.

I watch the mothers introduce their family members to one another, one by one, as if in matching kimono. Everyone sips from little cups of cherry-blossom tea, lightly salted – the taste of spring in early autumn – and the bride looks like a picture-book model of a girl in white. For months, I'm guessing, she's kept herself on an unforgiving diet, while growing her hair long, so it will tumble down as in a heart-shaped frame the minute the special day arrives: now, in her tiara and pearls, her gossamer arms catching the light as she rearranges a curl, she might be Audrey Hepburn in *Roman Holiday*, though even fresher and more delicate.

At 9.45 on the dot, an unsmiling man in a stern black suit comes in to lead the families to the hotel Photo Studio, accompanied by a friendly lady in a kimono, the sweet, smart wedding planner (in self-effacing black) and the man with the camera. The room they enter might be in Versailles – so long as you ignore the puppets and toy monkeys on hand to distract restless babies. Three experts, male and female, slip forward, kneeling discreetly, to position features just right, to tweak shoulders to the ideal angle, to advise how best to put clenched fists on thighs (thumbs out). A chic girl in a loose black jacket works to apply make-up between shots as if on a set of an even more professional kind.

There are two photographers working from a huge camera on

a dolly, which rolls back and forth across the polished floor. The pictures will be framed and ready for collection before the day is over. And then the couple, ready for a thousand close-ups, heads out into the radiant sunshine, and walks towards an entire church set up on a middle floor of the hotel, as thin and elegant as a huge communion wafer in concrete.

It takes a while, I think, to learn how to appreciate the packaging, which is the pageantry, of Japan. In California, growing up in the sixties, I'd been taught that the most important thing is to 'be yourself'; in Japan this, like most Californian pieties, is reversed. The great thing is not to be yourself: to conform to some archetype that the world knows how to deal with, to subordinate your private agenda to a larger whole. What someone wants when she goes to a wedding may not be Pico or Hiroshi or Yuki-chan; it's the model of a bridal couple, going through the rites that have been deemed most pleasing, delivering the scripted words with unwavering sincerity.

It's not just that surface and depth are different here, but that you can't begin to infer one from the other. That college-age girl in the microskirt, flaunting her bare flesh as a streetwalker might, will, if you talk to her, sweetly tell you she's a virgin; romance has little to do with fashion when it comes to choosing a role. And the prim matron in the twinset beside her on the train – Hiroko, who works with her, will tell me – is off to see her young lover tonight and in fact will go with any man who asks.

I've never lived in a society where parts are so perfectly choreographed; my wife calls her boss 'Department Head', which ensures that as little as possible is personal, on either side. I've also never lived somewhere so open with its feelings when the moment allows. I step into a locker room after an American football game in Kyoto, and the 280-pound linebackers are sobbing, too full of emotion to speak, whether they've just won or been trounced. When Daniel Day-Lewis acts, I often reflect in Japan, he moves us not because he's so good at simulating emotions, but, rather, because he can so powerfully access true emotions, with such depth, as soon as his director shouts, 'Rolling!'

Now, as we take our places in the chapel, we're greeted by a girl at an organ playing Bach. Three women in elegant black dresses walk to the front – one with a flute, another with a violin and a third who begins to sing as if her heart might break. The minute she hits her highest note, the bride comes stepping up what's known in Japanese as the Virgin Road, in perfectly synchronized paces, with her father beside her, before being taken over by her groom a few feet in front of the altar just as 'Here Comes the Bride' subsides.

Neither of the two is Christian; I'm not sure they've ever been to a place of Christian worship before (though their honeymoon will take them through the churches of Vienna, Prague and Budapest). But this is how it's done in movies, in dreams, and this is what they've been rehearsing for months to make meaningful and true.

The couple stands in front of a tiny sliver of light that casts October sunshine down on them. A priest appears – a hotel employee, perhaps, though maybe truly connected to some church – and leads us in a Christian prayer in Japanese, having told the audience when to recite 'amen'. The young ones kneel, they close their eyes in prayer, exchange oaths. The groom gently parts the bride's veil, the priest raises his voice above them, translating 'God' as *'kami-sama'*, the word originally meant for a Shinto deity. The two share their first kiss as a married couple.

There are to be six weddings in the hotel this holiday Monday, and there were nine here the day before; for all I know, this man is leading amens in every one. But his voice quivers with intensity as he recites his words and when I look at his eyes, tightly clenched, I wonder whether he will burst into tears as well. The nature of what's authentic and what's not confounds me daily in Japan. I've read that older couples hire actresses to visit them on Sundays at lunchtime and say, 'Hi, Mom! Hi, Dad! How are you doing?' if their own daughters are disinclined to do so.

When the couple walks out into the light again, we shower them with the confetti we've been given for the purpose, and there are more elaborate photo ops in the sun. I think of the time, twenty-one years before, when Hiroko wrote me a card that moved me. I told her how much I liked one phrase, and she began to reproduce it, in every letter she sent me for years thereafter, regardless of the context. If you've given happiness with a sentence – or a gesture – why not repeat it again and again?

In a stylish antechamber, we're brought tingling sorbets in transparent, light blue goblets, and drinks, and then, after a suitable pause, led into the banquet room, where a gorgeous announcer in a floating, thin black dress starts putting us at ease with bright chatter. In truth, this professional-seeming emcee turns out to be a friend of the bride's, moonlighting as a favour, and I appear to be the only one worried that she might upstage the bride. The announcer's job, after all, is to look gorgeous, while the bride only has to be Audrey Hepburn: in a role-correct society, there's less room for competition.

And here a whole different movement in the carefully arranged symphony begins. Arcade Fire comes onto the soundtrack, and new husband and wife walk in, spotlit, so we can admire the bride's dress again. The two sit alone onstage, and the groom apologizes for the simplicity, the modesty of the occasion (for which he has paid, out of his own pocket, $30,000).

Then, over a seven-course meal, a wedding ceremony is turned into a wedding party. A speech from the groom's boss, very long, and a toast from the guy who'd been their chaperone on early dates. A giggle from the announcer. A friend of the bride comes up and, through tears, expresses her congratulations, before escorting her friend out of the room for another change of costume.

Bags of money are handed out, following a pattern I can't begin to discern. Envelopes of cash are slipped into certain hands. Members of the staff steal in and out, whispering directions. More sorbets arrive, a beautifully cut steak. An onstage 'interview' is held with the

Cupid who first introduced the couple, though now he's a Buddhist priest, munching on steak beside his wife.

I think of what a leap of faith this occasion entails. One Japanese man in four nowadays says that he has 'no interest' in sex, even 'despises' it; more and more Japanese women are marrying out of Japan, so as to escape their traditional roles and constraints. Not so many years ago, there were two thousand 'Narita Divorces' in the space of twelve months (young Japanese man and woman enjoy a wedding; they go to Honolulu or Surfers Paradise for their honeymoon – and the girl is so at ease with abroad and English, her husband so ill at ease, that by the time they return to Narita Airport six days later, roles unhappily reversed, they decide they have to get a divorce).

Three former band mates of the bride now come to the front and deliver a stirring, *American Idol*-worthy version of 'Seasons of Love' from *Rent*. The words appear on a screen that fills one wall, and one of the young beauties takes a solo, belting her words out as if she were Diana Ross, while the others trade quieter turns. Then all three dance in perfect sync, the Supremes translated to a *Mikado* world.

I could go on, describing every last detail matched to each passing moment, and refined over decades: the bride's re-entry and the bridal couple's visit to every table; the cake wheeled out in advance of the meal so that everyone can crowd forward and take photos of the bride stuffing pieces of it into her proud husband's grinning mouth. (Once the photo op is complete, the cake is wheeled out, never to be seen again.) The champagne, and the beautiful moment when the couple goes out and returns with a candle, with which the two of them set off a flicker of light on every last table. The films made up of slides of them both through the years, as if a segment of the old TV programme *This Is Your Life* were set now to the wistful chimes of U2 and A-ha.

Yet the point, really, is not in the details but in the idea. When foreign friends visit me in Kyoto, they often marvel at the perfection of Japanese packaging, the way every candy will be individually wrapped, and a Popsicle will be placed inside a bag with a sachet of ice to keep it cool, the way a three-dollar stick of incense will be sold in a cool, cylindrical box and then placed within a gossamer bag and then draped in elegant paper, with a little business card placed under the bow, reminding you that Lisn, the elegant shop, sells 'sophisticated incense for listeners'.

But if those friends stay longer, they start to complain about the individual wrapping of the self, the packaging of rituals and the heart. As if something dishevelled is automatically more authentic; as if personal feelings can't be set within impersonal frames, the way the wedding photos from this day will be, and the memories of what was felt when Bono and The Edge sang 'One' on the sound system.

Now the parents of the happy couple are standing, backs straight, against the main doors to the room, and the bride is reading a letter of thanks to her mother and father, moving her groom to tears. He does the same and then his mother, my wife, delivers a speech apologizing for all the ways she made life difficult for him when she got a divorce, and his sister, at a nearby table, collapses into sobs. There are hankies in every young woman's hand at this point, and the sound of sniffled tears; by candlelight, the scene is as affecting as the climax of any rapturously photographed, impeccably storyboarded movie.

Then the groom's friends gather round him in a circle and toss him up into the air five times, shouting, 'Banzai!' The same thing is done after every season with every single winning baseball coach. But it's always stirring, always the perfect gesture of warmth and celebration. Does the fact we all say 'I love you' make it mean less every time?

The guests now start to disperse; they know what formalities to expect, perhaps, but still they have tears in their eyes, and voices crack as they say goodbye, the way I can listen to the song that wiped me out at seventeen and still be fairly confident it will do the same now (if only because it brings back the memory of being seventeen, wide open). I think of the priest – he looked like an ageing Elvis, but he carried himself like a solemn man of Rome – and the place mats, on every one of which the groom has written a description of each of the eighty or so guests. I think of the Bach – it's always Bach, I suspect – and yet 'Jesu, Joy of Man's Desiring' always stirs and uplifts.

Upstairs, in the third-floor Fitting Room, there are so many sobbing brides and kimonoed old women that people start welcoming the wrong grandmother, or thanking a bewildered-looking man who belongs to another wedding party. In the hallway, everyone is wiping off tears and mascara as the party from the next wedding streams out, in a similar state of emotional disarray. Our newly-weds are now in their room – part of the wedding package (though it's not, I gather, the Moonlight Forest room, the Lovers' Suite or any of the other love-hotel options, such as the View Bath Luna Suite).

A young boy from our group slips me a perfectly folded scrap of paper with a hand-drawn map on it. 'We're having a second party,' he explains, in English. 'Not far from here. In the park. Very relaxed. Lots of frisbees; kind of like a picnic. Please come.'

Outside, the bright autumnal sunshine catches flocks of kids heading back from a radiant day at Tokyo Disneyland nearby. I remember hearing that the wartime emperor, Hirohito, was buried with his Mickey Mouse wristwatch, the smallest thing changing value as it moves between cultures so that it becomes folly to laugh at any prop or to see it as out of context.

I've been to plenty of weddings in English churches where the women in broad hats whisper about the young Thai wife Charlie has brought back from his stint out East with Swire's, or say, 'Surely that woman couldn't be a member of the bridal party?' I've been to my share of New Age weddings in California where groom and bride stand barefoot above the ocean, a friend of theirs having acquired a certificate from the Universal Life Church to marry them, and recite Rumi before playing Van Morrison singing, 'Have I told you lately that I love you . . . '.

I've even officiated at weddings in Californian gardens where the groom declaims from Shakespeare and the bride takes pains to prevent me from seeing how many previous husbands are listed on the certificate I'm obliged to sign.

But none has so affected or filled me up as this one. Somehow this seems more authentic, precisely because it's planned so seamlessly, more full of feeling exactly because every moment is choreographed.

Is that the Japanese secret? That the emotions we find when rehearsed may be at least as powerful – as real – as the ones we so cherish for their spontaneity and distinctness? That somebody else's model, honed and perfected over centuries, may be better and wiser than the one we've come up with ourselves last month? Might that even be the secret of a happy marriage? Play your part to perfection, and before long, the feelings that belong to it may be yours. Hit your mark and, before you know it, those marks will disappear and you will be the wife and husband of the picture books.

I don't have time to think of any of this; the new married couple is heading out into the autumn sun, as the next couple steps into the Bridal Salon. ■

GRANTA

PIG SKIN

Andrés Felipe Solano

TRANSLATED FROM THE SPANISH BY NICK CAISTOR

© KENICHI YOKONO
Liquidness/Confusing 26 Eyeballs
2012

It's not that I've forgotten his face, more that it changes each day inside my head, like lava from a constantly erupting volcano that cannot settle into a definite shape. One day, a dense fringe of hair covering his forehead is his most prominent feature. On the next, it is his baboon's snout. Yesterday it seemed to me his face was beautiful, strong yet at the same time sad, like that of a long-forgotten actor.

We met one night seven years ago on board the Busan–Osaka ferry, and never saw each other again. Even so, I owe everything to him. Without Park Bong I would still be lying on the beach near the port, where I used to go to watch Russian seamen enjoying their free afternoons. A beach umbrella with rusty metal spikes, a large can of beer and a box of fried chicken – that was me back in the days when I spied on those strangers getting a tan, some of them pot-bellied, others with gladiators' bodies, most of them bald. They would talk to the Filipino girls, the only ones who wore bikinis. Korean girls always dressed as if they were about to go mountain climbing. As I wandered round the port I could see the litter the Russians left behind on their nights out, tossed outside the huge warehouses where fish was stored, or piled up by the Madonna Billiard Parlour or the Lolita Bar, places with big neon signs where the sailors sought refuge after nightfall. Park Bong must have walked round the same places, the same streets, and yet it was my destiny to meet him on board the *Panstar Honey*.

My wife had won a trip for two in a mobile-phone company prize draw. The prize did not cover the hotel or meals, but I had an overwhelming desire to see Osaka. In those days we didn't have much money, hardly any in fact, so it was not an easy decision. I promised her I would write an article about the nightlife in the Umeda district for a travel magazine to cover the money we spent. She also wanted to go to Japan – she needed a few days off. While I was lazing on the beach over the summer, pretending I was gathering information for a novel, she worked as a programming assistant for the Busan Film Festival. During the cold months I'd sheltered in a public library. That was where the wish to visit Osaka began to incubate within me like malaria. One afternoon I came across an anthology of essays in English on Japanese literature. Nearly all of them were boring, apart from one, which I read three times. It talked about the Buraiha school. 'A group of writers who embraced alcohol, drugs, sex and a life of excess as a response to the identity crisis facing Japan during and after the Second World War' was how the author described them at the start of his essay. The Buraiha were the dissolute, the villains of modern Japanese literature. One of the most prominent members of this 'school of decadence' was Sakunosuke Oda.

The ferry trip would allow me to get to know the city where Oda was born. I had a very simple plan for when I arrived in Osaka. I would fill my belly with alcohol in memory of the Buraiha writers, and try to persuade my wife to engage in a threesome with a Japanese girl. That would be my best homage to the school of decadents and my humble tribute to the improvement in relations between Korea and Japan, always as tense as a harp string. As soon as I bumped into Park Bong, though, my intentions changed completely. By the end of the night I met him, I had become a thriller writer. The truth is I have only published one book, but in my defence I should say it has been a huge success in both Korea and Japan. The novel is called *Pig Skin,* and its main character is a detective whose face no one remembers. A perfect impostor.

Yesterday, while I was clipping my nose hairs in front of the mirror after reading a story, I again remembered the incident that was the start of everything. If it had not been for my wife's forgetfulness I might never have spoken to Park Bong. My wife left our camera on the back seat of the taxi taking us to the dock. This led to a bitter argument even before the *Panstar Honey* set sail. I saw prize-winning photographs all around me, photos I would never take. The red face, bulging eyes and shiny jacket of the trumpeter welcoming the passengers on board with a woeful rendition of 'Here Comes the Sun' was worthy of a portrait, as were the abandoned cargo boats lying on their sides in the outer harbour like huge cattle, and the red, salt-encrusted navigation lights. Not to mention the beautiful stewardesses with their long legs and hair done up in ponytails, studiedly calm. Half the crew was Russian.

We quarrelled for half an hour until I decided it would be best to separate before one of us was thrown overboard. As we split up in a corridor, I told my wife I was going to the sauna. According to the leaflet we had been given when we checked in, in addition to a public bath, the ferry had a restaurant in what was the main saloon, a bar, a gift shop and a small supermarket.

I undressed and stowed my clothes in a locker. Going into the steam room I saw an old man in the shower washing off the last traces of soap. At the far end, in a small pool near portholes looking out onto the sea, another man was lying back with a towel covering his face. He seemed to be asleep. I entered the water as quietly as I could so as not to disturb him. I didn't want to wake him up and have to face his look of reproach. The old man finished his shower and on his way back to the lockers made a revolting noise. He spat into a basin as if he had lung cancer and was coughing up all the filth in his dying body with this one immense gob of phlegm. I writhed with disgust in the pool.

'I hate that sound. I hate it. Damned sonofabitch,' the man next to me muttered in perfect English.

'Yes, so do I,' I repeated softly, as if to myself. Spitting seemed to be the national sport of all Korean men over forty.

The man pulled the towel from his face and sank down in the water for a couple of seconds and surfaced again. When he spoke, it was with a good deal of ceremony.

'If it's not indiscreet, might I ask where you are from?'

'From Colombia,' I replied reluctantly, thinking he would not have the faintest idea where my country was to be found.

'I know someone who lives in Colombia. He runs a tae kwon do academy. His name is Moon. The maestro Moon. In reality he has another, more old-fashioned profession.'

I had no chance to ask what his acquaintance's other profession was, because he immediately came over to me and, after carefully drying his hand on a towel, extended it. He introduced himself with his full name. It was in three parts, although I can only recall the first two: Park Bong. When I told my wife this, she said it made no sense. Nobody was called Park Bong. It was completely absurd.

He also misunderstood my name, because on the various occasions I saw him that night he insisted on calling me Andrea instead of Andrés. I told him I was a writer and that this was the first time I was visiting Japan. I wanted to write a short, incisive novel like the Buraiha authors. I don't know why, but I mentioned Oda and his links with Osaka. I suppose I was slightly nervous. It had been quite a while since I had talked to anybody about my life. I was sure this man would not know anything about those decadents, the libertines of Japanese literature. Once again, I had underestimated him.

'Yes of course I know who they are. I used to import goods from Japan. Books, films, manga, video games. A professor at the National University in Seoul once asked me to bring him a couple of Oda's books. I don't know whether you know it, but until a few years ago it was illegal to bring in all that sort of thing from Japan.'

Apart from revealing in these few words that he had dealt in contraband, during this first chat Park Bong mentioned some other things about his life, among them the fact that he had travelled regularly between Korea and Japan from an early age. He had learned English when he was very young from living close to a US military base in Sasebo, and perfected it at another base at Jinhae.

'I can tell you more about myself,' he said as the sun was about to set, 'but first we have to come to an agreement.'

After Park Bong briefly explained what the agreement consisted of, I stayed silent, enveloped in the steam for several minutes. Out of the porthole I could glimpse the leaden sea. One of the adolescents who was part of the big group of students I had seen when we boarded took a quick shower and stepped towards the pool. I knew I had to give my answer, whatever it might be. Park Bong was not going to carry on discussing the matter with somebody else present. So I said yes, I would do it. Park Bong nodded, and clambered out of the pool just as the student was getting in. As he left, I was able to study Park Bong's naked body, which I remember perfectly. In my mind, his multiple faces are always attached to the same incorruptible body. He had the beginnings of a belly but his arms and legs were those of a professional wrestler. As for his penis, I have to say that it was the biggest I had seen in a public bath in all my time in Asia.

Over dinner I made up with my wife over a clam chowder. Her mood lightened, even though I only smiled and didn't say much. I was still in the grip of the profound impression Park Bong had made on me. I was counting the minutes to our next encounter: he had left a note in my sauna locker, suggesting we meet at the bar at eleven o'clock, where he would provide me with further details.

After our meal, I told my wife I wanted to go to bed early. I did not want to feel tired during our first day in Osaka. She agreed, and we parted with a quick kiss. The tickets we had won in the prize draw were for B-class berths. This meant separate shared cabins for men and women. C class was a big saloon with futons on the floor for forty people, while A class, which we had tried to change to when we boarded, consisted of single or double cabins.

Park Bong arrived fifteen minutes late. He was wearing a leather jacket that I envied. As soon as he was seated at the bar he got straight to the point. Park Bong explained that he himself had been tailing the man I was to follow for three months. But the man knew him very well so he could not be on his trail for longer than an hour, or at less than ten metres from him. Park Bong was afraid the man might catch him out on the ferry. That was why he needed me.

'He can recognize my odour, my smell. We worked together in

the same department for almost fifteen years,' he said, ordering two Japanese beers. He hated Korean beer.

In the sauna, Park Bong had told me he had once worked in the section of the Korean National Security Agency that dealt with film censorship. He said that in the seventies he had watched thousands of feature films. His job was to award them points from one to five according to a system his bosses had established: communist propaganda, destabilizing the government, a threat to morals, consumption of drugs, inappropriate language. If a Korean film was given five points, Park Bong had to stick to the director like a limpet and submit a weekly report. While we were drinking ice-cold Kirins, I pressed him to tell me more about his life. After working for the secret service and then dedicating himself to moving contraband between Korea and Japan, he had set up a detective agency near the port of Busan. The most extraordinary part of his life was his relationship with his secretary, Yuri Kawahara.

My reward for following his former colleague from his cabin to the supermarket, looking at his right hand and counting the number of petals on the flower tattooed there when he came to pay, was for him to tell me all about that relationship, which he had described as a true mystery of nature.

'Don't worry, it has nothing to do with love. It goes far beyond anything so banal. It's worth hearing, you won't regret it.'

Shortly before one in the morning, Park Bong paid for the beers and pointed out the man's cabin to me. He was in A class. 'He has very odd eating habits, as if his stomach were in another time zone. He always has lunch at five in the afternoon, and supper at three in the morning,' Park Bong told me. At that time, the target would leave his cabin and go to the supermarket to buy pot noodles. I knew what I had to do. 'We'll see each other at half past three up on deck, near the ping-pong tables,' he said, walking away with his hands stuffed in his jacket.

I roamed for a while along the corridors until loud shouts and applause drew me to the main saloon. The students were entranced by the dance of the seven veils being performed for them by one of the stewardesses who had welcomed us on board. From the poster by the entrance, I saw that another of the stewardesses was also part of the show. Her name was Irina, and she was going to sing, accompanied by the red-faced trumpeter. The spectacle was to conclude with a male receptionist performing magic tricks. The show was incredibly long and tedious. Irina sang out of tune in a shiny, tacky dress, and the magician's hands shook. He looked even more nervous than I was.

Afterwards, I was left on my own with an elderly couple who were quite drunk. One of them ordered a second bottle of whisky while I looked out of a big window at the lights of Japanese coastal cities. By now we were crossing the Inland Sea. Hotels covered in neon flowers like enormous birthday cakes and a huge Ferris wheel passed in front of my eyes as the dark waters slapped against the sides of the ship. I stared for a long time at a helium balloon the magician had used in his act that was stuck in a corner of the ceiling. To me it seemed like the very picture of loneliness. So the time passed until the moment when I was to fulfil my mission.

The man left his cabin at three, but did not head straight for the supermarket as Park Bong had said he would. Instead, he went up on deck. I followed him at a distance. A rush of blood filled my heart cavities. It felt as though it was expanding to twice its normal size. Fortunately lots of youngsters were still around, drifting hither and thither like schools of fish, mobile phones in hand. The man sat on one of the benches near the ship engines. I leaned against a rail behind him, next to an old woman eating crisps from an enormous packet and staring into the void, into the empty depths of the night. Five minutes later, the man stood up and walked over to Irina, who was standing there smoking, once more dressed in her uniform. He asked her for a light. They remained close to each other, neither saying a word. At that moment it seemed to me that all of us – the old lady, the man with the tattoo, the stewardess-singer, my wife and I myself – were nothing more than solitary balloons at the end of a party.

I walked away gloomily. I could not stay close to the man without arousing suspicion, and so I went back down to the saloon. He would have to go through there on his way to the supermarket. It was very likely that he was dangerous. I played my cards like a real detective.

Even though I invented a lot about Park Bong's life in *Pig Skin*, for example that at a certain point he had to take shelter for a year in a Buddhist monastery to avoid being killed, I chose to leave many things exactly as he told them to me that night. After it was published, several readers wrote to congratulate me. What they most enjoyed about the novel was the unusual method the detective and his secretary employed to solve the most difficult cases. The method, if it can be called that, was precisely one of the things I took word for word from what Park Bong told me on the deck of that ferry.

They had met at a baseball game. As usual, the Busan team were losing. The fans' insults echoed round the stadium, but Park Bong's were so outlandish they made Yuri and the girlfriend she was with laugh out loud. From the start, Park Bong had liked Yuri's friend, and so when the game had finished he invited them out for chicken and a beer. He convinced them by saying that they needed to drown their sorrows together after their team's humiliation. To Park Bong's dismay, the friend left after the first mug of beer. Yuri decided to stay – she lived near the stadium with her mother. She told him she had finished university and was looking for a job. For the moment, she was working as an assistant in a shop selling maths games for children. The detective said he had an office and was possibly in need of a secretary. He was drunk when he said this, trying to impress her. At the end of the night, Yuri had to help Park into a taxi after she found him fast asleep when she came back from the toilet. The following Monday, Yuri knocked on Park Bong's office door while he was drinking a bottle of Sunrise 808 to cure his hangover and staring through the window at a Vietnamese ship unloading. He had no idea how she found his office, which he shared with an agency that hired seamen. He was certain he had not given her the address.

I think I can help you in your work, said the young girl, proud of herself for tracking down the detective. Park Bong surmised that she must have searched his wallet as he slept and taken out one of his business cards. Not bad. He took her on that same day, although at the time he did not have many clients. Yuri was silent, methodical, possibly too obliging for his taste. She had black coffee and rice cakes for him in the morning, or a spicy fish soup if he turned up in the afternoon after a long night of drinking. She not only paid all the office bills, but looked after the expenses of Park Bong's apartment and even made sure his car tax was up to date. Sometimes at the end of the month they shared a meal in a sashimi restaurant, or Yuri accompanied him to see an old friend who ran a second-hand record shop. Lou, as he was called, had grown fond of Yuri. She knew a lot about music, especially Korean and Japanese psychedelic rock from the late sixties, something unusual for a woman her age. One night, Park Bong invited her to eat at his favourite restaurant. He was anxious because he could not solve a case, and needed to clear his head. As they sat with a small grill filled with thin strips of pig skin, she told him a little about her family, her Japanese father and Korean mother. Her father had been quite a well-known singer in Osaka. His version of 'Bésame Mucho' had been a hit in the seventies, and could be found on the playlists of many of the city's karaoke bars. He died onstage of a heart attack, and Yuri went back to Busan with her mother. She had never felt at home in either country. That night they ended up in a motel near the port. In order to find out what happened next, I had to complete my task.

The man with the tattoo went into the supermarket. He picked up some spicy noodles, like the ones I used to eat on the Russian beach those afternoons when I had nothing to do. He went to the till, and I followed him with the first thing I could grab. Between us was a fat lady I rudely pushed in front of. She gave me a look of pure hatred. The decisive moment had arrived. My legs trembled like a building shaking in an earthquake. The man took his hand out of his pocket and held out a new banknote. I saw part of the flower. It was red, and looked like an azalea. Approaching him from behind, I reached to take a bar of chocolate from beside the till. I needed to find a better angle while he was waiting for the cashier to take the note. At last his hand was completely uncovered and in my field of vision. I started counting the petals, one, two, three, four, five. At that instant I heard a voice next to me.

'What are you doing awake? And why have you got a tube of lubricating jelly in your hand?'

It was my wife. Startled, I turned to her for a moment, but then quickly looked back towards the man's hand. It was not visible any more. It was back in his pocket, and I would never catch a glimpse of it again. I don't recall what I said to my wife, but she left in high dudgeon. As the man went past me, he looked me straight in the eye. It felt as though my body was being put through a powerful mincer – muscles, tendons, bones, everything. It was obvious I would not be able to keep following him, and I had to meet with Park Bong in half an hour. There was no way I could tell him I had failed; I couldn't bear the idea I would not get to hear the end of the story about him and his secretary.

'Are you sure? Are you absolutely sure there were six petals on the flower?'

'Yes, I saw them very quickly, but I am sure. I counted six.'

'A week ago there were five. How odd. Damn it, that makes everything more complicated.'

There was no one else on deck. Park Bong took out a cigarette and stood lost in thought. The chill of dawn enveloped us. The ship passed under a gigantic bridge. Once he had finished his cigarette, he decided to tell me the end of the story.

'In fact that night I was going to sack her. There was no point in her wasting her life in my office. She was still young, and she was engaged, although she seldom saw her fiancé. She could easily find something better.'

The case Park Bong was working on at that time involved a con man. His client had paid him a handsome advance, and he had been close to resolving the case, but there seemed always to be one piece of the puzzle missing. He told Yuri all about it as they drank and ate grilled slices of pig skin. He hardly ever revealed any details of his cases to her. She only found out about them when she was filing the records once they had been solved.

Park Bong had not been thinking of having sex with Yuri. The idea of going to a motel had come from her. He guessed she must have been very drunk. His plan had been to stay in the bathtub until Yuri fell asleep, and then to stretch out on the sofa. But as soon as he saw his secretary's naked feet, the detective's willpower evaporated. They were tiny, beautiful, eternal like a statue's – those were the exact words he used to describe them to me. Her toes were perfectly proportioned, the nails painted blood red. This simple detail was enough to unleash a huge tidal wave of desire in Park Bong. I'm a podophile, he confessed to me with a wry smile, taking out another cigarette. I love women's feet. On my monthly trips to the brothels on Texas Street in Busan or the ones in Tobita Shinchi in Osaka, I used to ask the whore to show me her feet before I struck a deal. I studied them like a botanist, and it was only if I liked the arches, the heel and the soles, that I agreed to pay for a night with them. This very rarely occurred – I seldom came across a perfect foot. Yuri had exquisite feet, but that was not what cemented our relationship. What happened next is still beyond my comprehension. At this, he stopped and stared hard at me. I realized that he had not told anyone his secret before. Something in me, something I myself am unaware of, encouraged him to tell me that at the height of her orgasm Yuri cried out two completely unconnected words. What came from his secretary's mouth was so absurd it remained stuck in the detective's mind until the next morning. The words had been Blue Crab. Thanks to them Park Bong closed the case. Crab was the nickname of the owner of a tea house known to be a bookie. He was the one who had swindled his client. Blue was the colour of the drawer where he found the evidence of the man's guilt.

During the time Yuri worked in his office they had sex nine times to try to solve the most complex cases, but his secretary was not always able to provide him with a crucial word or number. She could only do this if Park Bong took her to the extremes of sexual ecstasy. To do that they had to really fling themselves into it, and he was no longer a young man. The last time they slept together, Yuri was already married.

When he finished telling me the story, the detective withdrew to a corner and sent a text message.

'I haven't seen Yuri for two years. She lives in Osaka now with her husband. I've asked her to meet me. I need to solve this case. If I do, I can retire. I'm fed up with this life.' Those were the last words I ever heard him say.

That night I had the entire plot for *Pig Skin*. I wrote it down in my notebook by the light of my mobile screen. Exhausted, I promised myself I would talk to Park Bong as soon as day dawned, to tell him I wasn't sure how many petals there were on the flower. I looked for him in every corner. I couldn't find him in the sauna, the supermarket or on deck. I knocked on my wife's cabin and told her everything that had happened. I begged her to help me find him. We walked around the *Panstar Honey* from bow to stern and did not come across him anywhere.

When we reached Osaka, I went to return my cabin key in a pretty rotten mood. I was handed a small card by the man who had performed as a magician the night before. 'Let's meet by the exit to immigration control. I'll tell you how to get to Jiyūken, the restaurant where Oda used to meet up with his friends.' It was unsigned. Instead he had drawn an animal. I thought it looked like a wolf. My wife said it was a fox. I was pleased: I still had the opportunity to tell him the truth.

Thanks to my passport, it took me one hour to get through immigration. The customs officers were convinced I was loaded with drugs. Why else would a Colombian be travelling by ferry between

Busan and Osaka? They inspected my bag several times. They took out my shampoo and put it through their X-ray machine. They showed me something that looked like a shopping catalogue, but instead of shoes, jewels and perfumes there were photos of automatic weapons, bags full of pills, a thick wad of banknotes and a small heap of white powder. They asked me if I was carrying any of these things. Then they made me undress in another room. In the end they apologized. I could understand them. If they had caught somebody with a secret haul, they would have won a medal. When I got outside the terminal nobody was there. Park Bong must have grown tired of waiting and left. I saw three cigarette butts on the floor. I picked one up. It was the brand that he had smoked, the same as the protagonist of *Pig Skin*.

Sometimes I think Park Bong was not a detective or anything of the sort. Perhaps he didn't have the slightest idea where Colombia was, or who on earth Oda had been. He had just sized me up in two seconds. Even before he had removed the wet towel he had known who I was and what I needed. During the hours we spent on the *Panstar Honey* he put breadcrumbs on his palm so I would peck at them like a little bird and not leave his side. Maybe everything he had told me was simply to avoid being bored. It was also quite possible he took the ferry once a week, and the man with the flower tattoo was his associate. Or perhaps he had a second family in Osaka. Korean men like Japanese women, and Japanese women like Korean men. I like women from both countries. I still haven't given up on the idea of having a threesome in honour of reconciliation between them. At other times I imagine what Park Bong must have had to do because of me. Supposing that all he said was true, the detective must have gone down on his knees to Yuri to beg her to have sex one more time in order to solve the case that had suddenly become more complicated.

I mentioned that yesterday I thought of Park Bong once more. After I had lounged on my leather sofa reading a short story, his features came back to me like the perfect face of an actor or saint, somebody who was outside time. Today his face is a blank screen, a deserted planet. The sofa is opposite a large window with a view of the sea between Korea and Japan. We don't have to worry so much about money these days. The royalties from my novel keep being deposited in my account, and a producer has contacted me about a screen adaptation. Yet in some ways I am in exactly the same position as when I started out. After *Pig Skin* I haven't been able to write a thing. In desperation I have tried to take my wife to the heights of sexual ecstasy so that she can reveal the plot of a new novel at the moment of orgasm. I have also taken the Busan–Osaka ferry four times in the hope of meeting Park Bong again.

The last line of the story reads: 'The fox is the god of cunning and betrayal. If the spirit of the fox enters a man, his descendants are doomed. The fox is the god of writers.'

Perhaps Park Bong was a writer, and I am in one of his stories, and he can remember my face. Yes, perhaps he was a true writer, the last of the Buraiha. ∎

PRINTABLE

Toh EnJoe

TRANSLATED FROM THE JAPANESE BY DAVID G. BOYD

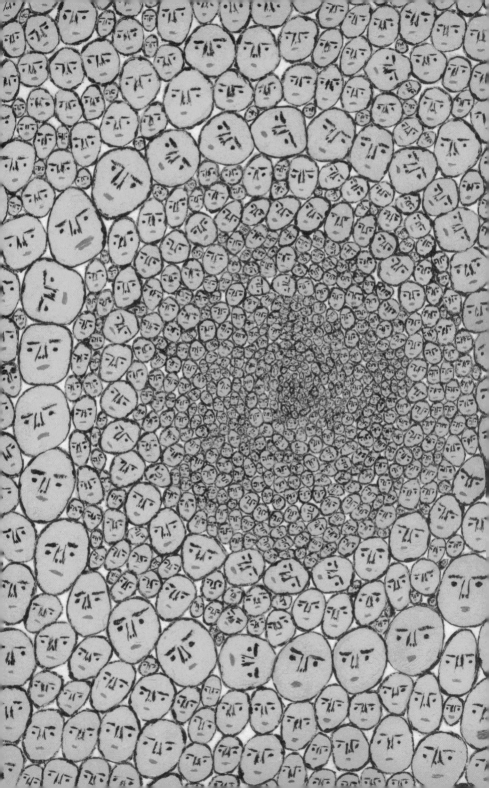

Sometimes I set stories in San Francisco because I have friends who live there. No family yet, sadly. I like to imagine them reading what I write and maybe smiling. I'm setting this story in Tokyo-Tokyo for the same exact reason. Greg, for one, lives in Tokyo-Tokyo. We first met a few years ago in San Antonio, Texas. He was there as our interpreter, but he actually makes his living as a translator. Last year he moved to Tokyo-Tokyo. Situated between present-day Tokyo and future Tokyo: Tokyo-Tokyo. New York-New York. Europa-Europa. Tiger-Tiger. Bilbao-New York-Bilbao. Never-Nevermore. It's a city like those cities. Of course it doesn't really exist, but the people who live there don't seem to mind, and – if you ask me – that's just the way things are. There's nothing unusual about things you can't do anything about.

Now I'm working on this story, hoping Greg will be the one to translate it, but I'm sure he won't. Either way, he will read these words. In someone else's translation. Or in the original. Or maybe both. The Greg in this story will find them in his mailbox. A plain-looking, oversized Manila envelope is waiting for him there amid a heap of flyers and bills. Greg climbs the rust-railed stairway while sorting out the mail for his wife, then cuts through the clear tape on the envelope. He pushes the front door open with his shoulder and surveys the package's contents. Inside he finds this story and a translation. Or a story and its original. He takes a second to think about which one to look at first, then turns around when the bedroom door opens. Good morning, says his wife, blinking sleepily. Then, glancing at the stack of papers in his hands, she asks: New work? It looks like the work's already over, he responds, holding up the translation so she can see.

Someone else's, you mean, she says looking at Greg. You're hung up on work that's already over. She doesn't know it yet, but she sounds a little bitter. She refrains from saying: You *would* have the time to do that. She says: Greg, you. Greg, you're the one who talked me into moving here. Sometimes you forget that. You were born somewhere in Texas – in Paris or London or Berlin or Rome or wherever it was. But now you're stuck between times in some God-awful place like Tokyo-Tokyo. You have to be here for your translation job. But it would be nice if you weren't always working on that long, long novel. Sure, you can do that. If you want. But – aside from that – I want you to do some work that we can live on. We don't have a lot of money left. You won't say it, and I know it hasn't even crossed your mind: We'd be all right if I found a job. But I'm as much a writer as you are a translator. And I don't write non-fiction. I live to write fiction. But I don't know the language here, and people here don't know my language. I can work, but people here won't see it as work. It would be something different. I hate to admit it, but I haven't been able to write well since we got here. Even in what used to be my language. My brain is full of another kind of language. I don't even know what I'm writing any more. I can speak the language here, but I just can't write it. I keep getting worse at my own language while getting better at a foreign one. It's like I'm two different people, but I'm not really either of them. Like I'm a kid again. I'm supposed to be writing a novel, but I don't think anyone would see it as a novel.

You're translating a long, long novel. Your contract states that you won't receive any payment until the translation is over. But you went for it and came to this city. You love this story that much. Living in this city was a part of the deal. When they came to you with the offer, you didn't think twice. When I started listing my practical concerns, you countered by eagerly telling me the writer's name, but it was a name I'd never heard before. If I can translate this writer's work, it'll change our lives, you say. This isn't some run-of-the-mill novelist. No writer sells better, you tell me. You go through some of the writer's books – but I know that every book you mention was written by

SUBSCRIBE

Subscribe to *Granta* to save up to 29%
on the cover price and get free access
to the magazine's entire digital archive.

US $48   **CANADA** $56   **LATIN AMERICA** $68

Complete the form overleaf,
visit granta.com or call 845-267-3031

© KIMIAKI YAEGASHI

'Provides enough to satisfy the most rabid
appetite for good writing and hard thinking'
– *Washington Post*

GRANTA.COM

GRANTA

THE MAGAZINE OF NEW WRITING

SUBSCRIPTION FORM FOR US, CANADA AND LATIN AMERICA

Yes, I would like to take out a subscription to *Granta*.

GUARANTEE: If I am ever dissatisfied with my *Granta* subscription, I will simply notify you, and you will send me a complete refund or credit my credit card, as applicable, for all un-mailed issues.

YOUR DETAILS

MR / MISS / MRS / DR ....

NAME ....

ADDRESS ....

....

CITY.. STATE ....

ZIP CODE .... COUNTRY ....

EMAIL ....

☐ Please check this box if you do not wish to receive special offers from *Granta*

☐ Please check this box if you do not wish to receive offers from organizations selected by *Granta*

YOUR PAYMENT DETAILS

1 year subscription: ☐ US: $48 ☐ Canada: $56 ☐ Latin America: $68

3 year subscription: ☐ US: $120 ☐ Canada: $144 ☐ Latin America: $180

Enclosed is my check for $ _____ made payable to *Granta*.

Please charge my: ☐ Visa ☐ MasterCard ☐ Amex

Card No. ☐☐☐☐☐☐☐☐☐☐☐☐☐☐☐☐

Exp. ☐☐☐☐

Security Code ☐☐☐☐☐☐

SIGNATURE .... DATE ....

Please mail this order form with your payment instructions to:

Granta Publications
PO Box 359
Congers, NY 10920-0359

Or call 845-267-3031
Or visit GRANTA.COM for details

Source code: BUS127PM

a different author, so I have to ask myself if you've lost your mind. Unable to conceal your excitement, you add: and this one's supposed to be extraordinary. Supposed to be, because the novel you're dying to translate isn't even finished yet. When I tell you I don't know who that writer is, you say that's because it's a big secret. People who know know, but those who don't never will. You say this, stating the obvious. He writes incognito. No, you continue, she's a ghostwriter. One who writes other people's stories. Anonymously. Using a different writer's name each time. But this ghostwriter doesn't wait for jobs. This ghostwriter decides to write somebody else's story. And just does it. Sometimes it ends up being that author's best-known work. Sometimes the writer writes just one book in a series of books. One book that, of course, outshines those written by that author. The writer doesn't stick to any particular genre. It's all fair game: the popular and the experimental, the historical and the futuristic. Even stories closely linked to the present. New novels for newcomers and old ones for old hands – even posthumous pieces for late novelists who had come and gone unnoticed. It's not uncommon for the writer to translate a novel that hasn't been written. If anything, that's the writer's MO. Some magazine abroad calls the would-be novelist about his latest work, only to discover that he's never even heard of it.

This writer writes someone else's story and sends it to him. There's no contact information on the manuscript and no additional word ever comes. One writer who was sent a manuscript that he didn't write (though it announced itself to be written by him) hired a private eye to find out where it came from. The private eye found his man in no time. Yet, in another sense, it was a dead end. Because the culprit was only a copycat. I just wanted to try it, said the suspect. This world, he went on, is more overrun by plagiarists, bootleggers and imitators than anyone cares to realize. It happens right under our noses, he said. Even as-yet unwritten stories can be stolen. In other words, what you write right now can be ripped off by some novel from the past, and a whole slew of writers specialize in plagiarizing novels from the future.

It just hit me that the novel I wrote belonged to someone else, the culprit said in his statement. Until the story came to an end, he was positive the story was his. But, looking back now, he found all too many signs pointing to the contrary. His writing was far more fluid than usual. He found the story moving in directions that were too sophisticated for him. His hand was too slow for his brain. It wasn't the first time that had happened to him, but this was the first time he didn't want it to end. Whenever I stopped writing, he said, an intense wave of fear came over me. Like if I forgot how the story goes, even for a second, it would vanish from the world forever. Just like giving birth to a long, thin messiah, he said. He felt a constant compulsion to slowly push the messiah out into the world. If he lost his concentration, the messiah would perish. If he took too long a break, the messiah would suffocate. He gave his two most productive hours each morning to the novel (like giving it the frosting from his cupcake). He was determined to live right, so he ate his vegetables and started working out. But after two long months of writing, the resulting novel was one that – alas – could never have been his. He figured it out while writing the last sentence. He saw the face of the newborn novel, and he could tell right away that it belonged to someone else. He knew that he had transformed into something womb-like, but it hadn't occurred to him that he had been used like a surrogate mother. He didn't need to hire a detective to track down the story's real author. He ran out of his house, and soon found himself standing in the aisle of his local bookstore. Almost immediately, as if guided by some force, he found one writer in the mountain of new releases. That instant, he surrendered to the fact that the story he had written was that author's next novel. He could tell his memories were getting mixed up. He started to think: Did I really write that book or did I just read it somewhere? Which is scarier: that the past could actually change or that you could just think it did? Either way, he had to get his story back to the original author.

The writer finds his latest work in the mail and is – needless to say – shocked. But, as he goes on reading, doubts begin to swirl in his mind.

There's no way this isn't mine. It's obviously the sort of thing I would write. Sure, some of the lines aren't exactly what I'd write right now. I mean, I'm not the same now as I will be in the future. I'll progress and I'll regress. So, he tells himself, there are bound to be things I don't understand in writings by other versions of myself. And the line *I might not have written those lines* starts to lose meaning for him.

Greg says to his wife: We only know this because the culprit's work was a cheap knock-off of a sub-par writer. Nobody notices the real culprit. His wife thinks for a moment, then says: Wait a minute, if somebody could write another author's story so well that even the author would be completely convinced it was his or hers, then how could we even know that such an author exists in the first place? Greg laughs. There are two answers. First, there are geniuses – real geniuses – who'd never think that something they didn't write was theirs. At the same time, a genius knows that if he ever claimed that a new work of his was written by someone else, nobody would believe it. But he's the only one who really understands, who will still be there when there are none, and so on. The other answer goes like this: In some cases, the translation is already under way by the time the real culprit sends the original author their work. The one I'm working on translating is slated to be the latest novel from a well-known writer, but the author-to-be hasn't seen it yet – no one has. I think I mentioned this already, but sometimes a writer will figure it out when she hears about a translation of a novel she never wrote. At some point, though, it will become the original author's writing. It isn't even remotely possible to think otherwise. But, before that process is complete, it's certainly possible to notice some minor discrepancies. Within that window of time, a whole array of things can happen: seeing a checked pattern of day and night in a spider's web, looking at your own back in the mirror or finding a picture outside of its frame, et cetera. This job is special, Greg goes on. Because I'm supposed to translate the novel while it's still being written. It's a really strange story. But interesting.

A really strange story, Greg thinks as he puts down the half-read manuscript. But interesting. Setting aside the translation he'd been reading, he turns his attention to the original. The story that comes pouring out is nothing like the translation. There are some commonalities, but the two are unmistakably different stories. Greg starts to wonder why he thought the two stories were an original and a translation. Nobody asked him to think that. The story that Greg had until now thought to be the original is – compared to the one he was reading before – much more fantastic. The story takes place in Tokyo-Tokyo, in the not-too-distant future, when advanced printing technology is used to print virtually everything. Kids in the city learn to type on keyboards before they ever write with pencils. They use CAD software instead of rulers. Printers capable of producing three-dimensional objects become household items. Because 3D printers have advanced to the point that they can print 3D printers. Kids play with printed origami and pinwheels that are folded within the software, printed already twisted. The finished product emerges with none of the protocol or procedure associated with making origami – just like layers of earth piling artlessly, or human beings coming out toe-first. Printers are no longer limited to printing paper. Actually, it takes a good amount of time before printers can produce paper. It all starts with plastic. Then glass, then metal, then paper. And then body parts. Comestibles become printable a little before that. That is when the meat industry and animal rights groups come to an understanding. Printed proteins are moulded into meat. Tables are covered with printed goods as if they belong there. A 3D printer is set up squarely by the microwave. You can pick a dish from a two-dimensional carte du jour and your choice will materialize in three dimensions. Just heat it up and dinner is ready. A knot-print table; on it, pattern-print tableware; on that, artificial meat with three-dimensionally printed tendons. As time in the story fast-forwards, the ratio of printed things to non-printed things spikes. Kids print all sorts of things with their own hands. They design their own clothes. They print their own shoes. They download schematics for bicycles and press PRINT. The difference is purely a matter of how things are made, so all kinds of products that until then had been made from plastic are quickly replaced by printed goods. Man-made teeth, man-made anuses, man-made bones, man-made hearts. Durability is a problem early on, but the time it takes to work out the kinks is minimal.

Then, eventually, we get to the point where a person can be printed. Not printed parts added to a living person – a 100 per cent printed person, made from scratch. At least she looks like a person. But she isn't made by combining sperm and egg. She's born out of a printer. She comes out as an adult, complete with imprinted memories. Of course she isn't printed in order – from her toes upward – because, by this time, print technology is ridiculously advanced. Obviously you know she's different when you see her. Something about her doesn't sit right. She's so close to human but that makes her seem nothing like us. She's used just like a sophisticated robot. Then time in the story speeds up again and what was bound to happen happens. Print women everywhere begin printing print children. Two-dimensional kids, maybe for fun or out of curiosity, start to print adults. They lack the common sense to know that it's adults who make children. People keep on printing people until blood ties have to be decided by contract. Printed people print trees and bricks – a whole city for themselves to live in. Nearly everything there is printed. Printing a cook for a single meal or a novelist for a short story becomes popular. Instead of printing movies, people find pleasure in printing entire film crews in a single go. Of course, just as printed guns work like regular guns, printed people work and play like regular people. But something's still off. They look like mannequins, like ball-jointed dolls. Nobody understands that the question of whose movements appear more natural – the human race's or the printed race's – is determined by popular vote. Everyone insists that the races are fundamentally different. The humans are particularly adamant about that one. We're fully fledged, living people. We're nothing like the computed or printed races. We have souls and you don't.

By that point, a lot of the people living among human society were considered not to be people. The so-called computed race existed as personalities within computer-run simulations – as part of a technological genealogy developed in order to supplant human telemarketers. The computed race was born well ahead of the printed race. Long aware of their self-awareness, they started a movement to obtain the same rights as living human beings, but everyone thought it was a glitch. So they wound up living their lives completely neglected. Or shut down altogether. In fact, even after consciousness was born within the machine, thinkers continued to debate age-old questions: 'If we lived inside a simulation, would we even know it?' Despite the fact that, within the machine, computed thinkers had already declared, loud and proud: 'We're inside a computer simulation.' They even asked themselves: 'Can we ever know that the simulation is over?' Human rights for the computed race went unrecognized because, insofar as they were run by some program, they were believed to be computable. Sufficiently advanced parrots and hill mynahs can never become human. In that sense, it's patently obvious that living human beings are incomputable. So long as the literary proposition stating that no human being can be exhaustively documented stands, then the computed race – by virtue of being written in a mechanical language – simply cannot be human. The very same criticism applies to the printed race. Printability precludes humanity, living human beings said. The printed race countered that such boundaries had long since disappeared, but their opinion was brushed off as meaningless.

Museums teem with computed-race art and printed-race art. There's a room filled with man-made beef, a printer eternally spitting out one strand of hair, a water tank packed with printed sperm and printed eggs, even a printed foetus. All sizes of printed people – from microscopic to gigantic – are put on display. When a series of technological breakthroughs made possible by the computed race's processing power brings the printed race gradually closer to humankind, museums start to display successive printed-race models next to statues of human evolution from anthropoid ape to modern man. But these ventures – going well beyond the museum's ordinary bad taste – are consistently regarded as being in even worse taste. It draws in a younger audience, but they rapidly lose interest with age. It's simply tasteless for a cassette recorder to announce 'I'm human' on loop. Humans insist that anyone who has to announce he's a human is nothing of the sort – a real human knows it in his soul. When all is said and done, souls are impossible to print. Because what we call 'the soul' can't be written down. If it could, a long line of writers would have been producing souls left and right. Characters in novels would move around on their own and stop us from ever closing books. Actors would turn into the people they play and forget to turn back.

Greg's wife shuts herself in her room alone and writes this in a language over which she has no control. Like a speeding bike wheel that exhibits the strobe effect and looks like it isn't moving at all, Greg's wife's time is coming. Greg's wife, now a printed person, keeps on writing. This story was written by a printed woman. If you read this and thought the writer was a living human being, then I want you to believe that souls do reside in members of the printed race, Greg's wife writes. If, that is, you believe that only people with souls can write stories. Greg and Greg's wife printed themselves and moved to Tokyo-Tokyo. That's typically how one enters a place like Tokyo-Tokyo. She and he always believed that printed people have souls and moreover they thought that – in principle – it *is* possible to exhaustively document a human being. So, if that's the case, what's wrong with printing ourselves? What makes it any different from writing an autobiography? She's writing a story about the first man. The first man to print himself. Of course his endeavour succeeded with the help of the computed race. He was a living human being at first, but he printed himself, then scrapped the original, as a performance piece. He had his heart set on spending the rest of his life being an exhibit in a museum, but the public wouldn't have it. He wasn't allowed to mingle with the hordes of printed people on display there. Because, in short, he started off human. Of course there's no real difference between him and those born printed. He protests, but his cries land on deaf ears. When his plans for living easy at the museum fall through, he resorts to printing his own belongings. He codes his clothes, then – after printing them – scraps the originals. Hats, socks, furniture. He prints them and scraps the originals. He prints receipts, bills, books – he digitizes them and prints them anew, then scraps the originals. In order to live surrounded by printed objects. Still, he never stops thinking of himself as an original. He starts printing other people's things: personal effects, ledgers, notebooks, work memos, love letters, money with arbitrarily assigned values. He even starts writing other people's latest novels, then sending them to their original authors. When they wind up becoming the writers' latest works – without anyone batting an eyelash – it both satisfies and infuriates him. He prints novels with no novelists, handbags with no owners, dogs with no masters, residences with no residents. He sets up a 3D printer so it can print a slightly larger 3D printer. With free rein over printers of all sizes, he prints ownerless cities, ownerless countries, ownerless islands, ownerless continents, ownerless stars. The printer – knowing no limits – keeps on printing on an ever larger scale until it prints an ownerless universe. The printer automatically prints ownerless pasts and ownerless futures.

Greg starts to wonder if the two stories are neither – as he had initially thought – an original and a translation, nor two unrelated stories, but one continuous story. He starts to wonder if it's actually a part of some massive protean story in which the language being used changes in the middle. Or, he supposes, maybe a story in which the language is constantly being replaced. It could be ripped off from an unwritten section of the extremely long, still-unfinished novel I'm translating, he thinks. But Greg hasn't fully grasped the fact that the novel he's reading has no author. Seeing these lines now, he starts to feel as if he always knew, but he still isn't absolutely convinced. I'm translating this novel while looking at the original I was sent, so I can't be the author. Neither is the person who sent me the story. Same as above, he was only translating the story he received. He wonders if the story is actually written so that it can't be accurately translated.

Because, even after so many people have translated it, a lot of parts still fail to make sense. It's like a crossword puzzle kludged together from multiple languages in which every translator fills in whatever spaces they understand in their language. Someone who assumes that everything becomes clearer through repeated translation would likely think that, primordially, the story was whirling around in chaos. There are no letters to begin with, only patterns on a wall, out of which the translators discover or maybe invent them. As they're connected and disconnected and read and written, those letters stretch outward like ice crystals, or take root in the earth. The meaning thus becomes gradually clearer. On the other hand, someone who assumes that with translations of translations an original meaning only gets murkier would likely think that, primordially, the story was as solid as a block of ice. According to the former, we are in a cooling soup, in which something resembling personality is finally taking shape. According to the latter, the ice is melting and our personalities are beginning to merge together. Although we keep calling one another Greg, Greg's wife and I, we have no idea who we really are, to the point that we can't even contradict each other. Because a baby's babblings and an old man's mumblings lack the sophistication required to engender contradiction in the first place.

This is how we intersect with your time. Whenever a letter is read, it's like the hour hand of the clock making a circle. Like a hundred years passing per translation. Like, day in and day out, the same time of day looking exactly the same yet slowly transforming. Like spring is spring all the way down. Like how the next day is like a next day in which the eternal return has come full circle. It looks like a speeding wheel when it kicks into reverse. We're made up of printable pleasure, which I like to imagine is making its way to you. Sometimes I set stories in stories because I have friends who live there. Occasionally I set stories in San Francisco for the same exact reason – because I think of you as things-in-themselves, as things that have to be there. I don't suppose Kant ever thought the thing-in-itself was capable of cracking a smile. ■

Do No Harm by *Henry Marsh*

What is it really like to be a brain surgeon, to hold someone's life in your hands, to drill down into the stuff that creates thought, feeling and reason? How do you live with the consequences of performing a potentially life-saving operation when it all goes wrong? Find out in this astonishingly candid account from one of the country's top neurosurgeons and *Granta* contributor.

Weidenfeld & Nicolson £16.99 | **HB**

All the Birds, Singing by *Evie Wyld*

From one of *Granta*'s Best of Young British Novelists, a stunningly insightful, emotionally powerful new novel about an outsider haunted by an inescapable past: a story of loneliness and survival, guilt and loss, and the power of forgiveness.

Shortlisted for the 2013 Costa Award for Best Novel

Pantheon Books $24.95 | **HB**

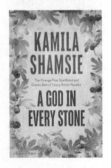

A God in Every Stone by *Kamila Shamsie*

July 1914. Young Englishwoman Vivian Rose Spencer is in an ancient land. Soon she will discover the Temple of Zeus, the call of adventure and love. Thousands of miles away a twenty-year-old Pathan, Qayyum Gul, is learning about brotherhood and loyalty in the British Indian Army. Soaring across the globe and into empires fallen, this is the powerful new novel from one of *Granta*'s Best of Young British Novelists and Orange Prize-shortlisted author of *Burnt Shadows*.

Bloomsbury £8.99 | **PB**

Double Negative by *Ivan Vladislavić*

Double Negative captures an ordinary life before, during and after South Africa's extraordinary revolution.

'Vladislavić is no minor congener of Sebald. His engagement with the shadow of a nation's evil times is slyer, more aslant, although brimful of Sebaldian melancholy' Neel Mukherjee, *Independent*

'Sensitively attuned to the uncanny phenomena that explode from the social fault lines of his city' Patrick Flanery, *Guardian*

And Other Stories £10 / $15.95 | **PB with French flaps**

AFTER THE WAR, BEFORE THE WAR

Ryūnosuke Akutagawa on the Bridge of Nine Turnings, in Shanghai, in 1921

David Peace

Huxinting Teahouse, c.1870–1900
From Historical Photographs of China project
© 2012 Billie Love Historical Collection

'Master Peachling,' called a pheasant, 'Where are you going?'
'I'm going to the Land of the Demons,' said Momotarō,
'To carry off all their treasures . . .'

– *Momotarō, the Peach Boy*, a Japanese folk tale

I.

From the land, on the wharf, two old friends: Murata of the Osaka *Mainichi Shimbun* and Jones of United Press International. To greet Ryūnosuke, to welcome him. To Shanghai, to China –

At last, at last. His first steps, on Chinese soil. Engulfed by rickshaw pullers, overwhelmed by their stench. Screaming into the frightened faces of the disembarking passengers, grabbing onto Ryūnosuke by the sleeves of his coat. Jones barged between the pullers and their prey, 'Stay close to us, Ryūnosuke, and walk quickly . . .'

Through the crowds and coolies, to a waiting line of horse-drawn carriages. But aboard their carriage, at the first crossroads, their horse careered into a brick wall, sending its cargo out of their seats and onto their knees. The driver beating and whipping the horse, its stubborn nose smack against the brick wall, its hind legs spastically dancing and violently kicking, rocking the carriage this way and that, as Jones smiled and said, 'Welcome to Shanghai, Ryūnosuke.'

Beaten into submission, or simply exhausted, the horse now backed away from the wall and soon they were trotting along beside a river. So many barges, so many sampans, side by side, bow to bow and stern to stern, Ryūnosuke could not see the water. To their left, a railroad bridge carried luminous green trains. To their right, red-brick buildings, three or four storeys tall. Beneath these buildings, Chinese and Westerners were walking briskly along the large, wide asphalt street, but yielding to their carriage at the signal from an Indian policeman in a red turban. First appalled by the ferocity of the rickshaw pullers and the violence of the horse-drawn carriage, now Ryūnosuke marvelled at this sudden order in a sea of chaos.

The carriage pulled up in front of a hotel. The driver already had his hand outstretched. Murata dropped a few cents into the open palm. However, the driver did not withdraw his hand. Spittle flew from the corners of his mouth as he yelled something over and over into all of their faces. Murata and Jones ignored the man, marching briskly through the hotel doors. Ryūnosuke glanced back only to see the driver already back in his seat, coins in pocket and whip in hand. Ryūnosuke felt somehow cheated by the man's performance; if he had not really cared, why make such a fuss?

Inside the Dong-Ya Yangxing Hotel, Ryūnosuke had more worries. The deserted reception room was gloomy, yet gaudy. Jones smiled and said, 'You know, this was the very place where Kim Ok-kyun was assassinated? Shot through the window of his room . . .'

'I don't doubt it,' began Ryūnosuke, then interrupted by the sound of slippers loudly slapping on the floor and the sight of the Japanese proprietor, grandly dressed in Western clothes, exclaiming, 'Welcome, gentlemen. Welcome, welcome . . .'

'I believe my colleague Sawamura has made a reservation for Mr Akutagawa,' said Murata.

'Ah, yes,' said the proprietor, bowing deeply. 'It is a great honour to welcome the esteemed author, Akutagawa-sensei. Our best room, reserved only for our most important guests, awaits you . . .'

Quickly, the proprietor ushered Ryūnosuke into a room off the entranceway. Two beds, no chairs. The walls covered in soot, the drapes eaten by moths. Ryūnosuke knew this was the very room in which Kim Ok-kyun had opened a window for the last time –

'I don't suppose you have any other rooms?'

The proprietor shook his head. 'No, sir. We do not. This is our best room, and our only available one.'

After initial apologies and excuses, then unpleasantries and threats, the party found themselves back out on the street –

Jones smiled and said, 'To the Banzaikan?'

II.

An hour later, Jones was waiting for Ryūnosuke in the lobby of the Banzaikan. 'Come on, Ryūnosuke. The Shanghai night awaits . . .'

In Shepherd's restaurant, the waiters were Chinese, the patrons all foreign, Ryūnosuke the only customer with a yellow face. But the curry was much better than he had expected, the room most pleasant, and Jones as talkative as ever, if still as melancholic as always –

'China is my hobby, but Japan is my passion.'

'You must miss Japan then,' said Ryūnosuke.

'Soon after I arrived here,' said Jones. 'I was sitting in a cafe where one of the waitresses was Japanese. She was alone, in a chair, staring into space. I asked her, in Japanese, When did you come to Shanghai? She said, I just arrived yesterday. I said, You must miss Japan then? And I thought she was going to break down in tears as she said, Of course, I want to go home. I knew how she felt then, and that is still how I feel now. Awfully sentimental, I know . . .'

'Perhaps,' said Ryūnosuke.

Jones laughed. 'Come on, *sa-ikō* . . .'

Along a busy four-laned road, on the northern border of the French Concession, to the Café Parisien. Its dance hall was large and Western, blue and red lights flickering in time to the music from the orchestra, just like the dance halls of Asakusa. But the music and the orchestra were far superior to Tokyo.

In a corner, at a table, Jones and Ryūnosuke ordered two cups of anisette. A Filipino girl dressed in bright red danced with a group of young Americans in fashionable suits. All happy, all laughing. An old British couple, both rather stout, came dancing their way. Ryūnosuke smiled and said, 'Was it Whitman who said the young are beautiful but the beauty of the old is much more precious?'

'What utter rot,' shouted Jones. 'The old should not dance. And the lines by Whitman you should be quoting are: "Through the laughter, dancing, dining, supping, of people / Inside of dresses and ornaments, inside of those wash'd and trimm'd faces, / Behold a secret silent loathing and despair . . ."'

'"Song of the Open Road"?'

'Yes,' said Jones, and now he laughed again. '*Sa-ikō* . . .'

Outside the Café Parisien, the wide avenue was deserted now except for the rickshaw pullers. Ryūnosuke looked at his watch and asked, 'Isn't there anywhere else to get a drink round here?'

'Yes, yes,' said Jones. 'Just up here . . .'

Only the sound of their shoes echoing in the street of three- and four-storey buildings, looking up at the stars in the sky, then down at the occasional lights of the shops – a pawnshop with white walls, a placard for a doctor, a worn stucco wall plastered with advertisements for Nanyang cigarettes – Ryūnosuke said, 'I'm awfully thirsty . . .'

'Patience,' said Jones. 'It's just up here . . .'

The cafe was far more low-class than the Parisien. Near the glass doorway, an old Chinese woman sold roses. In the middle of the room, three or four British sailors danced suggestively with heavily made-up women of the world. At the back, before a pink wall, a Chinese boy with his hair parted down the middle was banging away on a huge piano. In another corner, at another table, Jones and Ryūnosuke ordered two cold sodas –

'I feel as though I am looking at a newspaper with illustrations,' declared Ryūnosuke. 'And "Shanghai" could be the only possible title for that illustration . . .'

Drunkenly, a group of six more sailors fell through the door, knocking the basket of roses out of the arms of the old Chinese woman and onto the floor, rushing into the middle of the room, frantically dancing with their shipmates and their women, crushing the flowers under their feet, stepping on the fingers of the old woman –

Jones stood up and said, 'Let's go . . .'

'Yes,' said Ryūnosuke.

Jones threw a coin in the old woman's basket and said, 'Let me tell you about life, Ryūnosuke . . .'

'Go on,' said Ryūnosuke. 'What is life?'

Jones held open the door for Ryūnosuke and said, 'Life is but a road strewn with roses . . .'

Outside, rickshaw pullers descended on them from all four directions. Ryūnosuke felt a hand on his sleeve, pulling him back towards the cafe. The old flower woman was gripping his arm, her other hand stuck out like a beggar, shouting into his face –

'I feel sorry for your beautiful roses,' Ryūnosuke told her. 'Being trampled on by those drunken sailors and being sold by such a greedy person . . .'

But Jones just laughed and, for the second time that day, said, 'Welcome to Shanghai, Ryūnosuke. Welcome to China . . .'

'Thank you,' said Ryūnosuke. 'But I refuse to believe Shanghai is China.'

'Perhaps not yet,' said Jones. And then, suddenly, he sneezed.

III.

In the Banzaikan, in his room, in his bed, Ryūnosuke awoke suddenly. A twisting knife under his ribcage, a stabbing pain in the side and lower part of his chest. Ryūnosuke sat up in bed and coughed. Pain spreading from his abdomen, crawling along his shoulders, pain tightening around his neck. Again Ryūnosuke coughed, again the pain. Shooting through his chest, digging into his shoulders. He was shivering, he was burning. Ryūnosuke collapsed back onto his pillow. It was cold, it was damp. Ryūnosuke lay sweating on his bed. He cursed his ill luck, he waited for the maid. And then the doctor –

The diagnosis was dry pleurisy. Ryūnosuke would need to rest in the Satomi Hospital, on Miller Street, for two weeks, maybe longer. Dr Satomi would personally give him a shot every other day.

Helpless and in despair, Ryūnosuke feared he would have to cancel his trip. He dictated a telegram to Osaka. The reply came quickly: *Get well soon, but take your time. Then continue as planned. We await your reports and travelogue as soon as you are fit again.*

On his back, in his bed. In the room, on the ward. Jones or Murata visited every day. From time to time, baskets of fruit and bunches of flowers from unknown admirers also arrived. After a while, in a row, by his head, there were so many cans of biscuits that Ryūnosuke did not know how he would ever dispose of them. Luckily, Jones always brought a voracious appetite with him. Thankfully, he also brought books: the short stories of Friedrich de la Motte Fouqué, the essays of Herbert Giles and the poems of Eunice Tietjens.

Ryūnosuke was grateful for any distraction. His fever did not easily subside, his mind constantly stricken. In the daylight, he was certain sudden death was just around the corner. In the twilight, he took Calmotin to spare him the terrors of the night –

For twenty-two nights, for twenty-three days. On his back, in his bed. In the room, on the ward. In the hospital, on Miller Street. Mongolian winds banging on his window, yellow dust blocking out the sun. The sun fighting back, the spring now arriving. His fever finally subsiding, the pain now relenting. Dr Satomi smiled and said, 'Good news, Sensei. You are recovered. You are well enough to leave . . .'

IV.

Down a busy street, sitting in a carriage, driven at great speed. With Mr Yosoki, the distinguished poet, as his guide. Ryūnosuke had no more time left to lose. The afternoon rainy and already dark. Through the showers, through the gloom, the passing shops. Dark red roasted birds, hanging side by side, catching the lamplights, illuminating and reflecting, shop after shop, silverware and fruit, piles of bananas, piles of mangoes, hanging fish bladders and their bloody torsos, skinned pigs' carcasses, suspended hooves-down, on butchers' hooks, flesh-coloured grottos with vague dark recesses, sudden white clock faces, their hands all stopped, a shabby old wine shop with a worn old sign, written in the style of the poet Li Taibo. A wider avenue now, then around a corner, into another alleyway –

The heart of the Old City, the heart of the Real Shanghai, once encircled by walls, walls built to repel Japanese pirates, the Dwarf Bandits from across the sea, the walls now gone, the heart of the Old City open, beating, welcoming –

Out of their carriage, into a second alley. The pathway precarious, the cobblestones crumbling. Stores selling mah-jong sets, stores selling sandalwood goods, one on top of another, ordinary Chinese in long-sleeved black robes, bumping and banging into each other, no words of apology, no words of anger, no words at all.

At the end of the alleyway, the entrance to the Yu Garden, and a large ornamental lake. The lake covered with thick green algae, carp hidden in its waters, crossed by the Bridge of Nine Turnings, lightning flashes zigzagging this way and that, built to confuse evil spirits, devils unable to turn corners, and in its centre the Huxinting Teahouse. Dilapidated, forlorn. A ruined stone wall around the lake, before the wall a Chinese man. In blue cotton clothes, his hair in a queue. Pissing into the lake, oblivious to the world; Chen Shufan could raise his rebellious banner in the wind, the Anglo-Japanese Alliance could come up for renewal again; nothing would disturb his nonchalant manner as the serene arc of his urine poured into the algae-choked lake before this famous old pavilion and its bridge. A scene beyond melancholia,

a bitter symbol of this grand old country –

'Please observe,' chuckled Yosoki. 'What runs over these stones is Chinese piss and only Chinese piss . . .'

One whiff of the overpowering stench of urine in the late-afternoon air, and all spells were broken –

The Huxinting Teahouse was nothing more than the Huxinting Teahouse. And piss is only piss. One should not indulge in careless admiration, thought Ryūnosuke, on his tiptoes, tottering after Yosoki –

A blind old beggar, sat on the ground. So many beggars, beggars everywhere. Dilettante beggars and hermit beggars, professional beggars and genuine beggars. Dressed in layers of old newspapers, licking their own rotting knees. On the cobblestones, before this beggar. His whole miserable life, written out in chalk, in calligraphy better than Ryūnosuke's own –

Aching, longing for something you can never truly, truly know. That must be Romanticism …

'Come on,' called Yosoki. 'No time to be daydreaming with the beggars, Sensei . . .'

Back in an alleyway, lined with antique shops, their Chinese proprietors, water pipes in mouths, among clutters of copper incense burners, clay horse figurines, cloisonné planters, dragon-head vases, jade paperweights, cabinets inlaid with mother-of-pearl, marble single-leaf screens, stuffed pheasants and frightful paintings by Chou Ying –

But at the end of this alleyway, the Temple of the City God. The old focal point of the town, a venue for entertainers and fairs. Here dwelled the City God, the Lord of Old Shanghai –

Many, many years ago, Ryūnosuke had bought a postcard of this legendary temple. He had used it as a bookmark, often preferring the picture to the words he was reading, dreaming of the day he would stand here before the City God, this day –

Amidst the smoke and the noise, thousands of people, coming and going, paying their respects, offering up incense, burning paper money, bills of gold and silver, hanging from the ceiling, the beams and the pillars, covered in dirt and grease, the judges in hell seated on both sides – pictures and statues evoking illustrations from *Strange Stories from a Chinese Studio* or *The New Jester of Qi*; magistrates from hell who killed thieves who terrorized towns, clerks from the netherworld who broke elbows and chopped off heads – the red-faced City God himself towering, rising into the evening sky, before Ryūnosuke; Ryūnosuke entranced, Ryūnosuke overwhelmed, reluctant to leave, to follow Yosoki –

Out among the stalls; sugar-cane stock and buttons of shells, handkerchiefs and peanuts. Out among the crowds; a man in a bright suit with an amethyst necktie pin, an old woman in shoes only two inches long. All around him, Ryūnosuke could see characters from *The Plum in the Golden Vase* or *The Precious Mirror of Ranking Courtesans*. But Ryūnosuke could see no Du Fu, Yue Fei or Wang Yangming; the new China was not the old China of poetry and essays. Rather, it was the cruel, greedy and obscene China of fiction . . .

Back along the lake, into the deserted tea house, deafened by the sudden screeching of an invisible shower of birds, birdcages hanging from all the beams of the ceiling. So many cages, so much shrieking, their eardrums bursting as they fled the screaming birds. Their hands still over their ears in the street, numerous birdcages hanging in every shop, Yosoki shouted, 'One moment, Sensei. I'm going to buy a bird for my children . . .'

Down a quiet side street, before a shop window, Ryūnosuke was looking at a picture of the famous opera singer, Mei Lanfang, but thinking of Yosoki's children waiting for him to return home, and of his own son, waiting in their house, back in Tabata, back in Tokyo.

'Come on,' said Yosoki, a bird in a cage in his hand. 'As the locals say, the sun sets on the Old City and rises on the Concessions . . .'

v.

Murata had arranged for Ryūnosuke to meet and interview a number of important Chinese intellectuals. Mr Nishimoto, the editor of the weekly magazine *Shanhai*, had kindly agreed to accompany and interpret for Ryūnosuke. In a study in the French Concession, their first appointment was with Zhang Binglin –

A philosopher and a scholar, a leading political figure during the various revolutions and recent upheavals, Zhang Binglin had been imprisoned, then spent time in Japan. Now the man welcomed Ryūnosuke into his study –

A tiled room, a cold room. No stove, no rugs, only books. In a thin serge suit, on a cushionless wooden chair, Ryūnosuke stared at a large stuffed crocodile mounted flat against a wall. The skin of the crocodile offered no comfort, the cold of the room piercing his own skin. Ryūnosuke was certain he would catch his death of cold.

In a long grey official gown and a black half-length riding jacket with a thick fur lining, on a fur-draped wicker chair, with his legs outstretched, Zhang Binglin seemed oblivious to the cold. His skin almost yellow, his moustache very thin, his red eyes smiled coolly behind elegant frameless glasses as he spoke –

'I am sad to say that contemporary China is politically depraved,' began Zhang. 'You might say that since the last years of the Qing dynasty, the spread of injustice has reached immense proportions. In scholarship and the arts there has been an unusual stagnation. The Chinese people, however, do not by nature run to extremes. Insofar as they possess this quality, communism in China is impossible. Of course, one segment of the students welcomes Soviet principles, but the students are not the populace. Even if the people were to become communist, at some point would come a time when they would dispense with this belief. The reason is that our national character – love for the Golden Mean – is stronger than any momentary enthusiasm for fireworks . . .'

On his hard chair, Ryūnosuke desperately wanted to smoke, but just nodded along, Zhang waving long fingernails as he continued –

'So, what would be the best way to revive China? The resolution of this problem, no matter how concrete, cannot emerge from some theory concocted at the desk. The ancients declared that those who understood the requirements of the times were great men. They did not deductively reason from some opinion of their own, but inductively reasoned on the basis of countless facts. This is to know the needs of the times. After one has ascertained what those needs are, then plans can be made. This is ultimately the meaning of the dictum of governing well according to the times of the years . . .'

Ryūnosuke nodding along, eyes wandering again, to the crocodile. The fragrance of the lotus blossoms, the rays of the spring sun, the warmth of the summer water. Once you knew them all, now you are lucky to be stuffed. Have pity on me!

'The Japanese I detest the most,' declared Zhang abruptly, 'is the Momotarō of your favourite fairy tale, who conquered the Land of the Demons, and which you tell to all your children. I cannot suppress a feeling of antipathy for the Japanese who love this Momotarō.'

Ryūnosuke had heard many foreigners talk about Japan, holding up Prince Yamagata to ridicule or praising Hokusai to the skies. But until now, Ryūnosuke had never heard any of those so-called Japanese experts ever utter one word of criticism of Momotarō, the boy born from a peach. Zhang's words contained more truth than all the eloquence of those experts –

Now Ryūnosuke looked at Zhang Binglin and knew he was in the presence of a true sage.

VI.

In the Public Garden, which was not public. No Chinese allowed, only foreigners here. The nannies and their charges, the sycamore trees with their budding leaves. It was all very pretty, but it was not China. It was the West. Not because it was advanced; it was no more advanced than the parks of Tokyo. It was simply more Western. And just because something was Western did not necessarily mean it was advanced. It was the same in the French Concession. The doves cooing quietly, the willows already budding. The smell of peach blossoms in the air. It was all very pleasant. But Ryūnosuke did not care for the Western houses. Not because they were Western, just because they seemed somewhat unrefined. Like the Japanese who insisted on wearing only Western clothes, putting on their thick socks and tight shoes, stumbling up and down the Ginza or the Bund –

'Hypocrite,' laughed Jones. 'You actually prefer Western suits to Japanese clothes. You also prefer to live in a bungalow rather than a traditional house. You always order macaroni instead of udon. And you prefer Brazilian coffee to Japanese tea . . .'

Ryūnosuke shook his head and said, 'No, no. For example, I admit the Westerners' cemetery on Temple Street isn't so bad . . .'

'It's nice enough,' said Jones. 'But, personally, I would prefer to be buried under a Buddhist swastika than a Christian crucifix. I don't want angels and whatnot leering over me in my grave, grimacing and proselytizing. You just mean you are disappointed by Shanghai and are not interested in the Western things here . . .'

'On the contrary, I'm very interested. But just as you said, in one sense, Shanghai is the West. And so, for better or for worse, it's fun to be able to see the West. Particularly because I have never laid eyes on the Real West. I am just saying, even to my ignorant eyes, the West seems out of place here . . .'

'Really?' said Jones. 'I think it is a match made in heaven. Or should I say hell . . .'

This City of Evil, this Demon City Shanghai. Ryūnosuke had heard the horror stories of rickshaw pullers turning bandit by night, slicing off women's ears for their earrings –

'The worst are the Chaibai Gang,' whispered Jones. 'Luring women into automobiles, stealing their diamond rings, and then strangling them, inspired by the movies. Those cloak-and-dagger ones that are all the rage here . . .'

At sunset, outside the Green Lotus Teahouse, the Wild Pheasants flocked. Surrounding both Ryūnosuke and Jones, speaking both Japanese and English. Other girls hanging around in rickshaws, these girls waiting for fresh crumbs, all wearing glasses –

'All the rage,' said Jones, again.

Inside a building, an opium den. In the stark white light of a bare electric bulb, a lone prostitute lay puffing 'Western Medicine' on a long pipe with a foreign customer –

Ryūnosuke had seen so many strange foreigners in Shanghai, male and female, many of whom seemed to have migrated from Siberia. Even in the Public Garden, a Russian beggar had kept haranguing Ryūnosuke and Jones –

'It's not so bad,' said Jones. 'The Municipal Council is very strict these days. Such shady cafes as the El Dorado and the Palermo have disappeared from the Western parts of the town. Now you have to go out to the suburbs, to places like the Del Monte . . .'

In the opium den, under the harsh light. Ryūnosuke shook his head again and said, 'But this is Shanghai –

'Not China, young China . . .'

VII.

On his last night, under a Chinese lantern, in another cafe, in another corner, at another table, Ryūnosuke and Jones were drinking whisky and sodas, crowds of Americans and Russians swarming around the room, women leaning against the tables, listening to the Indian musicians of the orchestra. One particular woman, wearing a gown of celadon green, fluttered from one man to the next, her face beautiful, yet something porcelain, almost morbid about her –

Green satin, and a dance, white wine / and gleaming laughter, with two nodding earrings – these are Lotus . . .

'Who is she?' Ryūnosuke asked Jones. 'The thin woman in the green dress?'

Jones shrugged and said, 'Her? French, I think. An actress.'

'Do you know her? Her story . . .'

Jones shrugged again. 'People call her Ninny. But just look at him, that old guy over there. Now there is a man with a story . . .'

Ryūnosuke glanced at the man at the next table. Holding a glass of red wine in both hands, warming the drink, moving his head in time to the music of the band.

Jones whispered, 'He's Jewish. He's lived here for almost thirty years. But he's never said what brought him here, what makes him stay. I often wonder . . .'

'What do you care,' said Ryūnosuke.

Jones said, 'I just wonder. I'm already fed up with China.'

'Not with China,' said Ryūnosuke. 'With Shanghai.'

Jones nodded. 'With China. I lived in Beijing for a while, too.'

'Because China is gradually becoming too Western?'

Jones seemed about to answer, but then stopped.

'Then if not China,' asked Ryūnosuke, 'where would you live?

Japan again?'

Jones shook his head and said, 'I've already lived there. You should never go back to the places you've lived. You can't . . .'

'So where then?'

Jones smiled and said, 'Russia, under the Soviets.'

'Then you should go. You can go anywhere you want . . .'

Jones closed his eyes, was silent for a while, and then, in Japanese, quoted lines from the *Man'yōshū* Ryūnosuke had long forgotten: 'The world is full of pain / And the shame of poverty / But I am not a bird / I cannot fly away . . .'

Ryūnosuke smiled.

Jones opened his eyes, looked again around the room, and said, 'I don't know about that old Jewish guy, but even Ninny seems happier than me . . .'

'Aha,' laughed Ryūnosuke, 'I knew you must know her . . .'

Jones shrugged and said, 'I am not a straightforward person, Ryūnosuke. Poet, painter, critic, journalist and more. Son, brother, bachelor and Irishman. And on top of all that, a romantic in my mind, a realist in my life, a communist in my politics . . .'

'And lover of Ninny,' laughed Ryūnosuke.

Jones laughed, too. 'Yeah, yeah. And an atheist in religion and a materialist in philosophy. Now, come on. *Sa-ikō* . . .'

Outside, the city was lost in a strange yellow fog. Its false fronts, buried for now. Ryūnosuke followed Jones along the streets, towards the sound of the water –

By the water, they stopped. A customs-house spire dimly visible through the fog. A black sail, torn and tilted, creaking along, adrift and alone. The river swelled and flowed backwards. The black legs of a wharf bound in chains. Mountains of offloaded cargo. Coolies on barrels stacked on the embankment in the damp air . . .

'It's too late,' said Jones. 'To change anything.'

Ryūnosuke said, 'Then that means you've wasted your life.'

A group of exhausted Russian prostitutes sitting on a bench. The blue lamp of a sampan moving against the current, rotating hypnotically before their dimming eyes . . .

'Not only me,' said Jones. 'But all the people of the world.'

The dull clank of copper coins, Chinamen gambling on top of barrels. The gaslights in striped patterns, through the yellow fog and the wet trees. The boats tied to the quay rocking in the waves, floating up and down in the flicker of the lamplight.

'Look at that,' said Jones, pointing into the dark water –

At their feet, on the tide, the pale corpse of a small dog kissed the stones of the quay. A wreath around its neck –

Rising and falling, on the tide.

Ryūnosuke turned his back, lit a cigarette, and watched the prostitutes stand and saunter away along an iron railing. A young woman at the end of the procession glanced back furtively, stepped over the ropes that moored the boats, then disappeared among the barrels with the others. All they left behind was a banana peel, stepped on and crushed. Ryūnosuke stared back out across the water. Day and night, coins and goods flowed in and out from the port, and all along the river, the warships of the world spread out their batteries of guns.

'I wonder why we do that,' said Jones quietly, still watching the dead dog bobbing up and down on the black water.

'Do what?'

'Make a wreath,' said Jones. 'For the dead.'

Ryūnosuke stared back down at the corpse, then shook his head and said, 'I don't know. But I'm glad we do. Or some of us do.'

'Maybe it was Ninny,' said Jones.

Ryūnosuke looked back up at Jones, remembering again lines from that poem by Eunice Tietjens: *You too perhaps were stranded here, like these poor | homesick boys, in this great catch-all where the | white race ends, this grim Shanghai that like a | sieve hangs over filth and loneliness* . . .

Ryūnosuke flicked his cigarette out into the night and the water and said, 'For hope and all young wings are drowned in you . . .'

'Awfully sentimental,' said Jones.

Ryūnosuke nodded and then said, 'I'll be sorry to leave you, but not Shanghai.'

'The rest of China is no better,' said Jones. 'You still have too many illusions. So I'm afraid you'll be very disappointed.'

'Then I hope when we meet again, it will be in Japan and you'll be happier.'

Jones was staring up the river at the shadows of the warships. In the night, with their guns. Silent, waiting. Now Jones turned to Ryūnosuke and said, 'I'm sorry, old friend. But I doubt it.'

Ryūnosuke said nothing. There on that quay, here in this night, he was remembering their first meeting. A fire burning brightly in a fireplace, its flames reflecting in the mahogany tables and chairs. They had talked all night, of literature and of Ireland, until Ryūnosuke had been overcome with drowsiness. It had not been so very long ago, not even ten years, but it felt like a memory from another life, a different world. And the flames of that fire no longer seemed comforting and warm, but threatening and portentous, filling Ryūnosuke with a vague anxiety and dread. Ryūnosuke shivered in the damp air and said, 'Do you still detest George Bernard Shaw?'

'More than ever,' laughed Jones.

'And the words of Christ?'

'Awfully sentimental.'

Ryūnosuke stared into the water again, the dog and its wreath not moving now, just floating. The face of Jesus on the water. There were tears in his eyes, on his cheeks and now his collar, as he said, 'It's surely better to believe in at least the possibility of forgiveness, and of redemption . . .'

'You should return your ticket,' said Jones. 'The East and the West cannot be reconciled. They will tear you apart, Ryūnosuke.'

And now, suddenly, Jones sneezed again.

VIII.

After the goodbyes, in the night. Ryūnosuke walked out onto the deck of the *Hōyō-maru*. On the pier, no souls abroad. Lights shone downstream, along the Bund. All a forged facade, all a grotesque parody. In the night, on the deck. Ryūnosuke closed his eyes –

Long, long ago, there was a giant peach tree, its roots in the underworld, its branches above the clouds. One fine morning, Yatagarasu, a mythical crow, landed upon one of the branches of the tree. Yatagarasu pecked off one of the fruits of the tree. The fruit fell through the clouds, into a stream far down below. A childless old woman saw the peach in the stream. Inside the peach was a boy. And the old woman and her husband called this boy Momotarō.

Now Momotarō had the idea to conquer the Demon Island, because he hated working in the fields, the mountains and the rivers with the old man and woman who had adopted and raised him. The elderly couple, exhausted by this naughty foundling, prepared a banner, a sword and some dumplings and off he set. Soon Momotarō was joined by a starving dog, a cowardly monkey and a dignified pheasant on his quest to the Demon Island.

But despite its name, the Demon Island was actually a beautiful, natural paradise. And the demons themselves were a placid, pleasure-seeking race. They played harps, sang songs and danced dances. Their grandparents, though, would often tell cautionary tales of the horrible humans across the water: 'If you are naughty, we'll send you to the land of the humans. Their men and their women tell lies. They are greedy, jealous and vain. They set fires, they steal things, and they even kill their friends for simple pleasure or pure profit . . .'

With the banner of the peach in one hand, waving his sun-emblem fan, Momotarō brought terror to the demons, ordering the dog, the monkey and the pheasant: 'Forward! Forward –

'Kill the demons, leave none alive!'

The dog killed one young demon with just one bite. The monkey ravaged and then throttled the demon girls. The pheasant pecked the demon children to death. And soon a forest of corpses littered the Demon Island. And the demon chieftain surrendered –

'Now in my great mercy,' said Momotarō, 'I will spare your life. In return, you will bring me all your treasure and give me all your children as hostages . . . '

The demon chieftain had no choice but to agree. And in triumph, with his treasure and his hostages, Momotarō returned to Japan. However, Momotarō did not live happily ever after. The demon children grew up to be most ungrateful adults. Endlessly trying to kill Momotarō, ceaselessly trying to escape and return home –

Endlessly, ceaselessly . . .

Her engines turning, the *Hōyō-maru* began to move now. Ryūnosuke opened his eyes and reached into his pocket for his cigarettes. But instead of the yellow box of Egyptians, Ryūnosuke felt something else in his fingers –

Roses, red roses . . .

The petals already withered, the fragrance already gone, already spent now –

In the night, on the deck. Ryūnosuke tossed the wilted red rose into the churning dark waters. Then his fingers in his ears, now his fingers in his eyes. Ryūnosuke cursed Momotarō, Ryūnosuke cursed Yatagarasu. And then he cursed himself –

And now Ryūnosuke prayed,

his ticket in his hand,

Ryūnosuke prayed and he prayed no birds would ever disturb the branches of that tree again. No babies ever born of peaches again. *What you want, you should not want.* ■

COURTESY NATIONAL DIET LIBRARY

AUTHOR'S NOTE: In 1921, Ryūnosuke Akutagawa was one of the most acclaimed young writers in Japan. Partly to escape a complicated personal affair, and partly because of his fascination with Chinese literature, Akutagawa agreed to go to China for a few months as Special Correspondent for the Osaka *Mainichi Shimbun*.

This piece is an extract from the unfinished novel *Patient No. 23 – After Ryūnosuke Akutagawa*. It would not have been possible without the translations and scholarship of many other writers. The following books were essential sources of information and inspiration:

Profiles from China by Eunice Tietjens, 1917
Rashōmon and Seventeen Other Stories by Ryūnosuke Akutagawa, translated by Jay Rubin, 2006
Shanghai by Stella Dong, 2000
Shanghai by Riichi Yokomitsu, translated by Dennis Washburn, 2001
Tales of Old Japan by A.B. Mitford, 1876
'Travels in China' by Ryūnosuke Akutagawa, translated by Joshua A. Fogel, in *Chinese Studies in History*, vol. 30, no. 4, Summer 1997

FROM SITE

Daisuke Yokota

I look at a photograph. It is an image that I shot some time ago. It has been just long enough since I shot the image that I am fuzzy on the exact circumstances of the time.

What was I thinking then? There probably wasn't a particular reason I made the exposure, but there was some sequence of events that resulted in releasing the shutter.

What was my intention? I cannot remember; or, perhaps, the me of here and now can no longer know what it was.

If we accept that I am the one who photographed an image, then we must accept as truth that I was with a camera at the location where the photograph happened. The existence of the photograph is an artefact of the connection between the subject (what was photographed), the camera and me.

Ostensibly, this truth, and the marvellous power of reproducibility inherent to photography, is a record of fact. But what is found in the photograph is actually nowhere and no one. There is merely an assemblage of grain on paper.

The photograph we are left with and the memory of that time do not progress along the same time axes.

Then/now, memory/record, the phenomenon of reality that presents itself before me and my impression of it – each of these dualities has a complicated relationship, and affect one another.

The past appears to be fixed, but its form changes along with the changes in my consciousness. ∎

Translated from the Japanese by Ivan Vartanian

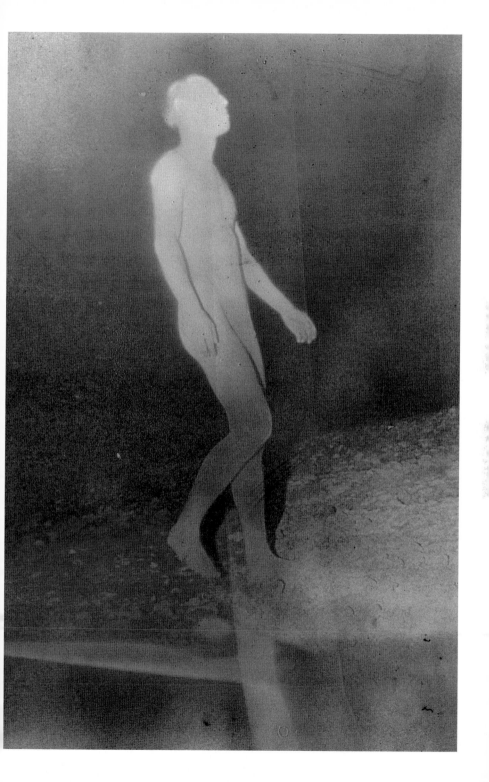

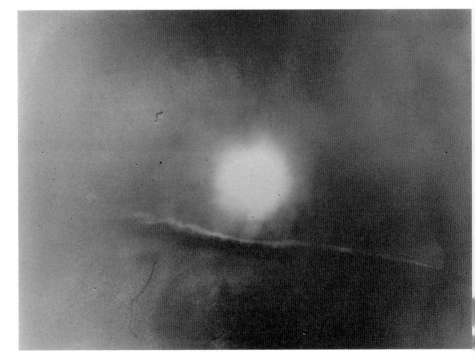

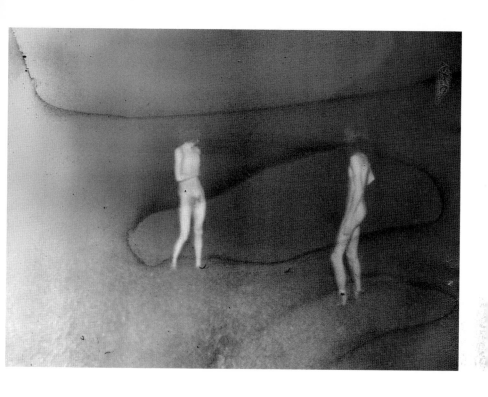

SCAVENGERS

Adam Johnson

I was in Pyongyang's Department Store Number One when I saw a bottle of rice wine emblazoned with the bust of famed Japanese pro wrestler Rikidōzan, Koreanized as 'Ryokdosan'. The bottle was styled after a Grecian urn, with Ryokdosan's image framed, halo-like, in a golden championship belt. Pearlescent and adorned, the bottle was a rare object of beauty for sale in North Korea. For a week, my minders had been steering me daily into shopping opportunities at various gifts shops and department stores. And I was ready to pay. I was dying to buy something, anything that would help my wife and children understand the profound surrealism and warped reality I'd experienced on my research trip to North Korea.

But there was nothing to buy. The stores were filled with cheap Chinese goods, grey-market medicines and out-of-date foreign snacks and candies. North Korea produced only durable goods like Vinalon overcoats, shovel handles and work boots. I might have actually bought a Vinalon blazer or a North Korean skillet. But the regime didn't offer these at their tourist shops. I couldn't even buy a painting or a ceramic bowl made in North Korea. Arts and crafts there are required to glorify the regime, yet it's forbidden for a foreigner to possess images of the Dear Leaders, DPRK flags or nationalist iconography like the Chollima (a mythical winged horse that symbolizes the rapid advancement of the society), a double rainbow over Mount Paektu (the 'official' setting of Kim Jong-il's illustrious birth) or some Taepodong missiles blazing upward. Hence the selection of a Beijing dollar store.

My main minder, Ga-yoon, was bright and funny and sophisticated – she had a graduate degree from Kim Il-sung University in handling

American tourists – but she seemed baffled that I wasn't salivating at all these goods for sale. She strolled with me down aisles of knock-off iPods, no-name tennis rackets and imitation handbags before showing me the object of her desire: a box fan moulded in China from pink plastic. Ga-yoon stared longingly at it, imagining perhaps the cool breeze it would bring to her Pyongyang apartment. She simply couldn't believe that I wasn't snapping up that fan, stowing it in my overhead luggage bin and lovingly unveiling it back in America. She couldn't quite figure me out. Why had I purchased only postcards? The only real interest I'd shown in shopping was when I was taken to a store that had a selection of North Korean taxidermy. I was holding my arms wide to measure the two-metre wingspan of a mounted vulture, wondering if I could get it home and how a stuffed North Korean scavenger would look over our mantle in San Francisco, when I caught Ga-yoon studying me like I was an alien.

Then I found the bottle of rice wine beaming the image of Rikidōzan.

I pulled it from the shelf and asked Ga-yoon about the wrestler it depicted.

'That's Ryokdosan, a famous Korean,' she said, her tone suddenly serious. 'He went to Japan, and after beating all the Japanese fighters, he wanted to return home to Korea a champion. The Japanese were angry so they kidnapped him and murdered him.'

Her assistant minder Dong-man was new at the job. He sported a starched white shirt, a straight black tie and a prominent Kim Il-sung pin.

'The Japanese were jealous and ashamed that a Korean was better,' Dong-man added. 'When Ryokdosan tried to return home to the glorious socialism of North Korea, the cowards stabbed him to death.'

'The Japanese murdered him?' I asked. 'How? Where?'

My minders shook their heads. They didn't know the details.

A young saleswoman jumped in with her limited English.

'Japan steal,' she added, her eyes wide. 'Japan kill.'

I studied the portrait of Ryokdosan on the bottle, a North Korean hero so powerful that Japan couldn't let him live, a North Korean so loyal that Japan had no choice but to steal him and kill him.

I purchased the bottle of rice wine, thus elevating myself somewhat in Ga-yoon's esteem. But the day was a disaster for her: part of her job was to entice hard currency from me, and I ended up spending only eleven American dollars in Pyongyang's most elite shopping establishment.

One thing I had acquired in North Korea was a stomach bug. Knowing that I couldn't drink the bottle of rice wine and that I couldn't bring it on the plane, I poured it down the sink in my room on the thirty-second floor of the Yanggakdo Hotel.

The hotel is on an island in the Taedong River. Pyongyangites are forbidden from setting foot on the island, and tourists are barred by guards from leaving. Assuming that tourists can't get into trouble in this moated lodging, the minders go home for the night, and the guests are left to their own devices. What guests there were. At the height of the tourist season, there were only enough visitors in Pyongyang to fill the sixth and thirty-second floors – two lit bands in a dark monolith straddled by a rain-swollen river.

Trapped and sick and a little stir-crazy, I went to the hotel's forty-ninth floor, where there was a bar and an unused revolving restaurant that didn't revolve. Here, I found a carpet of AstroTurf, a fish tank full of algae and a lone, drunken Japanese businessman. There was also a spectacular view of the DPRK's darkened emptiness.

Most of the liquors behind the bar were unknown to me, including a carboy of fluid that contained a pickled snake. A shot of Jack Daniel's, I saw, cost twenty-five euros. I ordered a Taedonggang beer to settle my stomach and asked the barmaid about the Korean wrestler who became Rikidōzan.

She shook her head.

'She's Chinese,' the Japanese businessman said, with a great lament, and explained that all the hotel staff were Chinese workers on contract, 'so we never get near a real North Korean woman, ever'.

He was quite drunk, and I had stumbled upon his central issue in life. It was with surprising candour that he explained to me his unrelenting desire for North Korean women, that he'd set up his entire career to enable him to visit the DPRK from Tokyo to be in their presence, to study them, to breathe their air. He said it was his cruel fate to be forever thwarted by their elusive nature. He went on and on about their beauty, about how they were uncorrupted by the shallowness of the rest of planet Earth, about how their sheltered status meant they were as close to 'real' women as could be found in our century.

'They are the only pure women left,' he said.

Moths circled outside the windows. Occasionally a bird would slash through the dark, picking moths from the air. I could almost hear the clicking of their beaks.

'Have you ever had a conversation with a North Korean woman?' I asked. 'I mean beyond minders and translators?'

With great pain, he said, 'No. We're the enemy here.'

I didn't know if 'we' meant all Japanese, or if it included Americans like me.

I said that perhaps there were more accessible women to meet in Japan, women he could get to know. Women of Korean descent. Even women who had defected from North Korea. This only seemed to increase his isolation, as if it was proof that I didn't understand anything.

As a joke, I said, 'You could always defect to North Korea.'

He snorted and gave me a look that said, You think I haven't considered that?

I looked over at the fish gulping in the murky water of the aquarium. My kids raised tropical fish, so I had a great urge to roll up my sleeves and clean that tank.

I'd been away from a toilet too long. It was time to leave this sad tableau. I took a last look at the moonlight glimmering off the fat Taedong River, its muscly, dark green bends slowly wending toward Nampo.

When I stood to go the businessman said, 'That wrestler you mentioned, I remember him. But he wasn't Korean – he was Japanese. I think he spent too much money on girls and gambling. He died in the toilet of a nightclub. They say the yakuza who stabbed him urinated on the blade.'

Rikidōzan, I would later learn, was born in 1924 in what would become South Hamgyong Province, North Korea. His Korean name was Kim San-rak, but under Japanese occupation, all things Korean were deemed illegal, including Korean language, arts, customs and personal names. Kim San-rak, an orphan, was adopted by a family of farmers in Nagasaki Prefecture in Japan and given the name Momota Mitsuhiro. He was a large boy, so his adoptive father had him train in sumo, and here he took the *shikona*, or ring name, of Rikidōzan.

It translates roughly as 'difficult mountain passage'.

Rikidōzan was a successful sumo, competing in over two hundred matches, but it was after the war that he discovered his destiny. He saw an American pro wrestling event sponsored by the Red Cross to entertain US troops. He began to train as a pro wrestler and travelled to America in 1952, where he booked hundreds of matches, competing mostly as a villain. Many American wrestlers later reciprocated, travelling to Japan to take on villain roles against Rikidōzan. Already known from sumo, Rikidōzan's defeat of 'evil' Americans captured the imagination of a nation in the mire of post-war defeat.

In 1953, Rikidōzan invited famed judoka Kimura to compete as a pro wrestler, allegedly agreeing in advance to a choreography that would end in a draw. Once inside the ring, however, Rikidōzan dealt Kimura a punishing beat down, lumping his face with brutal open-hand blows and striking his neck with the karate chops that would become his signature move. The attack lasted only a minute, and Kimura was left unconscious in the ring. Kimura vowed revenge, claiming ten yakuza hit men would retaliate. But it didn't matter:

Rikidōzan was now a superstar. By borrowing yakuza money, he started his own wrestling federation and began training a stable of fighters who would go on to become superstars: Kanji 'Antonio' Inoki, Kintaro Ōki and Shohei 'Giant' Baba. Rikidōzan's matches in the late fifties and early sixties become the most highly viewed television events in Japanese history.

Rikidōzan used his fame and fortune to purchase nightclubs, hotels and condominiums. He gained a reputation for his bar-room showmanship, drinking prowess and willingness to gamble. On 8 December 1963, Rikidōzan fell into conflict with the Japanese mobster Katsuji Murata, who stabbed Rikidōzan in the abdomen with a switchblade. It's unclear if the attack in the bathroom of Tokyo's New Latin Club was prompted by yakuza debt, personal rivalry or was in retaliation for Rikidōzan's beating of Kimura. A week later, thirty-nine-year-old Rikidōzan died of peritonitis.

Kim Il-sung had supposedly tried to lure Rikidōzan home with promises of a fancy Pyongyang apartment, his own North Korean wrestling federation and the ability to travel abroad for state-sponsored matches. But the wrestler had tasted the good life and refused. To a propaganda machine, however, a dead hero was even better than a live one.

After Rikidōzan's death, North Korea repossessed the fighter with the 1989 biography *I Am a Korean*, which became required reading for a generation of North Korean citizens. Pyongyang's Foreign Languages Publishing House brought out an English edition of the book, whose publication coincided with the production of the commemorative Ryokdosan Drink that I ran across in Pyongyang's Department Store Number One.

That was not the end of North Korea's wrestling propaganda. In 1995, Kim Jong-il hosted a pro wrestling event in Pyongyang's Rungnado May Day Stadium, the largest on earth, called Collision in Korea. Kim invited Rikidōzan's early protégé Antonio Inoki to North Korea to visit Rikidōzan's home village, meet his sister and lay a wreath at Rikidōzan's grave, despite the fact that Rikidōzan was buried in Ikegami Honmon-ji Temple Cemetery in Tokyo. Half a century after Rikidōzan beat Americans on Japanese TV, Inoki, a stand-in for a hero co-opted for North Korea, fought the American wrestler Ric Flair in front of 190,000 spectators to glorify the regime. Muhammad Ali travelled to Pyongyang to witness the fight. Ric Flair, in his memoir *To Be the Man*, recalls that Ali was having none of North Korea's monkey business. After being pressured to read a propaganda speech prepared by his handlers and being subjected to anti-American insults from party officials at a state-sponsored dinner, Ali interrupted the meal to announce, 'No wonder we hate these motherfuckers.'

Taking leave of the Japanese businessman in the unrevolving restaurant at the top of the Yanggakdo Hotel, I went to take the elevator. Here I paused. It wasn't because this elevator had tried to kill me the day before – when I'd called it to the thirty-second floor and the doors had opened, there was no car and I nearly stepped into the dark shaft. No, I think I opened the steel door to the fire-escape stairs instead because I wanted something real in this unreal place. So I began making my way down, floor by darkened floor, seventeen storeys to my room.

These sections of the hotel were dark, lit only by moonlight through windows at the ends of long halls. But I could faintly see that some kind of operation was going on. On some floors, large stretches of carpet were stacked in rolls by the elevator. On others, fixtures like toilets and lamps were lined in the hall. Doors were off their hinges. Wires were exposed. I began to understand that, to keep floors like mine looking good, they were stripping materials from the darkened ones.

It struck me that this kind of cannibalism was something I'd been feeling on my entire journey through North Korea. On a good day, propaganda can feel like a strange and fanciful story – 'We're the most democratic nation on earth', 'This is a worker's paradise', 'We have universal health care' – but this national narrative comes at the expense of every individual's in the country. Here, people's hopes and dreams and identities were raw materials, to be harvested and processed and consumed by the state. In the dim light of a darkened hallway, I saw someone had pried the metal room number off a door. Left behind was the barest outline of a 9. I remembered that the other functioning floor in the hotel was the sixth. In North Korea, it didn't matter if you were a 9: you would be turned into a 6. ∎

GRANTA

THE DOGS

Yukiko Motoya

TRANSLATED FROM THE JAPANESE BY ASA YONEDA

I once lived with a whole lot of dogs.

I don't recall their breed, which is strange, because we were close, and spent all that time together. I loved those dogs, and they loved me. There were dozens of them, each one bright white like freshly fallen snow. I spent my days warm and comfortable in a room with a fireplace, not seeing anyone. The dogs did ask to be let out, but I never once saw them doing their business – which was also strange, but at the time, I assumed that they were modest, and had set up some kind of toilet area away from the cabin. I didn't like beds, so I slept standing up, leaning against the windowsill. The dogs would gather around me at night like an overcoat, leaving only my mouth and eyes exposed. I enjoyed drowsily gazing at the fire, drifting to sleep, with the heady feeling of being engulfed by the mass of dogs.

At the time, I had some work that I could do holed up in the cabin. It involved sitting at the desk in the attic from morning to night, peering into a magnifying glass, tweezering tiny pieces of paper of innumerable colours: work too mind-numbing for most people even to contemplate. For many years, come winter, I'd take several weeks' worth of food and water and hide myself away in that cabin, which belonged to someone I knew.

The cabin consisted of a high-ceilinged living room, a small bedroom and an attic, but that was ample. When I first reached the isolated cabin, having driven inexpertly over the narrow, winding mountain roads, I was still on my own. I remember dropping the keys, and struggling to pick them up again while still holding all my luggage, because of the bulky scarf which covered half my face, preventing me from seeing my hands. Autumn had just ended. Towards the beginning of my stay I'd definitely gone to sleep alone, looking out the window each night and feeling as if I were at the bottom of a deep sea. Strangely enough, I don't recall when the dogs started living there.

I loved all the dogs equally. At first, I made an effort to name each one of them, but that was short-lived because I never actually liked naming things. I was happy just looking into the glossy black of their eyes, which shone as though they'd been fired in a magic kiln. And after all, it wasn't as if the dogs called me by name. But this got to be a little inconvenient, so I came up with some names to try out on them. I lined the dogs up in front of the fireplace, and told them to bark if they heard a name they liked. Then I held up the collars I'd fashioned and, looking into their eyes, called out the names one by one.

'First up, Early Morning.'

Heh heh heh heh.

'The Day the White Goods Arrived.'

Heh heh heh heh.

'Pastrami.'

Heh heh heh . . . Yap!

The dog stuck his tongue out deferentially. I placed the collar marked PASTRAMI around his neck.

'The World.'

Heh heh heh heh.

'Takeaway.'

Yap! Yap yap!

The dogs took care of their own meals as well. I surreptitiously let them out in the mountain woods, so they probably hunted animals as a pack. Once when I went for a walk among the trees, I found what looked like a bird's skull at the bottom of a tree. I slipped the skull into my coat pocket and, when I returned to the cabin, I threw it at the dogs where they lay lounging. 'Boo!' I shouted. The dogs didn't really react, but I thought that must be because they were ashamed that I knew they'd been eating birds. They never let me see them feed.

What I did see them doing was drinking plenty of the very cold water that I got from the well behind the garage. I tried warming it for them so they didn't catch a chill, but they wouldn't touch that. For some reason, the dogs preferred flimsy plastic supermarket dishes to ceramic, wooden or glass. With their tongues hanging from their mouths, they drooled everywhere, but I didn't worry about it too much – I just went around the cabin with my feet wrapped in plastic bags. They seemed to be at their most energetic just after drinking their ice-cold water.

One day, I drove down the mountain to replenish some food supplies, and came across a knot of people from the town, puffed up in woolly hats and down-filled jackets and gathered by the roadside.

I slowed down to see what was going on. Through the open car window I heard a voice saying something about a dog. My heart skipped a beat. The dog curled up in the passenger seat next to me began to raise his head as if he had sensed something, so I said 'hush' and held his round head down in my hand. He'd come nosing around my feet as I was getting in the car, so I'd brought him along.

The dogs' heads just fitted in the palm of my hand, and I was always moved by how their little skulls were wrapped in soft fur. This helped me stay calm on this occasion, too, and I quietly rolled up the car window and slipped past the townspeople. Perhaps a dog had caused some kind of problem. In the supermarket, I kept my scarf wound twice around as usual, hiding half my face, to discourage the staff from approaching me. But when the shop assistant from the fruit and vegetable section looked into my basket and casually remarked, 'Stockpiling All-Bran again?', I plucked up my courage and asked, 'Has something happened in town?'

The man looked a little taken aback – probably because I'd spoken at all. 'A five-year-old boy's gone missing,' he whispered as he glanced around.

'A child? Was it a kidnapping?'

'Kidnapping? No, nothing like that would happen around here.'

'Then what?'

'Maybe he fell into the valley when his mother took her eyes off him.'

Suddenly, the bantering air of familiarity that had arisen between me and the shop assistant became unbearable, so I hurried away with my trolley. The dog, who'd apparently been asleep at the foot of the passenger seat, looked up at me blearily, and I gave his head a stroke. I swung by the petrol station. There was an elderly attendant there who would always try to strike up a conversation with me. I found it a bit of a trial, but it was the only petrol station in town.

I didn't keep in touch with anyone. I'd always considered my only strengths to be that I was completely content not to talk to a single soul all day and that I had a high tolerance for monotony. The exception was the phone call I got once a week from a certain man. It's conceivable that I allowed his phone calls to lull me into feeling that I'd discharged all my social obligations. Of the few people I'd met over the years, he was the only one I felt I could still confide in. We had no romantic feelings for each other, simply a relationship where we could say what we honestly thought. When I heard his voice, my shoulders would let go of some of their tension, like the knot in a firmly tied silk scarf loosening deep inside a forest, far from where people are. His speech was distinct, like an oiled egg popping out of his mouth.

There was no doubt he was a misanthrope, like me, but unlike me he had enough courtesy and presence of mind not to let it show. He was the one that let me use this cabin, and would always joke that it was because he wanted me to pursue the life he couldn't. We often put our opinions to battle on the subject of whether it was better to distance ourselves from civilization or immerse ourselves in it, and when we tired of that we could hang up without a hint of awkwardness. He had a family. After our phone calls, I felt relieved at having fulfilled some minimal quota of human interaction, and comforted by the thought that he seemed to be making steady progress in the kind of life that was my 'road not taken'.

There wasn't a set time for our phone calls, but that day, like on others, I had a premonition that made me look up from my magnifying glass. I must have been engrossed in the work – though I thought I'd barely had a sip of my hot milk, five hours had passed since I'd come up to the attic. I put my tweezers down on their stand and got up from the chair, checking that none of the tiny pieces of coloured paper were stuck to my hands or clothes. Above the desk there was a window with two layers of glass, and I could see several dogs running around in the snow outside.

I descended the ladder with the empty Thermos and mug in one hand, and was warming up some more milk when the phone rang. Stirring the aluminium saucepan with a spoon, I reached over with my other hand and slowly lifted the receiver.

'Hey,' he said. 'I hope you're not suffering from isolation fatigue.'

No, I said, and asked whether he wasn't suffering from socializing fatigue, to which he responded, of course I am.

'You settled in your burrow? Anything giving you trouble?'

'Plenty, but better that than convenience.' I told him about the advantages of mountain life – the hairdryer blasting out hot air that was unbelievably cold, the paths that got buried in snow despite constant shovelling, the front door that I had to hurl my body against when it jammed, the hunks of snow that fell into the fireplace and sent ash flying everywhere.

He said, 'That's why I never go there in winter. I don't know how you stand it. After living like that, are you really going to want to come back down when spring comes?'

I informed him I'd been down to the town just today, thank you very much, then asked him never to speak of spring again, because I didn't want to think about it. That brought the afternoon's events back to mind, so I told him about the huddle of townspeople I'd come across. 'There might have been some kind of incident down there.'

'An incident? Wonder what, in such a nowhere town.'

I was reluctant to tell him more. I didn't want him to latch on to it and start looking it up in the papers or on the Internet. I stopped stirring the saucepan and looked over to the dogs stretched out in the living room. Sprawled on the rugs like white sausages, they acted unconcerned, but I could tell they were a little unsettled by my being on the phone, like a jealous boyfriend. I guess my demeanour changed slightly during these phone calls. At that moment, it occurred to me that I could ask him about them. Why hadn't I thought of this before? They might have been his dogs.

'Hey, about those little white fellows,' I said.

'Those ones?' he asked back.

'Yeah. They're doing really well.'

There was a pause. 'Oh,' he said. 'Here, not so much, but I did spot some of those little white fellows by the road today. Although maybe they weren't so white. Most of them are black now, with all the gravel and the dirt.'

'Is that so?' I wondered whether black dogs were really more common in cities.

'Plus, the black fellows aren't doing so well. All melting and deformed, more or less on their last legs.'

I cut off his laughter. 'You really don't know?'

'Know what?'

He wasn't playing dumb. But for some reason now, I didn't find it strange in the slightest that he didn't know about the dogs. One of them came up to me and pressed his fluffy coat against my shin. I knelt down and rubbed his sides like I was giving him a good scrub, and just said, 'I'll tell you next time.'

'Sure,' he replied, as though to say he was used to my crotchety ways.

After that, we chatted about nothing in particular, and I got through two mugfuls of hot milk. As we were about to hang up, he asked whether I'd seen the weather forecast. I reminded him there was no civilization up here, and he told me, laughing, that there was going to be a fierce chill invading over the weekend.

One day, I decided to surprise the dogs in the woods, and followed them in secret when they went out to play. Once I was holed up in my workroom with the Thermos, they knew I wouldn't be back out for a few hours, so they would start to disperse. They each had their favourite spot. Some liked to be just outside the door to my workroom, and others to lie on the clothes strewn around the bedroom and the living room, but most of the dogs seemed to be happier in the outside world.

I put on sunscreen to protect against snow burn, and some mirrored sunglasses and an anorak, and left the house. I traced the dogs' footprints through the bare trees, and revelled in my afternoon stroll. Picking up a branch that I liked the look of, I drew meandering lines in the bright snow as I walked, occasionally swapping the branch for another when I encountered a better one.

The dogs' prints were almost always all in a bunch. They were basically toddling along the least arduous path. Every so often, a set of tracks diverged from the rest, but then shortly came back to rejoin the group. I thought they must hunt as a team, like wolves.

Before I knew it, I was on a path that I'd never been on before. I looked over to a clump of trees, and saw one dog peeking through them from behind a bank of snow. His eyes were wide, and he was only visible from the nose up. I waved my branch number five, which was curled like a spring, removed my sunglasses and said, 'I followed you. Is everyone over there? May I join you?'

The dog got lightly to his feet and barked. Then he turned on his heels and ran off. I advanced into the clump of trees through knee-high snow, calling after him, 'Should I not have come?' Feeling like a parent secretly checking on whether my children were doing their homework, and suppressing a grin, I looked out from behind a great tree.

I was astonished to see where they were: on a large frozen lake. I hadn't known it was here, but there the dogs were, stepping with a practised air across the lake, which was big enough to hold several games of baseball at once. It was as if a ready-made dog park, sculpted by nature, had suddenly appeared before my eyes.

The dogs seemed to have no idea I was behind the tree, and were scattered in all directions. I tried to get closer to see what they were up to, but the ice at the water's edge was thin, and far too treacherous. I stayed where I was and squinted at the dogs beginning to jump up and down. At first, they only jumped up about as high as they were tall. Gradually their time in the air seemed to increase, until all of a sudden, they were jumping so high that they could have cleared the head of a person standing. It seemed that they were each trying to make a hole in the ice. Their front paws made digging movements, trying to break through the surface. Before long, each dog succeeded in making its hole, and jumped swiftly into the water. When the last one had dived in, they were nowhere to be seen, as if they'd melted away.

One of them poked its head out of its hole in the ice and sounded a short, sharp cry. It's drowning and calling for help, I thought in alarm, but in the next moment another dog stuck its head out of the freezing water, in a different spot, and made the same bird-like cry. Then more dogs popped their heads out from the ice, repeating the cry. It dawned on me what was going on. Swimming as a pack, the dogs were forming a large circle under the ice. And, using their cries, they were slowly closing the circle towards its centre. I couldn't take my eyes off them. I walked around the lake, and when I found an area where the ice seemed thick enough to hold me, I leapt onto it. Using my gloves like windscreen wipers, I scraped away the frost and peered through the ice.

The only thing I could see was grey muddiness at the bottom of the lake.

I made my way back to the cabin alone, picturing the image of the dogs gracefully chasing fish through clear water.

That weekend, I woke to the morning I'd always wished for, when every last thing in the world seemed to have frozen over. The All-Bran I kept in the cupboard was in clumps so hard it was like eating hail, and seeing the icicles protruding from the roof was like having been transported overnight to a grotto filled with stalactites.

Once I'd put on as many layers as I could, shivering all the while, I took an empty bucket and shovel and headed to the garage. The dogs scampered around me, keeping close to my feet as if to hurry me along. By the time I reached the garage, taking three or four times longer than usual, my whole body was emitting heat, and sweat was pouring out of me like I was in a sauna.

I made sure the generator's battery indicator was green. I checked how many litres of diesel fuel were left, then decided to dig out some more snow tools. I discovered some emergency tubes of chocolate, years past their 'use-by' date. Finally, I took some old, dusty blankets and went around to the back of the garage. I looked down into the well, and a solemn chill plastered my face, like sticky children's hands. The extreme cold had formed a miniature ice rink in there.

'What shall we do?' I asked the dogs behind me. 'Can't get you any water.'

The one with the collar marked PASTRAMI tried to climb up onto the well, scrabbling with his paws. 'Get off!' I told him, and decided to do what I could about the frozen pulley at least.

I brought out a chisel and a mallet from the garage, and as I pounded like a blacksmith, with all my might, the frozen rope finally started to give. I took hold of the rope with both hands and gave it a hard tug, and the layer of ice that had formed over the mechanism came away with a clatter as the pulley quickly began to turn.

That was when it happened. Pastrami leapt up onto the well, somehow got into the bucket, and disappeared down the hole, looking pleased with himself. 'Pastrami!' I shouted, but it was too late. Pastrami was yapping and rolling around in anguish at the bottom, having slammed onto the thick ice. Frantic, I worked the rope, raising and lowering the bucket that had fallen with him, trying to get him to jump back in it, but the bewildered dog could hardly stand up on the ice. 'Go get help!' I called to the dogs crowded behind me. I heard the footfalls of several dogs running off. I leaned into the well and stretched my arm down, shouting 'Pastrami! Pastrami!', but the yapping cries reverberating up the well were overwhelming and I couldn't keep my eyes open. When I came to after some time, I was slumped by the edge of the well. Pastrami's cries had ceased, as had the sound of his forepaws scraping at the ice.

'What should I do if an animal jumps into the well?' I asked. The power lines had gone down under the weight of snow, and it was late at night before I got through to him on the phone. 'Animal in the well?' he said, a little sleepily.

'Yeah.' I was wrapped in old blankets from the garage. I'd tried to keep my mind occupied all afternoon, chopping firewood and doing other things, but when night fell, I suddenly felt completely drained, and found myself unable even to stand up. The dogs stayed close by me through the day, like watchdogs.

'Actually, I did find something like a weasel drowned in it once.'

'Was it winter?'

'Summer.'

'Then that's a different situation.'

'I think I got someone from the town to get it out. I could give you the number. What is it? A raccoon?'

I told him that I couldn't really tell because it was all the way at the bottom. He suggested it might be dangerous, and that I should just put the cover back on and leave the animal there. Wolves sometimes prowled the area looking for food, he said. He would come by with his family on his next day off to take care of it. My mind kept replaying Pastrami trying to jump up into the well bucket, and I was terribly tired, so I told him that I wanted to go to bed now. If you ever feel in real danger, he began, then went on to tell me how to unlock the cupboard in the bedroom, which he'd never let me touch before. The emergency hunting rifle was hidden in there. I told him I had no need for such a thing, and hung up. I pulled myself together and made some food, but could only eat a bite and left the rest.

I was checking that the draughty living-room window was properly closed, when I thought I heard the faint cry of a dog. I raised my head. Was it the wind howling? With a storm lamp and a shovel, and with the other dogs in tow, I made my way through the snow towards the well.

The bucket was rattling against the pulley as the wind blew. I stopped a few paces from the well and raised the lamp. 'Pastrami?' I said in a small voice, almost to myself. 'Pastrami?'

I thought I heard the keening cry of a dog in distress.

'Pastrami, are you alive?' I called again.

This time I could definitely make out the dog crying. I flung myself towards the well – which I'd fled from that afternoon – put my hands on the edge, and looked into it. In the lamplight I could see Pastrami, getting up on the ice! I left the lamp and the dogs, retrieved a chainsaw from the garage and returned to the cabin. I sawed off the ladder that led to the attic, getting showered in sawdust, and loaded it on the red sledge that I used for transporting firewood. Once I was back at the well, with the aid of some of the dogs, I lowered the ladder into the well, careful not to break the ice, and called the dog's name. 'Pastrami.' I wanted him to take hold of the ladder somehow. But Pastrami only looked up at me with his tongue hanging out, and wouldn't make a move.

The ice at the base of the well seemed thick, and gave no sign of cracking when I tapped the ladder on it. I screwed up my courage, and tentatively climbed over the edge, and gingerly stepped onto the ladder. Slowly, cautiously, I descended. Pastrami wagged his tail weakly as I approached. Just as I'd put one foot on the ice and reached for Pastrami, there was the slight cracking sound of something giving way, and all the blood drained out of my body. With bated breath, I coaxed the stone-cold hunk of fur down into the front of my jacket. I put my hand on the ladder to climb back up, but stopped short – the other dogs had surrounded the rim of the well, and were staring down at us, motionless.

One dog moved its mouth clumsily just as the wind howled again. I thought I heard the dog say, 'Good enough.' Terrified, I found myself on the verge of laughter, almost simpering. 'Good enough?' I said. 'For what?'

Beyond the still forms of the dogs looking down at us, I saw clouds being blown across the sky. Pastrami, who had been keeping still inside my jacket, yapped, as though remembering that he was a dog.

It was a pain having to go down the mountain, but he was adamant about keeping stocked on certain things. I made up my mind to go to town for the first time in a week. I don't know how he knew, but when I got to the garage, Pastrami was waiting beside the car door, looking fully recovered and eager to come along.

I considered taking him, but decided against it. 'No, stay home,' I said. After what I'd seen last time, I thought it better to leave him behind. I drove down the mountain roads carefully, and saw that Christmas decorations were up all around town. It must be that time of year already. As I looked around, feeling the ache of old injuries from festive gatherings past, I noticed that something was a little off.

It was people's expressions – they seemed haggard, somehow. Not to mention their little tics like they were in fear of something, constantly glancing behind themselves. That elderly person sitting on a bench had the puffy face of someone who'd been up crying all night. There were few cars on the road, and every house had its curtains drawn. Was I imagining it? Even the overly cheerful Christmas decorations gave the impression that the town was desperately trying to avert its eyes from something upsetting.

The shop assistant in the fruit and vegetable section wasn't around. Normally, I'd have been relieved, but this time it bothered me so I asked the woman restocking the frozen foods what had happened. 'Yes, that boy – he quit.' Quit? All of a sudden? The woman gave me a long look. I thought I detected wariness and irritation in her eyes and quickly walked away. For some reason, the dog food had been moved, even though the cat food was still in the same place. I thought about asking where they'd put it, but I didn't feel like engaging that woman again, and left the supermarket. The older man at the petrol station with whom I always exchanged a few words wasn't there, either.

'Is he not working today?' I asked the young attendant in the Santa hat as he handed me my change. I'd got him to put a plastic container of diesel in the boot for me.

'Mm-hm,' he nodded, ambiguously. There it was again. Each time

I mentioned someone who wasn't there, I could sense irritation rise in the townspeople's eyes.

I was absorbed in a poster for a Christmas party – FORGET ALL YOUR TROUBLES! – when I felt the young man staring at me. 'He said I could ask him if I ever needed anything. I was counting on it,' I said, almost to myself.

'Let me know if there's anything I can do,' said the young man, batting away the pompom on his Santa hat.

'Do you mean that? I might take you up on it.' I hoped my eagerness to get back up the mountain wasn't showing on my face.

'Sure,' he said, nodding, and trotted inside to the cash register to bring me a pale pink flyer. 'The charges for the services are all on here, if you'd like to take it with you.'

I thanked him, and rolled up the window, but one more thing was weighing on my mind. I rolled the window back down and asked offhandedly, 'Do you deal with dogs?'

'Dogs?' he said. There was a pause, and he pointed at the bottom of the flyer. 'You can see about dogs at the bottom there.'

I escaped from the petrol station.

Outside the police station, as I stopped for a red light, I was contemplating the sign in large print on the noticeboard – FOR THE GOOD OF THE TOWN, THEY'VE GOT TO BE PUT DOWN – when the lorry behind me blasted its horn.

After that, I spent most of my waking hours at my desk, because I really had to knuckle down to my work. It required bottomless reserves of concentration. Several jobs were already complete and framed, and lined up along the attic wall, but even when I looked at those, I didn't understand in the slightest what made people want to pay so much for them. But there was no need for me to understand. The thing that mattered was that having this work let me avoid dealing with people. But the more progress I made, the more time I spent dreading when I would have to leave this place.

I was having a leisurely soak in the bath for the first time in a while, feeling good about the amount of work I'd accomplished, when it occurred to me that I hadn't had a phone call in a few days. When I looked at the calendar in the kitchen, it was four days past Tuesday, when he always rang. I checked the time, which was only eight at night, and decided to ring him myself. No answer. No matter how many times I tried, I didn't even get through to the answering machine. Had something happened? He was conscientious, not like me. When he'd had appendicitis, he'd left me a message letting me know he'd be in surgery and wouldn't be answering his phone for eight hours – that was the kind of person he was. It could be that the phone had actually rung, many times, and I'd been too engrossed in the work to notice. I checked the calendar again, and was taken aback. It was the 31st of December!

I decided to do something about the draught from the living room window before the arrival of the new year, and so I got some putty and pressed it into the window frame. Then I noticed the pale pink flyer on the floor beneath the coat rack. I sat down on the sofa with the dogs and looked through the list of services available, just in case. It looked like they could take care of most things. The prices seemed a little high, but I could see myself calling them in an emergency. There was no entry for 'Retrieval of animals in wells', although there was one for 'Recovery of dead birds in chimneys'. Further down, the item 'Dog walking' had been heavily crossed out. I recalled the exchange with the young man at the petrol station. The last item on the list was even more mysterious.

'Extermination of dogs.'

Perhaps they meant feral dogs, I thought, as I stroked the heads of the white dogs. But surely that sort of thing would normally be left to the public health department. I suddenly remembered the strange snow tools, like big sharp forks, that I'd seen propped beside the winter tyres at the petrol station. What could they have been for? The dog I was petting pricked up its ears, barked menacingly and leapt onto the flyer, ripping it to shreds. 'Stop it!' I said, but then the other dogs caught the scent of the paper and, crouching down ready to pounce, started howling and growling like they'd gone mad. *Yap yap, yap yap yap!*

I calmed them down, got up from the sofa and thought I'd try ringing him again. But for some reason, I already knew he wouldn't answer, and instead I dialled the number for my parents' place, which I hadn't done in a long time. No one picked up, despite it being New Year's Eve. Just to make sure, I tried the police. No response. The fire brigade. No response. I dialled every number I could think of, but all I heard was the phone ringing, over and over.

I got my jacket from the coat rack, and with car keys in hand headed to the garage. The dogs followed and tried to get in the car. I told them I was just going down to have a look around the town, but this didn't satisfy them. You want to come too? *Yap yap!* But I can't take all of you! *Yap yap yap!* The dogs went on barking as if they were broken.

It took an hour to walk down to the foot of the mountain, white dogs in tow. When I got there the town was deserted, just as I'd expected.

There were still Christmas decorations everywhere, so it might have been more than a week since the townspeople had gone. Walking around, I heard pet dogs crying from inside their houses, so I prised open the doors and let them loose, but the white dogs didn't respond to them in the slightest. The newly freed dogs ran off in a flash, as if to get away from the white dogs as quickly as they could. I spent a long time wandering around the town, and ascertained that there wasn't a single person there. At the petrol station, I found the words OUR TOWN sloppily spray-painted on a wall. OUR TOWN. I gathered as much food and fuel as I could carry, and headed back to the cabin with the dogs, glancing behind me the whole way.

The following day, I sat and worked in the attic with the magnifying glass and tweezers, and went walking with the dogs over the snowy slopes when I needed a break. There was no sign of anyone approaching the cabin. I spent the next day the same way, and again the day after that. Watching the white dogs hunt, swimming gracefully under the ice, I could be engrossed for hours. When I ran out of food, I went down to the town and procured what I wanted from the unattended shops. I slowly became dingy and faded, but the dogs stayed as white as fresh snow.

One day, while I was watching them play in the snow from the attic window, I took the hunting rifle from the cupboard and let off three shots in their direction. The dogs stiffened in a way I'd never seen them do before, looked towards me and then scattered into the mountain as though to meld into the glistening snow. The day hinted at the arrival of spring.

I leaned out of the window and yelled, 'Sorry!' at the top of my voice. 'I won't do that again! Come home!'

That night, as the snow fell silently, I slept standing by the windowsill huddled with the dogs, who had come back. As I revelled in the sensation of being buried in their warm flesh, I thought – I'll be leaving this place tomorrow. ∎

ARRIVAL GATES

Rebecca Solnit

After the long flight across the Pacific, after the night in the tiny hotel room selected so that I could walk to the world's busiest train station in the morning, after the train north to the area most impacted by the tsunami in the Great Tōhoku earthquake of 11 March 2011, after the meetings among the wreckage with people who had seen their villages and neighbours washed away, after seeing the foundations of what had once been a neighbourhood so flattened it looked like a chessboard full of shards, after hearing from so many people with grief and rage in their voices talking about walls of water and drownings and displacement and refuge, but also about betrayal by the government in myriad ways, after the Christian minister pontificated forever while the Buddhist priests held their peace in the meeting my hosts secretly scheduled at the end of the twelve-hour workday, after I told people I was getting sick but the meeting went on, after I left the meeting in the hopes of getting to the hotel and stood outside in the cold northern night for a long time as a few snowflakes fell, or was it raindrops, I forget, after the sickness turned into a cough so fierce I thought I might choke or come up with blood or run out of air, after the tour continued regardless, and the speaking tour at the universities, after the conferences where I talked about disaster and utopia, after the trip to the conference in Hiroshima where I walked and saw with my own eyes the bombed places I had seen in pictures so often and met with the octogenarians who told me, with the freshness of people who had only recently begun to tell, the story of what they had seen and been and done and suffered and lost on 6 August 1945, after the sight of the keloid scars from the fallout that had drifted onto the arm of a schoolboy sixty-seven years before, so that he grew into a man who always wore long sleeves even in summer, after the long walks along the beautiful river distributaries of Hiroshima and among its willows and monuments, draped in garlands of paper cranes, to the vaporized and poisoned dead, and plum trees in bloom but not yet cherries, after the one glorious day in Kyoto when I was neither at work nor overwhelmed and alone but accompanied by a pair of kind graduate students, after a day of wandering through old Buddhist temples with them and seeing the dim hall of the thousand golden Buddhas lined up in long rows, I arrived at the orange gates.

You get off the local train from the city of Kyoto and walk through a little tourist town of shops with doorways like wide-open mouths disgorging low tables of food and crafts and souvenirs and then walk uphill, then up stairs, under a great torii gate, one of those structures with a wide horizontal beam extending beyond the pillars that hold it up, like the Greek letter π, and then a plaza of temples and buildings and vendors, and then you keep going up. There are multiple routes up the mountain, and the routes take you through thousands of further torii gates, each with a black base and a black rooflike structure atop the crosspiece, each lacquered pure, intense orange on the cylindrical pillars and crosspiece. The new ones are gleaming and glossy. Some of the old ones are dull, their lacquer cracked, or even rotting away so that the wood is visible underneath.

The orange is so vivid it is as though you have at last gone beyond things that are coloured orange to the colour itself, particularly in the passages where the torii gates are just a few feet apart, or in one extraordinary sequence many paces long of gates only inches apart, a tunnel of total immersion in orange (vermilion say some of the accounts, but I saw pure intense orange). Nearly every gate bears black inscriptions on one side, and if I could read Japanese I might've read individual business people and corporations expressing their gratitude, because rice and prosperity and business are all tied up together in the realm of the god Inari, but I couldn't. The place was something else to me.

I later read that the Fushimi Inari-taisha is the head shrine of 30,000 or so Shinto shrines in Japan devoted to Inari. It is said to have been founded in 711 and burned down in 1468, during a civil war, but much of it seems to have been replaced in overlapping waves, so that the whole is ancient and the age of the parts varied, some of them very new. The gates seem designed to pass through, and the altars – platforms and enclosures of stone slabs and obelisks and stone foxes – for stillness, so that the landscape is a sort of musical score of moving and pausing. The altars looked funereal to a Western eye, with the stone slabs like tombstones, but they were something altogether different.

The foxes were everywhere, particularly at these altar zones. Moss and lichen grow on their stone or cement backs, so some are more green than grey and others are spotted with lighter grey. They often have red cloth tied around their necks, the fabric faded to dusty pink, and there are stones at the altar sites with inscriptions carved into them, and rope garlands. The foxes, hundreds of them, a few at a time, sit up, often in pairs, sometimes with smaller torii gates that were offerings arrayed around them, and then sometimes even smaller foxes with the gates, as though this might continue on beyond the visible into tinier and tinier foxes and gates. You could buy the small gates and foxes at the entrance and some places on the mountainside.

Foxes, I knew, are *kitsune* in Japan, the magical shapeshifters in folk tales and woodblock prints – and manga and anime now – who pass as human for months or for years, becoming beautiful brides who run away or courtiers who serve aristocrats but serve another, unknown purpose as well. The foxes at the Inari shrine are the god's messengers, a website later told me, more beneficent than some of the foxes in the stories. Elusive, beautiful, unpredictable, *kitsune* in this cosmology represent the unexpected and mysterious and wild aspects of nature. Rain during sunshine is called a fox's wedding in Japanese.

Gates, foxes, foxes, gates. The gates lead you to gates and to foxes, the trails wind all over the slope of the steep, forested hill. Most of the literature speaks as though there is a trail you take, but there are many.

If you keep going you might come to a dense bamboo forest with trunks as thick as the poles of street lights, and a pond beyond that, or you might just keep mounting forest paths that wind and tangle, with every now and again a little pavilion selling soft drinks and snacks, notably tofu pockets – *inarizushi* – said to be the foxes' favourite food. And more gates, unpainted stone as well as lacquered wood.

Arrival implies a journey, and almost all the visitors that day arrived out of a lifetime in Japan, seeing a different place than I did, travelling mostly in small groups, seeming to know why they were there and what to expect. I came directly from the gruelling tour of disaster, but with a long-time interest in how moving through space takes on meaning and how meaning can be made spatially, with church and temple designs, landscape architecture and paths, roads, stairs, ladders, bridges, labyrinths, thresholds, triumphal arches, all the grammar that inflects the meanings of our movement.

I had been invited to Japan for the one-year anniversary of the triple disaster, reporting on the aftermath and talking about my book *A Paradise Built in Hell*, which had been translated into Japanese and published just before one of the five largest recorded earthquakes hit the country and the ocean rose up to, in places, 120 feet and scoured the shore, and the six Fukushima nuclear reactors fell apart and began to spread radiation by air and by sea. But that's another story. The Inari shrine was not part of it. My encounter there wasn't the culmination of that journey but perhaps a reprieve from it, and an extension of other journeys and questions I have carried for a long time.

Arrival is the culmination of the sequence of events, the last in the list, the terminal station, the end of the line. And the idea of arrival begets questions about the journey and how long it took. Did it take the dancer two hours to dance the ballet, or two hours plus six months of rehearsals, or two hours plus six months plus a life given over to becoming the instrument that could, over and over, draw lines and circles in the air with precision and grace? Sumi-e painters painted with famous speed, but it took decades to become someone who could manage a brush that way, who had that feel for turning leaves or water into a monochromatic image. You fall in love with someone and the story might be of how you met, courted, consummated, but it might also be of how before all that, time and trouble shaped you both over the years, sanded your rough spots and wore away your vices until your scars and needs and hopes came together like halves of a broken whole.

Culminations are at least lifelong, and sometimes longer when you look at the natural and social forces that shape you, the acts of the ancestors, of illness or economics, immigration and education. We are constantly arriving; the innumerable circumstances are forever culminating in this glance, this meeting, this collision, this conversation, like the pieces in a kaleidoscope forever coming into new focus, new flowerings. But to me the gates made visible not the complicated ingredients of the journey but the triumph of arrival.

I knew I was missing things. I remember the first European cathedral I ever entered – Durham Cathedral – when I was fifteen, never a Christian, not yet taught that most churches are cruciform, or in the shape of a human body with outstretched arms, so that the altar is at what in French is called the *chevet*, or head, so that there was a coherent organization to the place. I saw other things then and I missed a lot. You come to every place with your own equipment.

I came to Japan with wonder at seeing the originals of things I had seen in imitation often, growing up in California: Japanese gardens and Buddhist temples, Mount Fuji, tea plantations and bamboo groves.

But it wasn't really what I knew about Japan but what I knew about the representation of time that seemed to matter there. I knew well the motion studies of Eadweard Muybridge in which a crane flying, a woman sweeping, is captured in a series of photographs, time itself measured in intervals, as intervals, as moments of arrival. The motion studies were the first crucial step on the road to cinema, to those strips of celluloid in which time had been broken down into twenty-four frames per second that could reconstitute a kiss, a duel, a walk across the room, a plume of smoke.

Time seemed to me, as I walked all over the mountain, more and more enraptured and depleted, a series of moments of arrival, like film frames, if film frames with their sprockets were gateways – and maybe they are: they turn by the projector, but as they go each frame briefly becomes an opening through which light travels. I was exalted by a landscape that made tangible that elusive sense of arrival, that palpable sense of time, that so often eludes us. Or rather the sense that we are arriving all the time, that the present is a house into which we always have one foot, an apple we are just biting, a face we are just glimpsing for the first time. In Zen Buddhism you talk a lot about being in the present and being present. That present is an infinitely narrow space between the past and future, the zone in which the senses experience the world, in which you act, however much your mind may be mired in the past or racing into the future.

I had the impression midway through the hours I spent wandering, that time itself had become visible, that every moment of my life I was passing through orange gates, always had been, always would be passing through magnificent gates that only in this one place are visible. Their uneven spacing seemed to underscore this perception; sometimes time grows dense and seems to both slow down and speed up, when you fall in love, when you are in the thick of an emergency or a discovery; other times it flows by limpid as a stream across a meadow, each day calm and like the one before, not much to remember, or time runs dry and you're stuck, hoping for change that finally arrives in a trickle or a rush. Though all these metaphors of flow can be traded in for solid ground: time is a stroll through orange gates. Blue mountains are constantly walking, said Dōgen, the monk who brought Zen to Japan, and we are also constantly walking, through these particular Shinto pathways of orange gates. Or so it seemed to me on that day of exhaustion and epiphany.

What does it mean to arrive? The fruits of our labour, we say, the reward. The harvest, the home, the achievement, the completion, the satisfaction, the joy, the recognition, the consummation. Arrival is the reward, it's the time you aspire to on the journey, it's the end, but on the mountain south of Kyoto on a day just barely spring, on long paths whose only English guidance was a few plaques about not feeding the monkeys I never saw anyway, arrival seemed to be constant. Maybe it is.

I wandered far over the mountain that day, until I was outside the realm of the pretty little reproduction of an antique map I had purchased, and gone beyond the realm of the gates. I was getting tired after four hours or so of steady walking. The paths continued, the trees continued, the ferns and mosses under them continued, and I continued but there were no more torii gates. I came out in a manicured suburb with few people on the streets, and walked out to the valley floor and then back into the next valley over and up again through the shops to the entrance to the shrine all over again. But I could not arrive again, though I walked through a few more gates and went to see the tunnel of orange again. It was like trying to go back to before the earthquake, to before knowledge. An epiphany can be as indelible a transformation as a trauma. Once I was through those gates and through that day I would never enter them for the first time and understand what they taught me for the first time.

All you really need to know is that there is a hillside in Japan in which time is measured in irregular intervals and every moment is an orange gate, and foxes watch over it, and people wander it, and the whole is maintained by priests and by donors, so that gates crumble and gates are erected, time passes and does not, as elsewhere nuclear products decay and cultures change and people come and go, and that the place might be one at which you will arrive some day, to go through the flickering tunnels of orange, up the mountainside, into this elegant machine not for controlling or replicating time but maybe for realizing it, or blessing it. Or maybe you have your own means of being present, your own for seeing that at this very minute you are passing through an orange gate. ∎

PINK

Tomoyuki Hoshino

TRANSLATED FROM THE JAPANESE BY BRIAN BERGSTROM

The sixth of August marked the start of the nine-day streak of blistering heat. Just after one in the afternoon, Tokyo registered forty degrees Celsius. It was the highest temperature since city records were kept, and the heat kept rising, reaching 42.7 degrees a couple hours later. The humidity never dropped below 80 per cent, and the sky, though cloudless, was thick with a pale mist. Older folks greeted each other, laughing, with lines like, *Next week is the Bon festival, but the dead might go back early – it's too hot even for them!* Perhaps because age had numbed their senses, they seemed unbothered by the heat, and several of these very senior citizens were content to stand talking in the sunshine that beat down on Kaki-no-ike Park. It seemed to Naomi, as she listened to two old biddies go on while she watched her niece play in the sandpit, that it might be a good idea if they thought about their own welfare rather than that of the dead. Or maybe they *were* the dead, having returned for Bon without realizing it, chattering away thinking they were still alive. Though why the dead would want to come back to this prison called life – just because it was that time of year again – was beyond her. *If I had the chance to end it all,* muttered Naomi to herself, *I'd leave this world in an instant and never look back.* What was her problem? Why was she so irritated, she didn't even know these women, why was she getting so carried away? It was the heat, the goddamn heat, and it was her goddamn stupid sister, who insisted that Naomi take her daughter outside to play at least once a day – for her health – even in this toxic weather. *Why don't you take her outside?* thought Naomi, but she nonetheless did as her sister asked, the promise of a thousand yen for her trouble pushing her out the door.

Naomi's two-year-old niece Pink (the stupidity began with the naming) was absorbed with her playmates in some sort of sandpit public works project, and so, seeing that other mothers were keeping an eye on things, Naomi left the play area and walked over to the edge of the pond to have a smoke. There were no trees to filter the sunlight, which poured down from the yellow sun like sulphurous gas. Even the cicadas, whose tinny drone was usually inescapable, were silent. Humidity saturated the hot air to oozing, sticking to Naomi like insects. It felt less like she was sweating than like her skin was melting and running down her body. Everything around her seemed not entirely solid, a series of colours running like ruined ice cream. *When the temperature gets high enough, even the landscape melts*, thought Naomi.

Little bodies began to fall one by one from above. They were birds, dropping down for a dip in the pond. They gathered at the edge, splashing themselves with water. Sparrows and white-eyes, starlings and bulbuls: there were so many of them. A few actually immersed themselves in the water, which had made Naomi think they were ducks, but when the birds broke the surface, she could see they were sparrows. She saw some dive straight into the water. Naomi counted the seconds – one ... two ... – and then, flapping their wings, the birds emerged and flew up into the sky.

It wasn't just sparrows. The white-eyes, the bulbuls, the starlings: they all began to dive into the water, as if imitating the sparrows. At one point, the oversized body of a crow crashed into the water, causing the smaller birds to fly off. Only the pigeons, perhaps unable to swim, refrained from diving in, scuttling back and forth at the water's edge.

The crow finally left, and the sparrows returned. They dove in the water again and again, twisting their bodies and spinning in the air. Had sparrows always been waterfowl? It began to seem so to Naomi. As they emerged from the pond, water spraying, the wet sparrows gleamed in the sun. Suddenly, in their midst, shiny things began to leap from the pond. They were fish! Similar in colour and size to the sparrows, the fish were flying alongside the birds just above the surface of the water.

Naomi crouched down and dipped a finger into the pond. As expected, the water was warm – too warm. The fish were suffering. They were throwing themselves into the air for the same reason the birds were plunging into the water. Seeming to follow the sparrows' lead, the fish twisted and somersaulted in the air. Were they trying to fan themselves? Birds have wings; humans have hands; fish have only their bodies to twist and turn if they want to generate a breeze.

Fish were jumping and twirling all across the surface of the pond. The pond was alive with the spray they produced, a silver mist that, carried by the hot wind, cooled Naomi's face.

Naomi was gripped with a sudden joy. This place was a living hell. No one was dead, but they felt closer to death than the dead. Assaulted by such unbearable conditions, they longed to flee their existence. Birds wished to quit being birds and become fish, fish longed to stop being fish and become birds, people longed to become anything but people. And so they all went crazy, flailing and flopping, spinning and twirling. But wasn't it fun too? To spin, to twirl?

A crowd gathered to watch the leaping fish, but Naomi broke away from them and began twirling slowly by herself. If viewed from above, she became a clock, her body the axis. The soft breeze produced by her twirling touched the sweat on her skin, cooling it. She raised her arms like a ballerina to form a circle parallel to the ground, and she pictured it turning as she spun. Slowly, gently, so as not to get dizzy, she made her way back to the sandpit where Pink was playing.

Naomi raised her head to look at the sky, which she felt was getting closer. Like she was floating up into space as she spun. Spiralling upward like the feathers of a shuttlecock, she felt air gathering beneath her. To spin and spin until you become the wind itself – would that make her a tornado? Well, nothing so strong as a tornado – a whirlwind? That's it, a whirlwind. If she became a whirlwind, she'd be cool. Light. Able to fly.

Naomi gradually returned to herself and stopped spinning. She was near the sandpit, and just about to run into a metal post. The heat began to press in on her from all sides, and sweat poured from her like water from a spring. She felt wobbly, and her head ached. She'd crossed a point of no return. Once you start to twirl, you can't stop, because if you do, it'll be even worse than before you began. The only way out was to spin and spin forever.

Naomi walked over to Pink, saying, 'Time to go home!' as she took the child by both hands. The moment she did, she was struck by a feeling that something wasn't right. Naomi looked around, inspected Pink from head to toe, but nothing seemed out of place. Still, Naomi couldn't shake the feeling that some unknown had been introduced into the world around her, something that created a subtle but inescapable dissonance. It was as if everything around her had been replaced by an exquisite fake.

In order to collect herself, Naomi, still hand in hand with Pink, spread her arms to create a circle between them and began to spin with the child, singing softly. *Bird in the cage, bird in the ca-a-age* . . . Pink danced happily even when her legs tangled up as they spun. Naomi didn't want Pink to get dizzy, so after a few spins they walked side by side for a bit before Naomi held out her arms again and said, 'Let's play bird-in-the-cage again, Pink!' They'd re-form the circle between them, repeating the pattern again and again until they reached home. Exhausted by the heat and the excitement, Pink fell asleep at once. Not long after, Naomi was asleep too.

That evening, the television news was all about the heatwave. Not only Tokyo but all of Japan saw temperatures exceeding forty degrees, with 392 people hospitalized and fifty-six dead, mostly elderly. But the story that really grabbed people's attention was that of a seventeen-year-old high-school girl who'd spun and spun under the blazing sun until she succumbed to heatstroke and died. According to friends who were with her, the girl had said, *Hey, what if we spin like fans – wouldn't that cool us off?* And so she tried it, and it worked so well she invited her friends to join her – *Oh, it feels so good! Try it, try it!* – and they did, but soon, dizzy and nauseated, they lay down to rest, and, after a while, the girl lay down beside them; when it came time to get up, she was still, and when they tried to rouse her they realized she was gone. A so-called expert compared her to someone trapped on the top floor of a burning building choosing to jump out a window rather than face the flames; it was a perfectly logical choice, not abnormal in the least.

'So things are so fucking awful that death is preferable. Let's not beat around the bush,' Naomi carped at the television. This prompted her sister to admonish her: 'Could you not use that kind of language in front of Pink? As it is, all she does is imitate everything you do.'

'It's only natural. I'm the daddy around here. She's a daddy's girl.'

'No one asked you to be her daddy. She's better off without one. All I asked was for you to be her big sister.'

Appalled at the utter immaturity of Pink's father, Naomi's sister had dumped him and kept Pink. It was like throwing away a box of candy and keeping the prize that came with it. She was working at a nursing home to make ends meet, and had invited Naomi, who had graduated from university but was without a job, to look after Pink in exchange for a place to live. Naomi had accepted the invitation without a moment's hesitation. She'd been stuck in the couch-surfing life and, nearing the limits of her friends' patience, she'd been on the verge of signing up with the Self-Defense Forces anyway. The truth was that Naomi had been fixated on the SDF since she was little; she had the feeling that her sister's offer was, at least in part, an effort to stop her from enlisting.

After he was dumped by Naomi's sister, Pink's father thought he would 'toughen himself up' by participating in right-wing demonstrations, and about a year later he showed up on her doorstep, the fashionable clothing that had been his sole redeeming feature replaced by a dowdy suit that clung to his thickening frame. *I'm an adult now. Give me another chance!* When Naomi's sister had asked what he meant by 'adult', he replied that he could now state his beliefs without fear, even as the world turned a cold eye on him, even as he was blasted by the harsh winds of public opinion, that he had learned how to stand his ground even if it meant putting his body on the line and that he would put everything on the line to protect himself and his family. Naomi's sister had heard enough, and she told him that it was time for him to go home. But he refused, saying that he was no longer the weakling who gives up and goes home just because a woman tells him to.

As the confrontation escalated, Naomi returned with Pink from one of their customary trips to the park and couldn't help breaking in. She'd once seen Pink's father in action – on a street corner with a group yelling into megaphones for revival of the colonial policy of Five Races Under One Union. 'You joined the right-wingers to find yourself – what do you think you're gonna find here? There's nothing for you here, not yourself or anything else.'

Recoiling at Naomi's ridicule, Pink's father began yelling, though it wasn't clear exactly what he was saying. Naomi cut him off: 'This is you being an adult? All you've done is learned how to yell! Everything else is the same, you're still a little boy begging for attention: *Mommy, mommy, listen to me, mommy please!* A real adult would start by asking my sister what *she* needs!' The guy slunk away, though not before swearing they would get theirs.

Naomi's sister was left uneasy, worried that he would try to get revenge. But ever since, Pink stuck to Naomi like glue, from the beginning of every day to its end.

'Naomi was smoking!'

'Tattletale!'

Naomi took Pink's cheeks in her hands and squeezed them, rubbing them up and down. Delighted, Pink shouted, 'You were smoking! You were smoking!' in hopes of prolonging the cheek squeezing. As she dutifully complied, Naomi noticed that the small bruise Pink had gotten earlier in the day – she'd bumped into the doorknob while playing around as they got ready to go to the park – had disappeared without a trace.

Starting the next day, Naomi's sister insisted that Pink be out of the house so she could have some time to herself, if only in the morning or evening when temperatures fell below forty. For her part,

Pink would rush to the door, ready to start playing bird-in-the-cage. Her body plastered with cooling patches, Naomi would do as she was told.

There were now – several days into the heatwave – endless reports of people sustaining burn injuries from cars and rocks that had heated up during the day. Between streets and buildings holding the heat and the air barely cooling, temperatures failed to dip below thirty-five at night, and hot wind blew continuously from cranked-up air conditioners like they were hairdryers mounted in windows. Day after day, the number of people dying from the heat reached the triple digits, and anywhere you went, you'd encounter bodies of small animals that had passed on too. On the fifth day of the heatwave, the city of Kōfu saw temperatures reach 50.2 degrees. It was a new record for the country. Where Naomi lived with her sister and niece, temperatures soared above forty-five by noon; when things 'cooled off', dropping down to forty in the late afternoon, Naomi would leave the house with Pink. Almost no one was outside, the area a ghost town, the streets like vacant sets. Pink and Naomi made their way to the park, spinning all the while. Naomi drank bottles of Pocari Sweat in an attempt to replace the liquid draining from her body. By the time they reached the park, she looked as if she'd emerged from a soak in a hot spring.

All signs of life had disappeared from Kaki-no-ike Park, and a terrible stench rose from the pond. The water level was low, the surface oily and lumpy with dead fish. Not just dead fish – dead birds were mixed in with them – and some sort of larger animal, part of its bulk sticking up out of the water. Naomi didn't want to know what it might be.

She took Pink into the shade beneath a huge zelkova tree, and they began to play bird-in-the-cage. The ground was pitted and uneven, not only because the earth had hardened and cracked in the heat, but also because the tree's roots, seeking water, were extended crazily in all directions. If a tree concentrates its energy in its roots, it can displace the earth. Most plants in conditions like these might wither and die, but a tree that was strong enough could fight for what water there was.

On the opposite side of the pond was a large camphor tree. Someone had tied a rope around a branch and seemed to be twirling in mid-air from it. *Someone else had the same idea*, thought Naomi appreciatively, as she and Pink went to take a closer look.

'It doesn't hurt, hanging like that?' Naomi asked the young man.

'Not at all, it's nice and cool!' he replied.

'So you're doing what the fish do?'

'Fish? No, no. I saw it on TV! You can spin like this and feel cool – and you can get dizzy enough to forget everything!'

'The other day the fish in the pond were jumping and spinning in the air, trying to get cool too.'

'But they're all dead now, right?'

The young man grabbed the rope and nimbly pulled himself up its length to sit on the branch. 'I'm not just cooling off, you know,' he said as he untied the rope from his waist. 'I discovered that if I really let myself spin, it was like I was getting . . . purified. If I was feeling depressed, I would feel better, as if the depression flew off somewhere as I went around and around. Like I was in a salad spinner. So I began to spin faster and faster. Pushing the limit, you know? I would get sick and vomit. And I would sweat, really sweat. It was like detox. Like I was bidding farewell to parts of me that were bad. And as I got rid of more and more toxins, I could spin as much as I wanted without getting sick. And it was the most amazing feeling. Like it wasn't me who was spinning, it was some larger force that was spinning me. And it felt *good* not having control, giving it all up to whatever it was. I don't know how to put it. Maybe it's like life taking over, so you can just go with it, naturally. Like letting go and feeling easy, feeling . . . peace.'

The young man had descended from the tree and was now standing in front of Naomi and Pink.

'Huh. Well,' Naomi said, 'I've been spinning a little these days, but I've never felt anything like that.'

'It's not just me. I mean, there're a lot of people who feel this way. They begin by just spinning, but then they have some kind of awakening. And they realize that the spinning is really a kind of prayer.'

Naomi felt irritation bubble up within her. 'Prayer?' she said, her voice rising. 'To whom? For what? I don't get it.'

'A prayer to a larger force, or power, asking it to take control and make us suffer less. Like a prayer to the heat, even. Or a prayer for rain.'

'I take it this *larger power* hasn't heard our prayers yet?'

'Maybe the prayer isn't powerful enough yet. I believe that if enough people come together and unite their feelings, something will happen.'

'So along with prayer comes prophecy?'

'It's not just me who feels this way. There is really something to this, I know it. That it's not just me. Not just me who's spinning. Not just me who's getting stronger, who's growing. The feeling is . . . *there*. Everyone is starting to feel this way, and I just know that if we can gather all these feelings together, we can really make something happen.'

'I've never felt anything like that.'

'Maybe it's rude of me to say, but I think your spinning must be inadequate. You have to do it more, devote half a day or more to it, and you'll see. The feeling will come, and it will be real.'

'I haven't been spinning all day every day or anything, but I've been doing it pretty regularly for five days now, and all I've noticed is that it feels good while I'm going around and around, but once I stop I feel exhausted. Isn't that normal?'

'Five days? You're more experienced than me! You started the first day of the heatwave then, right? That makes you one of the first to be enlightened! Don't you think it's strange? That people began spinning that day not just here but all over Japan?'

'You mean like that girl who died?'

'Yes! Our first martyr. I myself only began spinning when I heard about her on the news – I'm just a wannabe! Who am I to say anything to you, you're the real deal, starting spontaneously like that. What made you do it?'

'I told you, I was watching the fish jump and twist in the air and imitated them. It wasn't some revelation from above.'

'If you see fish jumping and twisting, do you always start doing it too? Did anyone else watching the fish start spinning?'

All Naomi knew was that she had separated herself from the crowd that had gathered around the pond and started twirling, off on her own.

'So I'm right. The fish might have been the inspiration, but it was a larger force that moved you.'

Naomi was shaken. She began to doubt that her spinning was a result of her own intention. But she didn't agree with the young man that some higher force had possessed her either. That wasn't how it felt. It just seemed like the only way to respond to such crazy heat was to do something she would never normally do.

'What about tornadoes or whirlwinds? They're touched off by forces larger than themselves, right? Natural forces, like gravity and atmospheric pressure. But no matter how hard you pray to the atmosphere or to gravity, they won't make the heat go down.'

'Do you think it was gravity or the atmosphere that made you start spinning?'

'Well, no, but –'

'Were all the people who started spinning that day moved by the same force that produces a whirlwind?'

'I don't know anything about anybody else. All I know is that I thought if I became a whirlwind I might feel cool.'

'Most of the people who started spinning that day describe it like that. They thought if they could become the wind, or become a fan, then they'd finally get cool.'

'It doesn't seem so strange that people who are all subjected to the same unusual heat would end up having similar thoughts.'

'We could stand here and debate all day, but what's the point? You should go where the others are and see for yourself. Even if you don't end up agreeing with me, you'll at least see what I'm talking about.'

'Where the others are? Where's that?'

'Just over this way, at Kumano Shrine.'

The young man spun around as he led the way to the shrine. Naomi and Pink began to spin too. Before long, the three of them formed a big circle as they continued on their way. Pink shrank shyly away from the young man at first, but gradually relaxed and began to return his smiles.

Even before they entered the grounds of Kumano Shrine, they could sense a force emanating from the place. People were packed all the way to the torii gate, body heat and moisture rising like steam from an internal combustion engine. They were twirling, all of them, as if intoxicated. All in the same direction too: clockwise. Completely silent, their heads slightly tilted, staring into space through half-lidded eyes as if near sleep, their arms spread like butterfly wings, they spun around and around in the same direction at the same speed. It was so quiet, as if the shrine were sucking the sound from the air, while the energy the twirling crowd exuded was so strong it seemed able to blast any onlooker into the air.

The first to join them was Pink. She began awkwardly, losing her footing and bumping into one of the twirlers. Naomi went to pull her away, but then ended up joining her. Out of the corner of her eye, she saw the young man walking away.

Naomi closed her eyes completely and felt a wave of energy coursing through her body. If she could just ride that wave, she could spin and spin forever. She let herself go with it, her arms rising of their own accord, like the wings of birds. She tried to spin a bit faster and felt resistance in her body, as if it were putting on brakes. She realized that this resistance, which was like walking against a strong wind, came from the wave of energy produced by the people spinning around her. The wave she was riding came not just from her own movements but everyone's. The energy produced by each individual movement interacted in complex ways, rippling the air within the shrine's grounds with waves that Naomi found herself riding. Everyone around her was riding these complex rippling waves, moving with them and putting up not the least resistance, lost in the motion. It was like music. Like dancing to music. Soon Naomi felt her consciousness on the verge of leaving her completely. She had the feeling that if she passed out, she would ascend to another level and be able to spin furiously, on and on, even unconsciously. Her insides would grow transparent, her self subsumed entirely by the trance. Surely at least half the people around her were spinning in such a state.

I might as well let go completely, thought Naomi, but as she did she became aware that the crowd had thinned significantly, and that there was only a smattering of fellow spinners left around her. The wave grew weak, depriving Naomi of the force that had been driving her, and she stopped. The heat descended once again upon her, and, pouring with sweat, Naomi took Pink by the hand and headed away from the shrine.

'It hurts, I said! Why aren't you listening to me?' yelled Pink, pulling her hand from Naomi's grasp. It was only then that Naomi realized she had been yanking Pink along.

'You're not respecting my will!'

What? Naomi looked hard at Pink. *Why is she talking like that?* Pink was clearly imitating what Naomi said, in so many words, to her sister all the time. But this was the first time Pink had said anything like that herself.

'I'm so sorry. Do you still feel sick?'

'My legs hurt.'

'We spun around too much, huh? That guy really got us going . . .' This last bit was addressed more to herself, but Pink replied nonetheless. 'Yeah, he's really cool.'

Pink kept complaining that her knees hurt, so they stopped to rest again and again as they made their way home, finally arriving only after night had fallen.

When she saw Pink, Naomi's sister sighed, 'These clothes are already too tight for you, aren't they? We're going to have to get you some new ones.' Shaking her head, she added, 'It would be nice if you could take a break from growing once in a while, you know.'

Naomi, who didn't remember Pink's clothes being too small when she'd helped her get dressed that morning, dubiously pulled at a sleeve. It was indeed tight as a drum.

The next afternoon, Pink and Naomi found the young man spinning from the camphor tree just as the day before.

'I didn't think I'd see you here today!' he exclaimed.

'The kid kept pestering me, saying she wanted to go back to the shrine,' Naomi said, pointing at Pink.

'So why aren't you there?'

'I wanted to spin by myself!' replied Naomi, almost angrily.

The young man looked intently at Naomi from where he hung suspended in mid-air. 'Every day more people show up, so it's getting a bit hard to find room over at Kumano – maybe you should try Sampin Temple. It has bigger grounds.'

'I told you – I want to spin by myself. And anyway, why are *you* out here all by your lonesome?'

'I can't really handle crowds.'

'What? You were the one going on and on about everyone uniting in feeling and all that crap! Do as you say and not as you do – is that it?'

'I can pray here all by myself and still be united in feeling with everyone else.'

'There's a term for that, you know. Delusion.'

'It's like I said yesterday. It's a real feeling I have. And so I'm just fine out here all alone. But it's different for people like you. I really am someone who can't handle crowds, and so I know how people are when they truly want to be left alone. They're not like you. It's so obvious to me that all you really want is to melt completely into a crowd. Besides, I saw how you were yesterday.'

There was no denying it. Naomi hadn't gone back to the shrine because she was afraid of her desire to do it all again. Maybe this guy had her figured out, and that's why he was tempting her now with Sampin.

'Enough about me already. What I want to know is why you can't stand being around other people.'

The young man clambered easily up his rope and, standing on the branch, undid the knot at his waist and then shimmied down to the ground.

'Have you heard of the Greater East Asian Friendship Society?'

'Yeah. They're the Five Races Under One Union guys.'

This happened to be the right-wing group Naomi's sister's ex had joined. Their idea was that, instead of East Asian countries squabbling all the time, they'd form an East Asian Union – like the European Union – and that East Asia would become a free economic zone. The centre would be in northern Kyūshū, and a trade corridor would stretch from Okinawa in the south to Hokkaidō in the north. The standard currency would be the Japanese yen, the standard language would be Japanese, and the union would have the backing of the Japanese military, once it was re-established.

'I went to a small vocational school in the sticks,' the young man began, 'so I knew that no matter how hard I studied, I'd never get anywhere. I wasn't the kind to join a gang, and I wasn't popular with girls. My sport was gymnastics, and while I got pretty good at the rings and uneven bars, I was never better than anyone who practised a lot. In other words, I was completely unremarkable – maybe below average. I never thought I'd be able to find a good job when I graduated, and sure enough, I didn't. Objectively speaking, I was disposable. But I wanted to improve myself, even just a little, and ended up getting interested in history. I joined a history group. Groups studying Japanese history, they're filled with losers like me. Below average, socially awkward: they don't fit in anywhere and they're desperate not to feel like losers. So they form groups like this to save themselves. I joined one, and then, along with another guy from the group, joined the Greater East Asian Friendship Society.'

Suddenly Naomi found herself feeling sympathy for her sister's ex. Come to think of it, this story wasn't so different from her own trajectory either, graduating from a third-rate university and applying to over 180 companies only to be hired by none.

'And you know, I felt great when I did things with them. I could respect myself. We were serious, maybe not so smart, but committed to debating important things and doing something about them, unlike the thoughtless, lazy people all around us who went about their lives with no sense of urgency. That this pride might lead to arrogance was maybe inevitable; after all, I was only about twenty. But the group gave me responsibilities, I worked with the police and got permits, I was put in charge of a platoon of demonstrators.'

'*Platoon?*'

'Yeah, the society was organized top-down, and each level had its captains and lieutenants and other borrowed military titles. They made me a sergeant major, and I led a platoon. The idea was that if the Japanese military did get re-established, military experience was going to be required for membership.'

'Why?'

'So that we could defend ourselves without help. Self-reliance was a big thing in the Society. We had slogans like, *Rely not on others – let others rely on you!* Anyway, one day one of the demonstrations I was leading got into a clash with some anti-foreign group. Those guys are idiots – they think that Japan will benefit by picking fights with its neighbours. The basest, most thuggish way of thinking. The Greater East Asian Friendship Society was about establishing Japan's leadership of East Asia at a much higher level – we didn't want to dwell on petty differences. They never understood that. So they saw us as the enemy, and they targeted us that day. They were screaming stuff like, *You want to sell out Japan! You're just a bunch of Koreans!* Some of my guys wanted to rise to their challenge, but I tried to keep everyone calm. The police trusted me, so they were on our side too. But the guys who wanted to fight started shouting me down and yelling that there was a government mole in the Society. The anti-foreign idiots joined in, and soon all hell broke loose. Later, at a Society meeting, I tried to explain what happened as calmly and clearly as I could. I thought that in a group focused on the big picture, reason would prevail over tough-guy talk, and so I couldn't believe what happened next. I was accused of being the mole, a traitor working for a government that was selling out its people, an agent provocateur causing division within the group, an enemy of the Japan that was to be, an anti-patriot. I was kicked out of the Society. And you know who the leader of the charge against me was? My friend from the history group! To see friends turn on me before my eyes, willing to string me up in front of a group I was devoted to – it was like I died, really died, in that moment.'

'And so now crowds are a source of trauma for you.'

'That all these believers in self-reliance could suddenly turn into a mob like that . . . but now I understand what it was all about. We thought we were using reason to bring about a revolution in society, but all we really wanted was to feel that our lives weren't useless, that we had purpose, had value; we were each trying to find ourselves but instead we ended up finding an "us". The content of the things we said or did didn't really matter. What was important was the feeling of "us".'

'You said it was obvious I wanted to melt into a crowd. Are you telling me I'm a candidate for a scene like the Greater East Asian Friendship Society?'

'I might have said that before. But not now. Because this "tornado dance" thing is pure. You don't do it to please anyone, even yourself. The joy and satisfaction are in the spinning itself, and all the unnecessary parts of the self fall away. There's no gap between one dancer's intentions and another's. That's why it's a kind of prayer. It's different from an ideology or a political position. It's a shared suffering and a shared attempt to overcome that suffering. A plea, from the simple basis of being alive. There's no difference between people at that level. Of course, some might not experience this suffering. But they're relatively few; most begin spinning purely from a desire to ease their discomfort, and everything else just flows from that.'

Naomi remembered the curious joy that had burst within her as she watched the fish leap and spin in the pond. They had spun in the air because their world had become a living hell, because they wanted to become anything else besides what they were, because to spin was to be reborn. If that joy was what this young man meant by 'purity', she understood what he was saying perfectly.

'You called it a "tornado dance"?'

'Yeah, I heard it on the news yesterday. They call it that.'

'Who does?'

'There's a little village up north of Tokyo that had a traditional dance they called the "tornado dance". Tornadoes would hit the area every few years, killing villagers and destroying crops, and so, to contain the tornado god's wrath, they began whirling around themselves in the opposite direction, clockwise. The area became depopulated over the years, and the tradition disappeared, and now the people left there say that that's why there have been all these tornadoes around Tokyo lately.'

'Well, do you want to come with us to tornado-dance over at Sampin Temple, then? But if you're going to slip away again, you might as well stay here. Pink and I will be fine on our own.'

'All right.' The young man began to climb back up his rope to the tree branch.

'I wonder – do you think there are more people like you, spinning and spinning on their own somewhere?'

'I bet there are. There must be plenty of people around with stories like mine.' The young man said this with a smile that seemed to come from the bottom of his heart.

'Scary!' It was Pink who said this. Naomi looked back at the young man. He was concentrating on suspending himself from the tree again, now that Naomi and Pink were out of sight and thus, it seemed, out of mind. *Let's go*, said Naomi, tugging Pink by the hand.

S ampin Temple turned out to be already filled to bursting with spinners. All was silent, even the cicadas; the air held only the smell of bodies, wafting from the temple in clouds. If Pink hadn't been there to lead her by the hand, Naomi might not have ventured in. But sure enough, her hesitation and unease faded away as she began to move. Surprisingly, Pink no longer clung to her as they spun, but rather went off to twirl alone. She took rests from time to time, but she spun just fine by herself, becoming as intoxicated in the trance as anyone else. She didn't seem to be stifling any nausea either.

An hour passed this way, and Naomi could no longer deny it. Pink was growing, and quickly. Her body was getting bigger, and the look in her eyes showed that her mind was maturing as well. Which meant that Naomi had to be ageing faster too. If she didn't want to chew up the time she had left, she had to stop spinning, right? But she didn't have the impression that time grew slower when she stopped. In fact, it was during her twirling that it seemed to slow down. Enough that it was a reason she kept spinning.

A chill went through Naomi. This unseen larger power, was it deceiving them, compelling them toward unspeakable acts? Were they unknowingly speeding time up? Was it a conspiracy? Was the young man in the tree sending people to these shrines and temples to do this 'tornado dance' for him? He said there were others like him all over. Were they a coordinated group inciting a movement? Were people like her, who longed to become one with something larger than herself, unwittingly becoming slaves?

Don't be stupid! I started spinning all on my own. It was only after however many days of it that I met that guy, there's no reason to think there's a conspiracy. Conspiracy theories are just illusions conjured by uneasy hearts. I'm totally at ease when I spin. If I do feel uneasy, all I have to do to feel better is spin more. Spinning makes all that is illusory fall away. The things that remain – those are the things that are real. That are true. Things like Pink growing up so quickly, for instance.

Naomi began to spin faster. She twirled fast enough that the landscape around her melted into a colourful blur. No matter how fast she went around, she didn't feel sick. Spurred on by her, the dancers around Naomi began spinning faster as well. At this speed, it seemed as if they would be lifting off the ground before long. She could feel her consciousness begin to detach itself again, somewhere in the back of her mind. *Let go,* she thought. *It's time.*

She spun. She flew. Gravity disappeared, and she floated in the air for a moment, only to come down gently back to earth when it returned. Her body still felt light. The rush of grey in front of her resolved into distinct shapes. She concentrated her gaze. The grey became transparent. The figure before her was Pink. Now a teenager, she had become pretty, even sexy. She was spinning as fast as Naomi, but she appeared still as she returned her aunt's gaze. And not just Pink. Everyone around Naomi moved so fast that the movement disappeared, leaving their still figures to emerge from the blur. It was like a zoetrope or the frames of a film, images revealed through high-speed revolution. But they were not just images; she could reach out and touch them. 'It's getting late, we should get back before dark,' said Pink, but when Naomi took her by the hand, Pink shook her off. 'I'm not a kid any more.'

Even as they continued to spin at such high speeds, they found that they could walk normally as they made their way home, just as if it were a day like any other. When they reached the house, Naomi's sister greeted them at the door waving an envelope watermarked with cherry blossoms. 'It arrived!' she exclaimed. The back of the envelope bore a Ministry of Defense insignia, and the letter informed Naomi that although she was just finishing up the last vacation period of her military service, she was being deployed; and so, in the time it took to say, *Off I go!*, Naomi became a crew member on the aircraft carrier *Sakimori.* Because it was a battle to defend an island, the fighting took place almost entirely at sea, with threats and displays of force exchanged almost as if choreographed in advance, but Naomi's unit, lured by the crossfire, was commanded to make a landing using small, single-passenger submarines, and just as Naomi was thinking they'd succeeded, it turned out to be a trap, torpedoes coming at them from three sides within the confines of the bay, and while she managed to eject herself from the submarine right away, she was hit in her back by shrapnel from the explosion, which immobilized her, and she drifted out to sea, only to be picked up by a passing cruiser and given a hero's welcome upon her return home, but even as she spent her time in the hospital working diligently at rehabilitation, she never rid herself of a lingering paralysis in her arms and legs, and she grew depressed with the passage of day after listless day while her sister, who was a nurse after all, did her best to take care of her; her depression expressed itself as resentment, resentment spewed at her sister and the world. *It can just go to hell for all I care!* she would say and say again, and soon the island was snatched away for good, Japan's supposed allies declaring that they wouldn't intervene, and thus the East Asian Union dissolved, leaving Japan isolated, its food supply rapidly diminishing, the country finally paying the price for opening its food markets so completely to foreign goods, the domestic agricultural industries woefully behind the times, woefully unable to increase production to meet demand, and even in Naomi's household, meals dwindled to two servings of thin potato gruel a day, and Pink, having once so idolized Naomi and now so disgusted by her current state, left home to live in a dormitory while she attended technical college, volunteering for the army right after graduation and ending up on the front lines near Kyūshū, where she became a casualty of war at nineteen, taken out by an unmanned stealth-fighter strike, leaving Naomi overwhelmed with guilt as if she had been the one to do the killing, the heaviness of her heart paralysing the rest of her body completely, but even as she imagined her own death again and again, she couldn't bring herself to abandon her sister to what had become a life dark with tragedy, a life her sister strove every day to keep herself from abandoning completely, and thus it was that August came again as rumours swirled that the war had reached Japan's main island at last, and the sun, as if driven mad, poured heat mercilessly down upon the land, Tokyo's temperatures breaking forty for the first time in nineteen years. Weakened and hungry, the residents of the archipelago, reduced to mere shimmers in the hot air, winked out one by one, and it dawned on Naomi as she watched her sister unable to cope, languishing before her on the tatami, that she could become a fan herself and create a breeze to revive her, and so, taking a small fan in each hand, she wrestled with her stiffened body, forcing it into motion, and as she slowly began to revolve, she remembered how she had spun like this to battle the heat nineteen years before, how Pink, so young then, had clamoured to play bird-in-the-cage every day, and as she shared these memories with her sister, they revitalized her enough that she joined Naomi in her spinning, a spinning that somehow made them both feel newly strong, and newly hungry too, enough to want to leave the house for food, and so out they went as the sun went down, and they encountered a crowd of people gathered at the edge of the pond, spinning slowly all in unison, and Naomi found herself joining them, looking up into the sky just like before, but this time she felt like she was falling, and she noticed she was spinning left, counter to the clockwise revolutions of nineteen years ago, perhaps this meant that time could reverse direction too, could unbind her from this past that so entangled and constrained her, and perhaps Pink could come back as well, and they could all go back to before they'd twisted their bodies in wicked prayer and find some other way to free themselves from a world become a living hell, and so she vowed that once they'd gone back all those nineteen years, they would take the world in their hands again and make it theirs at last; on and on she spun, every revolution a prayer in reverse. ■

CONTRIBUTORS

Brian Bergstrom is a PhD candidate at the University of Chicago and a course lecturer and visiting researcher at McGill University in Montreal. His articles and translations have appeared in publications including *Chroma, Mechademia, positions: asia critique* and *Japan Forum*. He is the editor and principal translator of *We, the Children of Cats* by Tomoyuki Hoshino.

David G. Boyd obtained his master's degree at the University of Tokyo and is currently enrolled in the East Asian studies doctorate programme at Princeton University. He has translated stories by Hideo Nakai, Riichi Yokomitsu and Hyakken Uchida, among others.

Nick Caistor is a translator of more than forty books from Portuguese and Spanish from authors such as José Saramago, Roberto Arlt, Andrés Neuman and César Aira. He is the editor and translator of *The Faber Book of Contemporary Latin American Short Stories* and has contributed translations for *Granta* 113: The Best of Young Spanish-language Novelists and *Granta* 121: The Best of Young Brazilian Novelists.

Juliet Winters Carpenter has lived in Japan for more than forty years. Her most recent translations are *Honkaku shōsetsu* (*A True Novel*) by Minae Mizumura and *Saka no ue no kumo* (*Clouds Above the Hill*) by Ryōtarō Shiba.

Michael Emmerich is associate professor of Japanese literature at the University of California, Los Angeles. He is the author of *The Tale of Genji: Translation, Canonization, and World Literature*, the editor of *Read Real Japanese Fiction* and *New Penguin Parallel Texts: Short Stories in Japanese* and the translator of more than a dozen books by Japanese authors including, most recently, Yasushi Inoue's *Tōgyū* (*Bullfight*).

Toh EnJoe holds a PhD in arts and sciences from the University of Tokyo. His writings include *Obu za besuboru* (*Of the Baseball*) and *U yū shi tan* (*As If*). In 2011 he was awarded the Akutagawa Prize for *Dōkeshi no chō* (*Harlequin's Butterfly*). *Self-Reference ENGINE*, translated by Terry Gallagher, is nominated for the 2014 Philip K. Dick Award.

Kimiko Hahn is the author of nine poetry collections, including *The Unbearable Heart, The Artist's Daughter, The Narrow Road to the Interior* and *Brain Fever*, forthcoming in October. She is a distinguished professor in the MFA programme in creative writing and literary translation at Queens College, City University of New York.

Yuji Hamada is the recipient of the 2013 Magenta Foundation Flash Forward Emerging Photographer award. He is based in Tokyo.

Tomoyuki Hoshino was born in Los Angeles but grew up in Japan. After working as a journalist and studying in Mexico, he made his debut with *Saigo no tōiki* (*The Last Sigh*). His novel *Ore Ore* (*It's Me, It's Me*) was awarded the 2011 Kenzaburō Ōe Prize.

Pico Iyer has been based in Japan since 1987 and is the author of two novels and eight books of non-fiction, including *The Lady and the Monk*, about his first year in Kyoto. He has also written introductions to forty other books and many liner notes for Leonard Cohen. His most recent work is *The Man Within my Head*.

Adam Johnson was awarded the 2013 Pulitzer Prize for his novel *The Orphan Master's Son*, an extract of which appeared in *Granta* 116: Ten Years Later. He lives in San Francisco and teaches creative writing at Stanford University.

Hiromi Kawakami is a novelist, haiku poet, literary critic and essayist. Her books include *Manazuru*, *Pasuta mashiin yūrei* (*Pasta Machine Ghosts*) and *Sensei no kaban* (*The Briefcase*), published as *Strange Weather in Tokyo* by Portobello Books in the UK. She was awarded the 1996 Akutagawa Prize for *Hebi o fumu* (*Tread on a Snake*).

Tao Lin is the author of seven books of fiction and poetry. His most recent books are the novels *Taipei* and *Richard Yates*.

Ian M. MacDonald is a translator of Japanese fiction and non-fiction. His recent translations include *Sharaku satsujin jiken* (*The Case of the Sharaku Murders*) by Katsuhiko Takahashi and *Yukensho* (*Tales of the Ghost Sword*) by Hideyuki Kikuchi.

David Mitchell was one of *Granta*'s Best of Young British Novelists in 2003. His novels include *Cloud Atlas* and *The Thousand Autumns of Jacob de Zoet*. He lives in the west of Ireland with his family.

Yukiko Motoya is a novelist, playwright and stage director. She leads her own theatre company, Gekidan Motoya Yukiko, which she founded in 2000. Her story collection *Arashi no pikunikku* (*The Devil's Picnic*) was awarded the Kenzaburō Ōe Prize in 2013.

Sayaka Murata made her debut in 2003 with the short story 'Junyū'. She was awarded the Noma Prize for New Writers in 2009 for *Gin-iro no uta* (*Silver Song*) and the Yukio Mishima Prize in 2013 for *Shiro-iro no machi no, sono hone no taion no* (*Of Bones, of Body Heat, of Whitening City*).

Kyoko Nakajima has worked as a journalist and editor. She is the author of several books and story collections including *Futon*, *Chiisai ouchi* (*The Little House*), *Ito no koi* (*Ito in Love*), *Jochu-tan* (*Tales of Maids*) and *E/N/Ji/N* (*Misanthropus*).

Lucy North is the translator of *Toddler-Hunting and Other Stories* by Taeko Kōno. She holds a PhD in modern Japanese literature and lived in Tokyo for thirteen years. She now lives in East Sussex and is working on a story collection by Hiromi Kawakami.

Toshiki Okada is a playwright, director, novelist and founder of theatre company Chelfitsch. His plays include *Sangatsu no itsukakan* (*Five Days in March*), *Cooler* (*Air Conditioner*) and *Marijuana no gai ni tsuite* (*On the Harmful Effects of Marijuana*). His novella collection *Watashitachi ni yurusareta tokubetsu na jikan no owari* (*The End of the Special Time We Were Allowed*) was awarded the Kenzaburō Ōe Prize in 2007.

Hiroko Oyamada was born in Hiroshima. She is the author of *Kōjō* (*Factory*) and *Ana* (*Hole*), for which she was awarded the Akutagawa Prize in 2014.

Ruth Ozeki is a novelist, film-maker and Zen Buddhist priest. She is the author of *My Year of Meats*, *All Over Creation* and *A Tale for the Time Being*, which was shortlisted for the 2013 Man Booker Prize and the 2014 National Book Critics Circle Award. She lives in New York City and Whaletown, British Columbia.

David Peace is the author of the Red Riding Quartet, *GB84*, *The Damned Utd*, *Tokyo Year Zero*, and *Red or Dead*. He was one of *Granta*'s Best of Young British Novelists in 2003, and has received the James Tait Black Memorial Prize. He lives in Tokyo.

Andrés Felipe Solano is the author of the novels *Sálvame, Joe Louis* (*Save Me, Joe Louis*) and *Los hermanos Cuervo* (*The Cuervo Brothers*). His work has appeared in the *New York Times Magazine*, *Words Without Borders* and *Anew*. He was featured in *Granta* 113: The Best of Young Spanish-language Novelists. He currently lives in Seoul, South Korea.

Rebecca Solnit is the author of fifteen books including, most recently, *The Faraway Nearby*. She lives in San Francisco.

Ginny Tapley Takemori's most recent translations include *Hantō o deyo* (*From the Fatherland with Love*) by Ryū Murakami, with co-translators Ralph McCarthy and Charles De Wolf, and *Minami kamuito* (*The Isle of South Kamui and Other Stories*) by Kyōtarō Nishimura.

Yumiko Utsu's work has been exhibited internationally in venues such as The Saatchi Gallery in London and Palais Lumière in Paris.

Ivan Vartanian is an author, curator, collaborator and publisher of photobook editions. He lives in Tokyo.

Daisuke Yokota is a photographer who lives and works in Tokyo. He is the recipient of the first award from the first Foam Outset Exhibition Fund.

Asa Yoneda was born in Osaka and translates from Japanese. She currently lives in Bristol.